Zelina Fang
– 1988 –

The ancient town of Saint-Emilion, historic central place for one of the world's great wine districts.

A Geographic Appreciation

Harm Jan de Blij

Foreword by *Robert Hosmon*

Cartography by *Margaret V. Post*

Rowman & Allanheld, Publishers

ROWMAN & ALLANHELD

Published in the United States of America in 1983
by Rowman & Allanheld, Publishers
(A Division of Littlefield, Adams & Company)
81 Adams Drive, Totowa, New Jersey 07512

Library of Congress Cataloging in Publication Data

de Blij, Harm Jan
  Wine—a geographic appreciation.

  Includes bibliographic references and index.
  1. Wine and wine making. I. Title.
TP548.D33 1983   641.2'22   82-20648
ISBN 0-86598-091-8

83 84 85 86 / 10 9 8 7 6 5 4 3 2 1
Printed in the United States of America

Contents

Tables and Figures

Foreword

Concurrent with the growing interest in wine in the United States is a thirst not only for new experiences from the bottle but also for new and expanded knowledge about the liquid itself. University and community college classes on the science and appreciation of wine are offered to overflow crowds; books on wine have become popular best sellers in the marketplace; wine clubs, where members taste and compare notes, have reached a peak of popularity in large and small communities alike. In all, those who have come to appreciate the better things in life have learned that the true satisfaction in wine comes from both tasting and studying the product.

No one appreciates that process better than Professor de Blij. His experience with wine is a lengthy one; his sense of taste and analysis is professional; and his knowledge on the subject is all encompassing. Clearly that knowledge of and sensitivity to the subject of wine is evident in this, his latest book, *Wine: A Geographic Appreciation.* Combining the elements of history, geography, sociology, science, and art, the book is a treasure of information for the experienced oenophile and the novice alike. Professor de Blij has shown us what he already knows: the appreciation of wine is a study of the culture of mankind; it is a science and an art.

Wine: A Geographic Appreciation is not just another book on the subject of wine. It is a unique contribution to the literature of dozens of books that have preceded it. With his own knowledge, Professor de Blij imparts to us his studied and cultivated appreciation of the culture of wine. Best of all, he invites us to follow him in his quest, to experiment on our own, and to realize that the study of wine is a never ending, lifetime challenge—and pleasure.

Robert Hosmon

Preface

A great bottle of wine is a noble creation, a work of art as well as science, a triumph of talent and initiative, a progeny of natural environment and cultural tradition. As complex as a Monet landscape and as intricate as a Bach partita, such a wine is to the senses of smell and taste what painting is to the eye and music to the ear. It creates indelible memories of brilliance and balance, distinction and excellence, complexity and depth. Quite naturally a great wine gives rise to anticipation—for another bottle of the same vintage or an even better one, or for a wine from another winegrower in the same region. It is an endless adventure of boundless joy, enlivened by discoveries of unexpected treasures.

Exploration and discovery once were the mainstays of geography, and filling blanks on maps of distant areas was an overriding preoccupation of geographers. Those days are over, but the curiosity about regions and places remains. Today geographers study interactions between human societies and natural environments, physical landscapes and social patterns, distributions and interconnections and their underlying causes. Such interests have many serious, scientific applications. But they also can enhance the appreciation and enjoyment of one of our highest cultural achievements: the glorious perfection of a winegrower's ultimate success.

If I write with enthusiasm for the accomplishments of winemakers, it is not simply out of admiration for their success against odds to be detailed in several chapters to follow; it also is a matter of gratitude for the way my life has thereby been enhanced. As the only child of distinguished musicians, I grew up surrounded by the quartets of Mozart and sonatas of Beethoven. From my father, a violinist and (later) conductor, I learned the importance of regional and social context in the appreciation of serious music. My mother, whose piano recitals gave me a unique insight into that literature, combined those talents with a remarkable sense of the visual arts.

What a discovery it was when—much later—I realized that similar absolutes of culture and quality could be found in wine!

By that time, my own musical aspirations having been relegated to amateur status, I had become a geographer. Now the connections that should have been obvious to me many years earlier finally clarified: viticulture undoubtedly is the most geographically expressive of all agricultural industries, and the making of wine is an art of such strong regional associations that a wine in a way constitutes a summary of a geographic region. In *Geography of Viticulture* (1981) I attempted to outline a course of study on this basis.

Wine: A Geographic Appreciation began as an updating of that first effort, but soon it developed into something rather different. In addition to geographic fundamentals of interest to serious wine consumers and students of the vine, this book also contains, in two concluding chapters, vintage information about wine regions in the Southern as well as the Northern Hemisphere. This information is drawn from numerous sources, including field observation, reports from local growers and observers, sampling of vintages, and materials cited. Some thirty new maps support the narrative. When used in conjunction with the discussion of developing classification systems and label contents, this may provide a useful practical guide, especially for wines from regions yet vaguely known to many consumers.

Acknowledgments

My first and greatest debt is to my wife, Bonnie, whose palate is far more educated than mine and who can discern nuances I could not detect without her direction. Her participation in this venture and her frequent advice were truly invaluable, and no simple record of it can adequately express my appreciation.

It is pleasant indeed to be able to acknowledge the assistance freely given by geographers and others who share my enthusiasm for this topic. While I was working on *Geography of Viticulture*, Dr. Donald G. Holtgrieve of California State University (Hayward) assisted me in several important ways, and I have again benefited from his expertise. Mr. Peter Saunders, Editor of the *New Zealand Wineglass* and author of *Wine Label Language* (1976), wrote me in some detail on particulars relating to New Zealand and Australia. Mr. David Hughes of the Stellenbosch Farmers Winery provided valuable information on recent Cape vintage conditions. In Argentina, Ing. Agr. R. Juan de Dios Morales of the Instituto Nacional de Vitivinicultura provided me with a superb dossier, and I am grateful also to Ing. Agr. Mario S. Toso for his followup. In Chile, Mr. Pablo Guilisasti Gana of Viña Concha y Toro S.A. forwarded information on several aspects of Chilean viticulture.

Mrs. Leigh Snider of McLean, Virginia, provided me with first-hand field data from her reconnaissance of the Chilean wine country.

Among colleagues who were kind enough to send me notes and other items of interest are Drs. David H. Kornhauser and Roland J. Fuchs of the University of Hawaii; Dr. Harold A. Winters of Michigan State University; Dr. Charles F. Kovacik of the University of South Carolina; Dr. William K. Crowley of Sonoma State University; Dr. John J. Baxevanis of East Strouds-burg State College; Dr. Richard J. Houk of DePaul University; Dr. Merle C. Prunty of the University of Georgia; Drs. Richard D. Kreske, Professor Emeritus, Peter O. Muller, and Donald L. Capone, all of the University of

Miami; Dr. Frank Whitmore of the United States Geological Survey; Dr. Dennis J. Dingemans of the University of California (Davis); and Dr. J. Douglas Eyre of the University of North Carolina. I also am grateful to Messrs. Sam J. Sebastiani, Jack E. Daniels (Society of Wine Educators), Ronald G. Small (New Zealand), Amram Surasky (Israel), Chip Cassidy (Miami), Stathis Sakellarios (Greece), and Silver Miller (Colorado School of Mines) for their interest and assistance.

The noted oenophile Dr. Edwin W. Snider of the National Geographic Society provided me with several of his photographs of wineries and vineyards in Chile.

I am especially appreciative of the work done on various drafts of the manuscript by Mrs. Helen Mogensen of the Colorado School of Mines and Mrs. Sally Kiernan of the University of Miami. Ms. Lynn Gannett, a recent graduate of the University of Miami, produced the attractive drawings from my tentative sketches. The cartography (including considerable research) was capably done by Mrs. Margaret V. Post.

It is a special pleasure to be able to acknowledge once again the interest and encouragement of my editor, Mr. Paul A. Lee, himself a professional geographer as well as an oenophile. At Rowman & Allanheld I benefited enormously from expert editing by the Associate Editor, Ms. Janet Johnston; production was superbly guided by Production Managers Ms. Kathy Rosenbloom and Ms. Tobi Krutt; and the art was handled by the Art Director, Ms. Linda Holzman.

As readers of WINE will be aware, there is much that is subjective about the topic and its numerous dimensions. I have received many suggestions and much advice, but remain solely responsible for substance as well as opinion in the pages that follow.

Harm Jan de Blij
Coral Gables, Florida
September 1982

1

Why a Geography *of Wine?*

The creation of a noble wine is one of civilization's highest achievements. An aristocratic wine ranks with great music and fine art as a supreme response to culture's most demanding and discriminating tastes. The world's greatest wines are products of a human endeavor of extraordinary intricacy, in which history and tradition, natural (physical) and social (human) environments, opportunity and adaptation, risk-taking and experimentation, and crucial decision-making all play their parts.

Certainly the rising value of notable wines confirms the place of wine among desired investments. The retail prices of the highest-ranked wines of Bordeaux approach (and will soon exceed) $100; California's premium wines are not far behind. Older wines of good vintage years can be found as collectors' items costing thousands of dollars. In 1981, a bottle of 1806 Lafite Rothschild sold for nearly $10,000 during a Washington auction. Even more startling was the $24,000 paid by a New York wine merchant for a case (12 bottles) of 1979 California wine, the first vintage resulting from a collaboration between two of the world's foremost winemakers, Robert Mondavi of California and Baron Philippe de Rothschild of France.

Viticulture (the growing of grapes) is perhaps the most geographically expressive of all agricultural industries. Not only does it involve considerations of climate and soil, the availability of water and the threat of disease, local and regional methods of cultivating the vine, and widely varying harvesting practices; the geography of viticulture also extends to the development of distinct cultural landscapes, the perpetuation of regional traditions and preferences, processes of diffusion, market competition, and even political issues. Viticulture and viniculture (the making of wine) can be studied from many viewpoints, but none provides the particular spatial perspective, so essential to both endeavors, as effectively as does geography. Choosing a bottle of wine is best done with some knowledge of region and place of origin, system of classification, and environmental conditions during the year of production. All three of these specifics are fundamentally geographic.

Exploration of the geographic literature for wine-related insights is a worthwhile venture in itself. Nothing quite matches Stanislawski's *Landscapes of Bacchus: The Vine in Portugal*, a book of penetrative insight that demonstrates the full force of geographic inquisition in the context of wine.[1] A later article by the same author traces "Dionysus Westward: Early Religions and the Economic Geography of Wine."[2] But the majority of geographers' wine writings are regional in focus, highlighting one of the discipline's chief components. These essays range from early studies now of great historic value[3] to current assessments of vintage conditions, cultural practices, and prospects.[4] The latter contain uniquely useful commentaries on matters political and economic as well as environmental in the wine country—always, as noted earlier, in spatial context.

Modern geographers were not, of course, the first to discern a close relationship between geography and viticulture. In ancient times (before geographers called themselves geographers) the Mesopotamians were fermenting grapes into wine while scholars etched maps into sun-baked clay, tracing the trade routes that would carry the wine to distant consumers. Those ancient cartographers knew that efficiency was important: wine had to be consumed soon after it was made, not aged as is now the practice. And they determined that river transport was efficient. In the days of old Babylon wine was brought to the city from the north by boat, along the Euphrates. It marked the beginning of a relationship between vineyard location, transport route, and market that was to endure for thousands of years. It is no accident, nor is it principally a matter of better soils or superior climates, that so many vineyards lie so near major river routes. It is a result of the spatial efficiencies prevailing at the time the vines were first planted.

As will be noted in more detail later (see Chapter 3), the art of winemaking diffused from its Armenian sources to Egypt; earthen jugs of wine filled the holds of Phoenician boats as they plied the Mediterranean. By the time of the birth of Eratosthenes, the scholar most often credited as the father of geography, vines had been planted on Mediterranean slopes from the Levant to Iberia, and Greece was the leading source of wine as well as knowledge concerning viticulture.

Roman geographers, including Strabo and Pliny the Elder, chronicled the emergence of viticulture as one of the two pillars of classical agriculture in ancient Rome. Wine and olive oil were the essentials of civilization, and more than two thousand years ago the outlines of Italy's modern viticulture map were taking shape. The expansion of Roman civilization carried with it the extension of viticulture and viniculture in Western as well as Eastern Europe; when Rome's power waned, so did the production of wine. During the Dark Ages of Europe's post-Roman misery, Christianity—the churches and the monasteries—sustained the industry.

Modern viticulture, like modern geography, began with a nineteenth-century resurgence. European missionaries and colonial settlers had spread the vine to the Americas, Africa, and Australia, but viticulture succeeded nowhere as it did in Europe itself. Horticultural techniques improved, the use of the cork was introduced and made long-term aging of wine possible, and wine quality rose markedly. The focus of the industry continued to lie in France, and French geographers, including De la Blache and Brunhes,

In the source region: vineyards at the foot of Mount Carmel, Israel. The vine stood here five millennia ago, as viticulture diffused from its Armenian beginnings toward Egypt, eventually to reach Greece via Crete and Anatolia.

were among the first to assess its modern development. During the twentieth century viticulture (again like geography) became a science as well as an art, supported by research in oenology (also spelled enology, the comprehensive term for the science of wine) and ampelography (science of the grapevine). California emerged as one of the world's leading wine-producing regions, its premium wines qualitatively in the same class as those of Europe's most prestigious areas. Argentina vied with Spain and the Soviet Union as the world's fourth-largest winemaking country by volume. Geographers in Europe as well as North America reported on these events from historic viewpoints, in environmental contexts, in economic terms, cartographically and, as will be seen later, in other perspectives as well.[5]

Viticulture and Wine in Geographic Perspective

Geography as a field of study and enquiry has physical as well as human dimensions. Among its uniting themes are its spatial orientation, its focus on the natural environment, its attention to human-land interactions, and its concern with the character of regions. It is thus not difficult to see why viticulture and viniculture would hold special geographic interest; the production of wine—its successes as well as failures—raises the kinds of questions that demand geographic solutions.

Environmental conditions, for example, are obviously crucial in the cultivation of the vine and the success of the harvest—but favorable climate and good soils do not necessarily produce healthy vines nor, for that matter, high-quality wines. It is one of the apparent anomalies of viticulture that certain of the world's greatest wines are produced from the grapes of vines that stand in soils that would, for other agricultural purposes, be described as "poor" at best. Every viticulturist would like to be able to predict where and under what conditions a particular species of the grapevine will do well, but although much progress has been made in this predictive aspect of viticulture, unexplained surprises still occur.

Quite another area of geographic-environmental interest lies in the effect of global and regional climatic variation on viticulture. The varying fortunes of winemakers in England over the past nine hundred years, for example, are mirrored by cooling and warming trends identified by climatologists from other sources of centuries ago. Where detailed records were kept of the dates when harvesting began (as in sixteenth- and seventeenth-century France), those dates also reflect prevailing growth and ripening conditions during the preceding summer, and whether it was warm, cool, or cold. Thus viticulture and viniculture contribute to the reconstruction of weather and climate maps of bygone ages.

Still another aspect of the geographic environment of viticulture lies in the origin, diffusion, and defeat of natural threats to the vine, especially diseases and pests. While much is known concerning the actual impact of various diseases that afflict the vine, the processes of their diffusion are less well understood. During the second half of the nineteenth century, a dreaded disease of the vine named *phylloxera* was carried from its North American source to Europe, where it devastated the vineyards, caused economic disaster, drove tens of thousands of French families to Algeria (at first believed to be safe from the onslaught), and required a massive program of regeneration once a solution was found. No biogeographic study of *phylloxera*'s worldwide diffusion exists today, more than a century later, although such a study would be vital to the determination of a cure.*

Within particular wine-producing regions microclimatic and micropedologic (soil) variations often have vital effect on the character of the wine, and some familiarity with these variations is useful. Regions such as the Médoc (and the entire south bank of the Gironde-Garonne in Bordeaux), Spain's Rioja, or California's Napa Valley are by no means homogeneous in terms of their physiographies (that is, their physical environments). In the Bordeaux region, for example, soils in the commune of Saint Estèphe contain much more silt than those to the southeast, until they become gravelly in the district of Graves. These contrasting soil characteristics are transmitted to the grapes and hence to the wines, and when buying a "Bordeaux" one should take such contrasts into account. In the case of Spain's Rioja region, there are three quite distinct environments, with annual average precipitation and temperature patterns varying widely. The "Upper" Rioja receives, in a normal year, more than 20 inches of precipitation; the

---

*The solution, as will be detailed in Chapter 3, was to graft French species of the vine onto American rootstocks, since certain American species proved to be highly resistant to *phylloxera.* Thus the French wines of today result from a remarkable combination of American vine roots and French scions. It is a solution—but not a cure.

The small town of Rüdesheim near the western end of Germany's Rheingau. The slopes face south; the Rhine River reflects sunlight and thus contributes to the ripening of the grapes.

"Lower" Rioja, about 12 inches. That difference is the difference between comparatively elegant and rather coarse wines. Rioja is a region, but not all Riojas are the same. Again it is a matter of geography.

Landscapes and Regions

Surely there are few human pursuits that generate as close a relationship between people and the land they cultivate as does viticulture. The well-tended vineyard is a hillside transformed, the soil turned and aired, the vines trained and pruned, the fields laid out for optimal benefit of sun or shade. Many a New World vineyard reveals, through the evident care and preferred methods of viticulture, the Old World origins of the farmer: traditions are durable. This is the essence of what geographers call viticulture's *cultural landscape,* the scenery of civilization, the layer of human works on the topography of nature. The cultural landscape of viticulture is embellished by the situation, architectural qualities, layout, and general ambience of the towns, villages, châteaux, and more modest wineries that are the foci of viniculture and the wine trade. The tangible attributes of this special cultural landscape are further complemented by a particular atmosphere, an appealing environment that is part of the reason why wine regions the world over attract endless streams of visitors, who come not just to sample the wines. The verdant hills where the promise of another vintage is being fulfilled, the attention to detail in the vineyards, the progress of the barreled wines in the winery, the preparations for the coming harvest—all bestow upon viticulture's cultural landscape a quality that is, simply, unique.

A cultural landscape gives identity to a region, and quite naturally the idea that the complex world can be made conceptually manageable through the identification of regions is a notion that appeals to geographers. The first designation given to a wine often is regional: it may be called a Bordeaux, a Rhône, or a Rioja. It is easy to identify a region by name; it is quite another matter to determine its extent and define its boundaries. One major reason why French winemakers have been displeased by American practices has been the American habit of naming California wines by French *regional* names, such as Burgundy and Chablis. There is, of course, no Burgundy in California, regionally or viticulturally. But comparatively few of the world's many wine-producing regions are legally delimited as are those of France. Yet, within the same wine-producing country, there will be regions that produce quality wines and other regions where the wines are, at best, ordinary. Again it is important to know the geographic detail: in Italy, for example, it is crucial. All wine labels should be read for the geography they convey.

It is therefore of some oenological interest to follow geographic reasoning when it comes to regions. Technically, regions are classified and ranked according to various sets of criteria, but basically two kinds of regions are most commonly recognized: *formal* regions, marked by a certain degree of visual and measurable homogeneity or sameness, and *functional* regions, which are tied together by a system (or several systems) of human endeavor. Areas in which the cultivation of vines and the production of wine are economic mainstays do tend to present an overall appearance of uniformity that gives veracity to the notion of a formal region: the cultural landscape of viticulture is unmistakable whether it exists in Bordeaux (France) or Barossa (Australia), in Mendoza (Argentina) or Marsala (Italy). The important, wine-related problem with formal regions lies not in the identification of the heart or core of such regions, but of their margins. Just where do the environments that produce the wines for which a region is famous begin to change so significantly that it is no longer proper to include them? In France, this problem was substantially solved by the *Appellation d'Origine Contrôlée* laws (see Chapter 5), which established legal boundaries within which a wine could, for example, be designated a "Bordeaux" but beyond which such a name would be illegal. In many other wine-producing countries, however, such regional precision has not yet been achieved. In the United States an American "Appellation" system is now being created, so that labels will have stronger geographic identity. Naturally any imperfections in the law, or vagueness of regional delimitation, can benefit the marginal wine producer and deceive the purchaser. Unless boundaries are clearly defined, the "Napa Valley" designation on a label might mean that the wine came from a winery near, but not within, that prestigious region, with a corresponding reduction in quality, that is, a quality palpably below what is expected of "Napa Valley" wines.

It is unfortunate indeed that geographers have not been more deeply involved in the developing "Appellation" system of the United States, but this merely reflects the general geographic illiteracy that characterizes our culture. In France and Germany, where effective regional systems have been created, geographers played critical roles in the process, and the results evince their effectiveness. Comprehensive and comprehensible, the *Appellation Contrôlée* system is one of French viniculture's chief assets in the maintenance of quality, regional and name recognition, and market competition.

As functional regions, wine-producing areas are oriented spatially toward central places whose services, especially during the critical harvest period, are indispensable. These towns have historic, often famous names: Saint Emilion, Beaune, Sonoma, Oporto. Many towns of lesser reputations nevertheless anchor viticultural regions in the same way, the domination of wine-related services and activities constituting evidence that a functional region exists around them. Not all viticultural regions are exclusively wine-producing regions: in Australia' famous Hunter Valley, for example, the vineyards lie interspersed with pasture lands, fields devoted to other crops, and stands of eucalyptus trees. Whether the Hunter Valley constitutes a formal region is thus arguable, but its central place, the town of Cessnock, leaves no doubt that a functional region exists here.

It was noted earlier that many of the world's major vineyard regions lie along or near large rivers. Even a small-scale map will suggest another association: many viticulture regions lie in the immediate hinterlands of large cities. This is a geographic reality of significant import, because the same urban centers which have long been the chief markets for the nearby winemakers now encroach, through suburbanization, on lands that were once comparatively remote and safe for viticulture. In France, expansion of the ancient Burgundian wine town of Dijon has overtaken nearby vineyards. In Portugal, the venerable districts of Carcavelos and Colares are threatened with extermination by urban growth. In the United States the urban sprawl of the San Francisco Bay area has invaded the Sonoma region and other vineyard areas nearby. In South Africa, several of the leading vineyards of the Constantia and Durbanville areas (see Chapter 9) lie within the municipal boundaries of the city of Cape Town, and a number of historic and famous vineyards have been destroyed by housing developments. Even in Japan, where viticulture is an important industry and winemaking is experiencing a strong growth period, some vineyards are losing at the expense of such cities as Osaka, Kurashiki, and Okayama. In Chile, city and vineyard compete on the margins of the capital, Santiago.

Other major viticulture regions, although situated within urban hinterlands, lie sufficiently far removed to escape such encroachment. These include the Hunter Valley (Sydney) and the Barossa Valley (Adelaide) in Australia, the vineyards of Paarl and Stellenbosch (Cape Town), the vineyards of Alsace (Strasbourg), and those of Champagne and Chablis (Paris). Proximity to a major domestic market constitutes a strong advantage, but the nearer the city, the greater the risk to the vineyards.

These are some of the salient reasons behind the geographical approach to the appreciation of wines, and others will emerge in the chapters that follow. Geography straddles physical and human worlds, regional and systematic viewpoints; viticulture and viniculture succeed where human skills, talents, and initiatives exploit the opportunities offered by nature and physiographic environments. Geography and wine: a fruitful alliance!

Additional Reading

On geography as a discipline, its emergence and development, and the role of the regional concept:

James, P. E. *All Possible Worlds: A History of Geographical Ideas.* New York: John Wiley & Sons, 1980.

English translations of two influential French geographers' works, with many references to viticulture:

De la Blache, P. V. *Principles of Human Geography.* Edited by E. de Martohe and translated by M. T. Bingham. New York: Holt, 1926.
Brunhes, J. *Human Geography.* Translated by E. F. Row. London: George G. Harrap, 1952.

An atlas of wine that contains far more than a set of maps of wine areas:

Johnson, H. *The World Atlas of Wine.* New York: Simon & Schuster, 1981.

The most useful alphabetical listing of names and terms associated with wine:

Lichine, A. *The New Encyclopedia of Wines and Spirits.* 3rd ed. New York: Alfred A. Knopf, 1981.

A regional summation of the wines produced around the world today:

Sutcliffe, S. *André Simon's Wines of the World.* 2nd ed. New York: McGraw-Hill, 1981.

2

From Ampelography to Ampelogeography

The ancient Greeks, who used the term *oinos* for wine (hence oenology or enology, the study and science of wine), also had a word for grapevine. They called the vine *ampelos,* and thus the field of ampelography is the science concerned with the identification, description, classification, and behavior of grape-bearing vines. It is not surprising that Greek names for wine and wine-related topics continue to be used: the ancient Greeks transmitted what was known of viticulture and viniculture from the Middle East and North Africa to Europe. Long before the Romans extended the wine industry in their imperial realm, the Greeks had brought the vine to Iberia, France, and, indeed, to Italy itself. And the Greeks, who studied and researched so many things so assiduously, also were the first ampelographers to leave a substantial record of what they learned.

Ampelography is a complex field of study, made more so by human intervention in the natural progress of the vine's worldwide dispersal. Species found growing wild in America were brought to Europe. European species were planted not only in America and Asia, but in the Southern Hemisphere from Argentina to Australia, regions the vine had never reached. Artificial and "accidental" natural hybridization produced hundreds of new varieties, the identities and antecedents of many still uncertain. It is estimated that about eight *thousand* grape varieties exist today, of which fewer than one hundred fifty produce the world's good wines.

When winemaking began in its most rudimentary form (see Chapter 3), perhaps as long as 8000 years ago, the vines on which the grapes grew probably were those native to the general geographical area of Armenia, possibly on south-facing slopes of foothills of the Caucasus Mountains between the Black and the Caspian seas. The species is likely to have been *Vitis*

Table 2.1. Subgenera and Species of the Genus VITIS

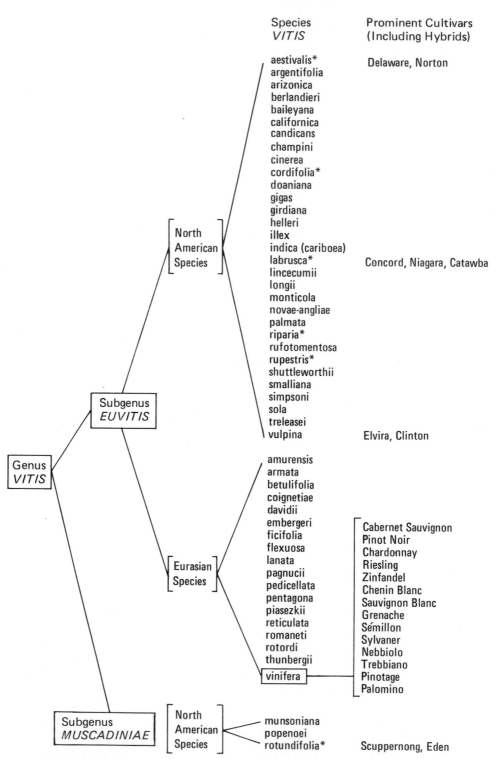

	Species VITIS	Prominent Cultivars (Including Hybrids)

North American Species:
aestivalis* — Delaware, Norton
argentifolia
arizonica
berlandieri
baileyana
californica
candicans
champini
cinerea
cordifolia*
doaniana
gigas
girdiana
helleri
illex
indica (cariboea)
labrusca* — Concord, Niagara, Catawba
lincecumii
longii
monticola
novae-angliae
palmata
riparia*
rufotomentosa
rupestris*
shuttleworthii
smalliana
simpsoni
sola
treleasei
vulpina — Elvira, Clinton

Subgenus EUVITIS

Genus VITIS

Eurasian Species:
amurensis
armata
betulifolia
coignetiae
davidii
embergeri
ficifolia
flexuosa
lanata
pagnucii
pedicellata
pentagona
piasezkii
reticulata
romaneti
rotordi
thunbergii
vinifera — Cabernet Sauvignon, Pinot Noir, Chardonnay, Riesling, Zinfandel, Chenin Blanc, Sauvignon Blanc, Grenache, Sémillon, Sylvaner, Nebbiolo, Trebbiano, Pinotage, Palomino

Subgenus MUSCADINIAE

North American Species:
munsoniana
popenoei
rotundifolia* — Scuppernong, Eden

Sources include Weaver (1976), Olmo (1976), Huang (1981), Takhtadzhian (1970), and others. Species marked by an (*) are represented on maps in this chapter.

vinifera silvestris, and if the first winemakers actually cultivated the vine, it was probably a variety of this species, *Vitis vinifera sativa.*[1] These vines were descendants of earlier species that emerged and dispersed during the Tertiary period of the most recent geologic era, the Cenozoic. The distribution of the vines before our distant ancestors began making wine was the result of about 60 million years of differentiation, and by the time Neolithic Man took an interest in *sativa,* wild grapes were growing in North America and Eastern Asia as well as Southwest Asia and Europe.

The environmental circumstances that prevailed during the genus *Vitis*'s evolving heterogeneity were crucial to the process. After its early Tertiary emergence, the vine spread latitudinally, *Vitis* separating into two subgenera, *Euvitis* and *Muscadiniae* (Table 2.1). Both subgenera were represented in Eurasia and North America when the Pleistocene Ice Age began, and the expansion of the ice had far-reaching consequences. In the first place, vines of the subgenus *Muscadiniae* were wiped out in Eurasia, whereas in North America they shifted southward during cold periods and survived. In addition, the separate isolation of North America and Eurasia caused vines of the subgenus *Euvitis* to acquire somewhat different characteristics in North America than in Eurasia. As a result of these events, North America is the world's only region where both subgenera of *Vitis* exist in their native forms: only the subgenus *Euvitis* remains in Eurasia. Not surprisingly, North America has by far the largest number of "original" species of the vine (about three dozen): just thirteen are native to Eurasia.

The Genus *Vitis*

The classification of grapevines and grapes is not a simple or even a clear-cut matter. Unraveling the relationships between species has proved a vexing task, and American and European scholars have disagreed on issues of detail, even to the name of the botanical family to which the grapevines belong. In the United States, a classification often employed is one developed by a Russian scholar, A. L. Takhtadzhian, which places vines that bear grapes in a botanical order called Rhamnales. This order includes three families of vines, among which one is Vitaceae. This family in turn has eleven genera, one of which, *Vitis,* is for grapes.

A different classification, developed by French scientists and long adopted in America as well, places the grapevine in a botanical family called Ampelidaceae, with ten genera including *Vitis* for grapes. Fortunately the apparent disparity matters little; the family name Vitaceae has taken precedence and the important genus has the same name in both classifications.

Among Vitaceae's genera, *Vitis* alone produces grapes suitable for winemaking. This botanical family encompasses a wide range of vines and climbing plants, and other genera also yield grapes and grapelike berries, but none of these has given an adequate wine. Only the genus *Vitis* is important in viticulture, and it thrives in moderate climates, mainly in two latitudinal zones between (very approximately) 30 and 50 degrees north latitude and 30 and 40 degrees south latitude (Fig. 2.1). Experimentation and hybridization have extended the environmental range of *Vitis,* and as noted previously the genus was diffused from its Eurasian source area around the world and to the Southern Hemisphere by human intervention. Thus Figure 2.1 represents only the zones in which lie the foci of viticulture; within these

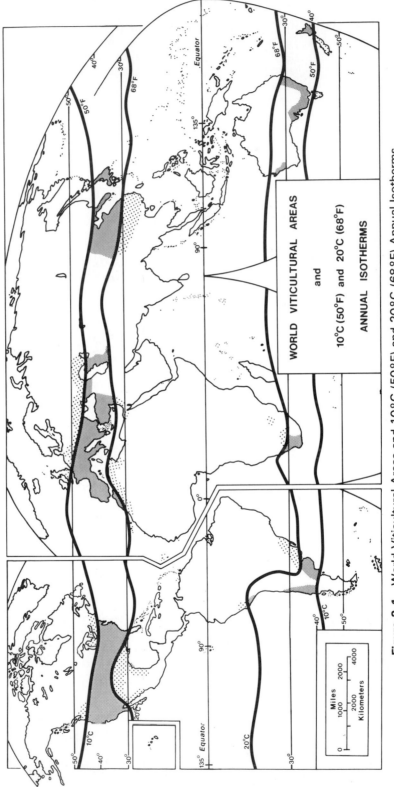

Figure 2.1 World Viticultural Areas and 10°C (50°F) and 20°C (68°F) Annual Isotherms

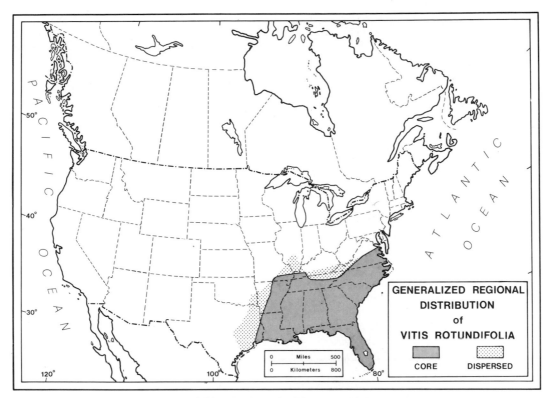

Figure 2.2 Generalized Regional Distribution of *Vitis rotundifolia*

zones vast areas are still unsuitable for grape growing, and beyond them, in areas where elevation moderates the heat and where water permits viticulture, the vines stand productively, even defiantly. Swiss missionaries in Tanzania, white farmers in Zimbabwe, Germans in Southern Brazil, Peruvians, and Mexicans are among those who have successfully cultivated the vine beyond its optimum range.

Botanists and biogeographers even differ somewhat on some aspects of the classification of species of *Vitis*, but there is no disagreement on fundamentals. *Vitis* has two subgenera, and of these, the *Muscadiniae* includes only native North American species, while *Euvitis* is represented in Eurasia as well as North America.

The subgenus *Muscadiniae*, whose grapes are properly called the Muscadines, is represented by three American species, *Vitis rotundifolia*, *Vitis Munsoniana*, and *Vitis Popenoi*.[2] *Vitis Munsoniana* grows in Central and Southern Florida, but the range of *Vitis rotundifolia* is much larger, extending from Virginia to Florida and from Georgia into Eastern Texas (Fig. 2.2). The map indicates a degree of inconsistency in the observations of ampelographers concerning distribution patterns; the core area on this and the maps that follow is the region identified by all authorities as the species' range, while the area of dispersal is mapped by some but not all observers as part of this range.

Vitis rotundifolia has many popular names, among which the Scuppernong is undoubtedly the most common, but it is also known, simply, as the

Muscadine, the Southern Fox, the Bullet grape, and, as a reflection of one of its locales, as the Roanoke. Its grapes hang in clusters like cherries, rather than in large bunches. There are black as well as white grapes, and both have a thick skin. These characteristics are important, and for several reasons. The small clusters save the Scuppernong from the rot that would set in if they were bunched more closely together in the heat and humidity of the southeastern summer; *Vitis rotundifolia* is known for its resistance to several serious grape diseases, including types of rot and mildew. When the grapes ripen, they are not harvested in the more traditional manner, but shaken off the vines to fall on a sheet placed on the ground. Because of their comparatively thick skin, this can be done without damage to the fruit.

The Scuppernong has a characteristic "musky" flavor as a table grape, and despite its low sugar content and high acidity it can produce a particular sweet wine with a unique aroma and an unusual taste. It is the basis for a small wine industry in the region of its occurrence, but the peculiar aroma and taste of the wine have not gained wide acceptance, even in its source area.

The taste of the Scuppernong and other Muscadine grapes is not, of course, the only basis for its classification as a distinct subgenus. The Muscadines are so different from *Euvitis* species that crossing them with non-Muscadines is extremely difficult and has, in fact, succeeded only recently.[3] Within the Scuppernong species, various crossings have improved the cultivated varieties (a *culti*vated grape *vari*ety is known as a *cultivar*), but ampelographers have long been interested in crossing *rotundifolia* with non-Muscadine species. A major reason for this, of course, is the strong disease-resistance of *rotundifolia,* which might thus be conferred upon the hybrid.

Euvitis in North America

The subgenus *Muscadiniae,* thus, is represented only in North America, having been extinguished in Eurasia. And its representation in North America, as Table 2.1 reflects, is quite modest. The great majority of the known species of the genus *Vitis* belong to the other subgenus, *Euvitis.* Again North America figures prominently: more than 70 percent of the species of *Euvitis* are native to this continent. The more important North American species of *Euvitis* are identified in Table 2.1, including *Labrusca, aestivalis, riparia,* and others of lesser rank.

The dominant North American species of the subgenus is *Vitis Labrusca,* also known as *Vitis Labrusca* Linnaeus after the famed botanist who first described it in 1763. Geographically, *Labrusca*'s native habitat extends from southernmost Canada to South Carolina and Georgia; it is, as Figure 2.3 shows, an eastern species, growing most abundantly in the Middle Atlantic states. This is North America's most productive native grape, contributing about 68 percent of all the cultivars on the continent.[4] The Concord grape, a *Labrusca* cultivar, in turn accounts for about 80 percent of the species' total production.[5]

Like the Muscadines, *Labrusca* varieties have numerous popular names, including Northern Fox, Plum, and Skunk. Its varieties have been exported to many areas of the world, where they have acquired additional names (such as the Isabella of Portugal, which returns to the United States on the labels of sparkling rosés). But unlike the Muscadines, *Labrusca* proved

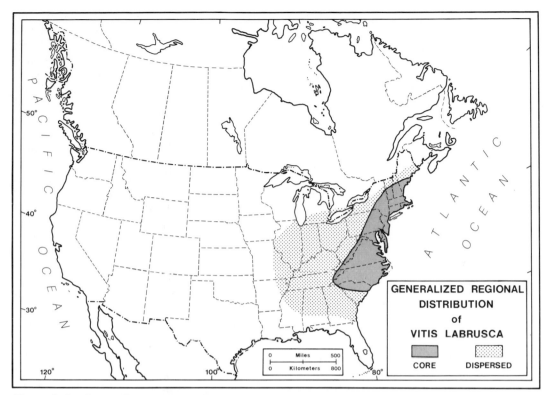

Figure 2.3   Generalized Regional Distribution of *Vitis Labrusca*

amenable to interspecific crossing, producing numerous hybrids of which some, such as the Catawba and the Delaware, will be familiar to oenophiles.

Along with the Scuppernong variety of *Vitis rotundifolia,* the grapes of wild-growing *Labrusca* were the first to be vinified by the earliest European settlers along the East Coast. Neither the grape nor the resulting wine had a flavor that was familiar to the Europeans. This flavor, described as "foxy," was among the factors that led to attempts to cross *Labrusca* with European varieties, thus to soften its pungency. But eventually a substantial segment of American wine drinkers became accustomed to this special character of *Labrusca*-derived wines, and cultivars and hybrids of the species continue to constitute a significant element of North American viticulture.

Labrusca's role in world viticulture has another dimension. It is probable that two dreaded diseases of grapes and vines, powdery mildew (*oidium*) and *phylloxera,* were carried on its vines and roots from source areas in North America to botanical gardens in Europe and hence into European vineyards during the nineteenth century. This diffusion had devastating impact; *phylloxera* destroyed millions of non-resistant European vines and spread to North and South Africa, to Argentina, to Australia and New Zealand, and even back to North America, where it attacked California's vineyards, in which European vines had been planted. When the solution against *phylloxera* was finally found, and resistant North American rootstocks were used to sustain European vines, *Labrusca* proved to be inadequate to that demand. *Labrusca* varieties are quite resistant to the effects of comparatively severe cold, but

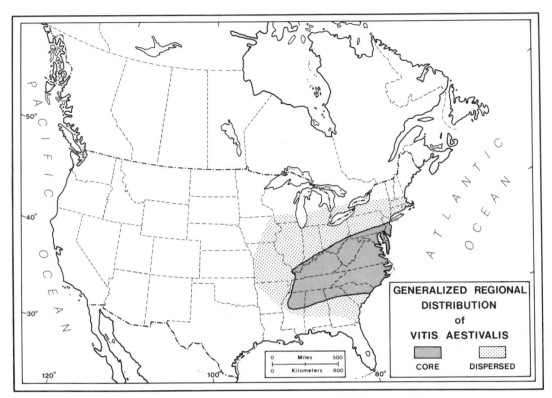

Figure 2.4 Generalized Regional Distribution of *Vitis aestivalis*

they have a low tolerance to a number of diseases of the vine—including the *phylloxera* of its own native habitat.

This weakness notwithstanding, *Labrusca* and its varieties and hybrids dominate the viticulture of North American native species. A measure of this is provided by the next ranking species, *Vitis aestivalis*, which has a much larger region of occurrence (Fig. 2.4) but which accounts for only 10 percent of the native cultivars. *Aestivalis*'s habitat extends from New England and Southern Canada to coastal states of the U.S. South, and westward as far as Iowa and Missouri. By itself, *aestivalis* is not an important or popular species, but its significance is based on numerous natural and artificial hybrids, some of which have become productive. One of its close relatives, for example, is part of the Delaware hybrid (in which *Labrusca* has the more important share). Another *aestivalis* descendant is a component of the successful Seibel cultivars grown in New York.

Neither *Labrusca* or *aestivalis* is especially resistant to *phylloxera*, but another North American species of *Euvitis*, *Vitis riparia*, does withstand the disease. As its name suggests, this grape also is known as the Riverbank, Riverside, and River grape; its geographic distribution is vast, extending from near the Gulf of Mexico well into Canada and from the Atlantic seaboard to the Rocky Mountains (Fig. 2.5). Rootstocks of *riparia* have been planted in Europe and in other areas of the world as well, and while it may not be an important wine-grape producer in its native habitat, its importance in viticulture in the defeat of *phylloxera* is secure.

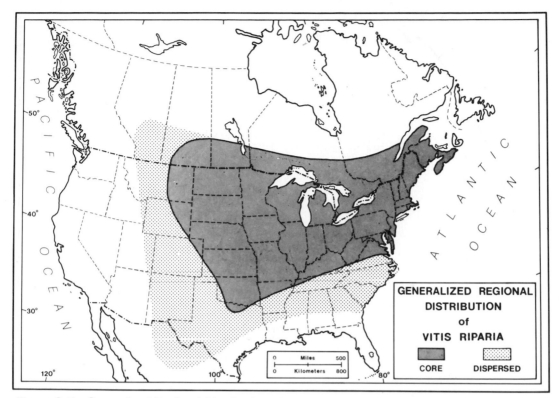

Figure 2.5   Generalized Regional Distribution of *Vitis riparia*

Vitis cordifolia, also resistant to *phylloxera,* is named after its long, heart-shaped leaf rather than its preferred growing environment. Nevertheless, where *riparia* and *cordifolia* overlap (in a substantial region, as Figure 2.6 indicates) it may be difficult to distinguish them from each other. *Cordifolia's* grapes, however, have a taste that is generally disliked, which limits its usefulness in hybridization; and its cuttings, when planted, have difficulty taking root.

Still another species that has played a role in the anti-*phylloxera* campaign, and one that also has an environment-related name, is *Vitis rupestris* (from the Latin for rock, *rupes*). It has various names including the Sand, Rock, and Mountain grape, and its preferred habitat is in the bright sun, on exposed hillslopes and open plains. It is important as a rootstock, but it also produces grapes used in winemaking from its cultivar named Rupestris Saint George. *Rupestris's* range lies in the south-central area of the United States, from the Ohio Valley to Texas (Fig. 2.7).

Although the species whose distributions are shown in Figures 2.3 through 2.7 have mainly eastern habitats, other native varieties of *Euvitis* in North America concentrate in the Southwest and West. Facing the Pacific Ocean in its Californian habitat, *Vitis californica* lay protected by distance and by the Rocky Mountains from the scourge of *phylloxera,* and never became a host to the disease. Just as *Vitis riparia* extends into Canada, so *Vitis arizonica, berlandieri, candicans,* and *cinerea* reach from the U.S. South and Southwest into Mexico. While the names of these and other native North American

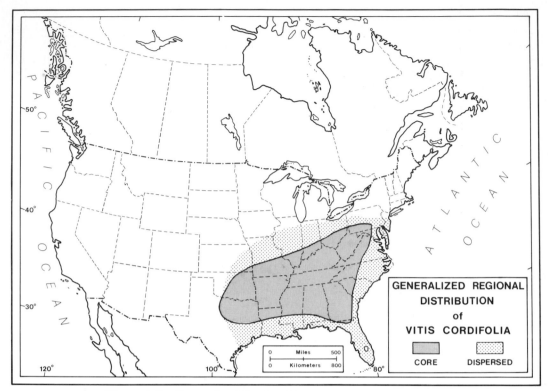

Figure 2.6 Generalized Regional Distribution of *Vitis cordifolia*

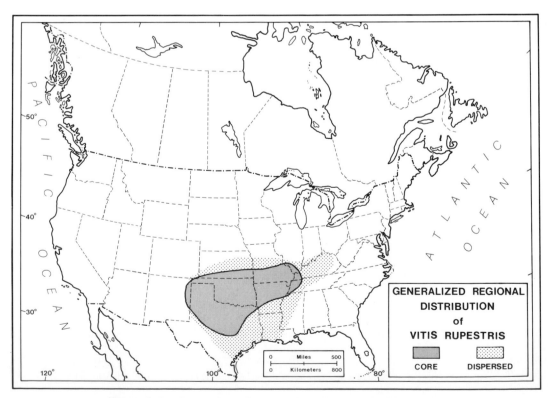

Figure 2.7 Generalized Regional Distribution of *Vitis rupestris*

species may not be as familiar as are the more prominent cultivars, their importance in hybridization and other kinds of experimentation should not be underestimated.

Euvitis in Eurasia

Eurasia is a much larger landmass than North America, but the number of its species of *Euvitis* is far smaller—less than 30 percent of the known total. Among this minority, however, is the species whose cultivars produce the grapes of the world's noblest wines: *Vitis vinifera*.

As Table 2.1 indicates, the subgenus *Euvitis* has Eurasian representatives in Japan and China, Southeast and South Asia, and Europe. Some cultivation and grape vinification of the East and South Asian species has occurred, including *Vitis cognetiae* and *Vitis thunbergi* in Japan and *Vitis amurensis* in China. *Amurensis* is the most cold-resistant species of the entire genus, tolerating temperatures as low as $-40°$C., but its grapes have high acidity and low sugar, so that hybridization with *vinifera* grapes has been attempted, recently with some success.[6] But none of Asia's eastern or southern species has become the basis for a major wine industry. A Southwest Asian species, *Vitis vinifera* spread westward and northwestward from its apparent source area on the southern slopes of the Caucasus Mountains to become Europe's dominant representative of the genus—and the foundation of the world's wine industries. Today, more than 90 percent of the world's winemaking grapes come from cultivars of this single species which, not unreasonably, also is called the European grape.

Vitis vinifera is represented by perhaps as many as 6000 grape varieties (including numerous hybrids), of which fewer than 150 are used to make the world's renowned wines. Cultivated varieties of the species are selected because of their particular flavor; capacity to resist pests and disease; adaptability to limitations imposed by climate, soil, or some other environmental element; high or dependable yield; especially successful growth in a certain region; or historic cultivation in specific, time-honored settings. Cabernet Sauvignon, Pinot Noir, Chardonnay, and Riesling are among familiar cultivars of *vinifera*.

If the exact origins of *Vitis vinifera* are somewhat uncertain (it is classified in Table 2.1 as a "*Eurasian*, or European-Eurasian" species), its European and later world-wide diffusion is well documented, a sequence of events that will be detailed in Chapter 3. In the process, the number of *vinifera*'s varieties multiplied, both by natural and by artificial crossing, giving rise to uncertainties about origins and relationships and, hence, about categories and classifications. Add to this the numerous results of interspecific hybridization with varieties of *Labrusca* and other North American species, and the complexities of ampelography become evident. (Technically, only the product of a crossing between representatives of two different species is a hybrid; when crossing of varieties occurs *within* a single species such as *vinifera*, the product should be called a *métis*.) The identification of grapevines and their botanical relationships is the most difficult of ampelographic work, and vexing questions always remain. The origin of a famous American wine grape, the Zinfandel, for example, has been the subject of decades of study and debate.

The anatomy of the leaves, flowers, bunches, individual grapes, shoots, canes, even the "hairiness" of the vines all play their role in ampelographic

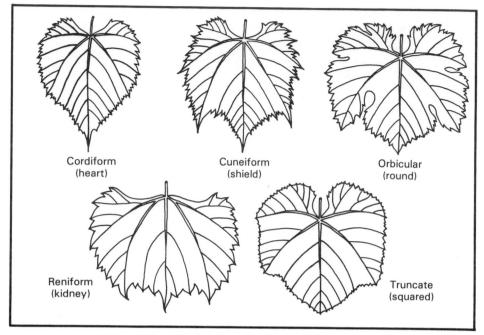

Figure 2.8 Prominent Leaf Shapes

study. Although the leaves of *Vitis* grapevines are nearly always palmate (that is, the major veins all originate at one point), there is quite a variety of overall leaf shape. As noted previously, the leaves of some non-*vinifera* American grapevines are markedly heart-shaped or *cordiform* (hence *Vitis cordifolia*). Another distinct shape is that of a shield, the *cuneiform* leaf, found in North America on *Vitis riparia*. Some leaves are very nearly round in shape and only slightly lobed, including several varieties of *Vitis vinifera*, and these are identified as *orbicular*. Still another leaf form is best described as kidney-shaped, or *reniform*, which can be observed on the North American species *Vitis rupestris*. And some of the cuneiform leaves seem squared off or *truncate*, as in the case of *Vitis aestivalis* (Fig. 2.8).[7] Not only the leaf shape but also its size, color, and surface are analyzed. Measurements of the length of the veins lead to mathematical calculations of statistically significant dimensions and proportions.

Similarly, the shape of the mature grape bunches has analytical value. Grape bunches develop consistent forms ranging from simple *cylindrical* or *conical* to more complex *shouldered* or *winged* (Fig. 2.9). Combinations of these shapes are of course possible. The Chardonnay (a *vinifera* cultivar), for example, has a cylindrical main bunch but is also winged. The Cabernet Sauvignon produces a long, conical cluster. The grape bunch of the Grenache is often shouldered. The density of the grapes in the cluster also matters. Some varieties produce dense, compact bunches with a minimum of space between the individual grapes. Others have loosely packed, more open clusters, permitting air circulation between the grapes and through the bunch—an important quality where the threat of rot or mildew prevails.

Other properties of the vine and its fruit also have analytical value. These include the color, size, shape, and flavor of the grape itself (wild grapevines

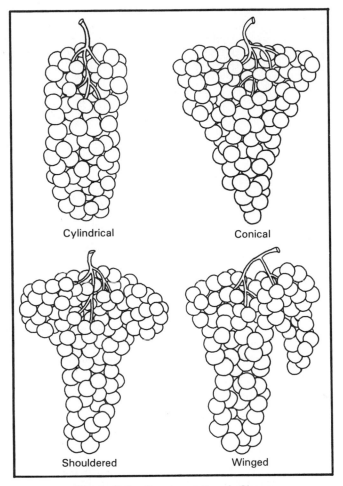

Cylindrical   Conical

Shouldered   Winged

Figure 2.9   Dominant Bunch Shapes

nearly always produce black or dark-skinned grapes), the size and weight of the seeds (small in *vinifera*, great in some American species), the length and other qualities of the shoots (those of *vinifera* usually much shorter than in hybrids), and aspects of the cane (a shoot becomes a more woody cane when the leaves have fallen). Even the "hairs" on the vines can be an asset, and are described with such terms as woolly, bristly, or felty.

The anatomy of the grape itself is important for theoretical ampelographic as well as practical vinicultural reasons. Since the grape produces the wine, its components are crucial. In the simplest terms, the grape is attached to the bunch by a short stem, and the berry itself has three main elements: the skin, the pulp, and seeds (Fig. 2.10). The proportions of these elements vary considerably by cultivar; as an average, the pulp constitutes somewhat more than 70 percent of the weight, the skin as much as 20 percent, the seeds about 5 percent, and the stem, when included in this measurement, about 3 percent.

The pulp makes up as much as three-quarters of the grape by weight, and of course this is the main source of the initial grape juice when vinification

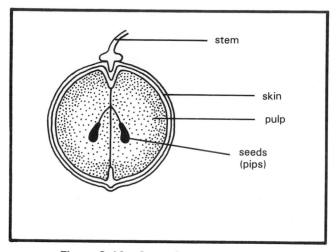

Figure 2.10   Cross-Section of a Grape

takes place. Approximately 70 to 80 percent of the pulp is water, about 10 to 25 percent is sugar, and the remainder is constituted by organic acids (5 to 15 percent), minerals, and various compounds. Thus water and sugar comprise more than 90 percent of the juice, although the other substances are crucial in the determination of the character of the wine. The sugar is converted, during fermentation, into approximately equal quantities of alcohol and carbon dioxide so that, as a rough estimate, the alcohol content of the "dry" wine will be close to one-half the sugar level in the grapes. The acids, tartaric and malic, when present in balanced amounts, prevent the wine's spoilage, give the color its "sparkle," and contribute to the wine's freshness and fullness. Tartaric acid is a constant property of the individual grape, and remains the same as the grape ripens. But the malic acid declines as the grape ripens and "sweetens," and optimum proportions produce a well-balanced wine. Too much acid, and the wine will be harsh; too little, and it will be flabby and flat.

The skin, by its color, provides an obvious clue to the identity of the grape; even more important, its pigments also color the wine. It is possible to make white wine from red grapes by removing the skins immediately upon crushing, but the skins, especially in red wines, contribute to the wine's character in other ways as well. Among these are the tannins derived from the skin; these help give the wine its body or substance, and serve to "clear" the wine by inducing the precipitation of particles that might otherwise cloud it. The sediment in an older bottle of red wine reflects in part the work of the tannins in it. Again, balance is important. Too much tannin makes a wine astringent and unpleasant, and too little causes it to be dull. The skin, furthermore, contributes to the aroma or bouquet of the wine, because aromatic substances are contained in it.

The seeds or pips, normally four per berry, vary considerably in size and proportion of the grape. They, too, contain small amounts of tannin that may be added to the juice. The stems often are separated from the grapes before fermentation, since they also contain some tannin and their presence may exceed desired levels. They are usually retained when white wines are made, since the tannin-poor white skins do not contribute to the juice as the red skins do, and the tannin is useful in the wine's clearing.

The dissection of the grape is an integral part of the analysis of legacies: what has been contributed by each participating variety in a métis or hybrid? Has an undesirable aroma been minimized or reduced? Has the acid level improved? Is the skin less susceptible to sunburn during ripening?

Thus the grapevine reveals its heritage. When a hybrid is created, the new variety will acquire some of the characteristics of each "parent," including not only the measurable qualities just discussed but also such properties as disease resistance, temperature tolerance, and so forth. When two known varieties are involved in the hybrid, the sources of the hybrid's properties are easily discerned. When the hybrid's origins involve three or even more ancestries, this becomes much more difficult. And when a variety is found whose antecedents are unknown, the search for its parentage may require true ampelographic detective work.

Vitis vinifera

The varieties of the single species *Vitis vinifera* produce the great wine grapes. These are the grapes of the familiar cultivars: the Rieslings, the Cabernet Sauvignons, the Pinot Noirs, the Chardonnays. It is appropriate to use the plural, because there is not just one, but several Rieslings, and more than one kind of Pinot Noir. Thus another aspect of ampelography: the way a variety develops a large number of closely related but not absolutely identical individuals or clones. In France, such an assemblage is called a *cépage*. Although it is said that *the* Pinot Noir is the great grape of Burgundy, several dozen Pinots have been identified in the Côte d'Or alone, and it has been suggested that there may be as many as a thousand representatives in the Pinot cépage today.[8]

This leads directly from ampelography to ampelogeography. The differentiation within a cépage, however subtle, has much to do with the varying environments under which members of the "family" develop. It is reflected by the various geographical names attached to many of the members, such as Pinot Noir d'Ambonnay, Pinot Noir d'Aunis, and Pinot Noir Bouzy. Over time, a grapevine adjusts to its environment, and this adjustment is obvious enough to be recognized and recorded. Over time, also, environments change (see Chapter 4), and again the grapevine responds. The result is a set of grapevines whose similarities and common properties are far stronger than its differences—but whose differences are sufficient to be noted.

In more general terms, the diffusion of cultivars of *Vitis vinifera* to environments that appeared (to the growers) to be approximately analogous to those of Western and Southern Europe proved more pointedly the sensitivity of particular grapevines to specific environmental conditions. A combination of climate, soil, and slope conditions similar to that of parts of the Bordeaux region proved to be no guarantee that Cabernet Sauvignon grapes would develop as well or yield comparable wines in California or Australia. Often the skills and talents of grower and winemaker overcame disadvantageous environments and produced remarkable wines that might not be equivalent to their European counterparts, but had quality and distinction nevertheless. And in some instances the environments of the New World proved to be at least as suitable as those of the Old, for certain varieties of *vinifera*. Whatever its uncertain origins (Hungary or Italy?) the Zinfandel does as well or better in parts of California than it does anywhere else in the world, and yields a characterful, long-lived wine.

Another consequence of the diffusion of *vinifera* relates to the apparent adaptation of certain varieties to new environments. Among seedlings introduced at an early stage in South Africa was the Chenin Blanc, the white grape of France's Loire Valley. In South Africa's Cape Province the Chenin Blanc was grown under conditions of greater summer heat and less moisture, but the vine thrived, producing a grape of high acid as well as sugar content, superior, in the view of many specialists, to the original. No attempt was made to hybridize or "clone" the vine; over the long period of adaptation it adjusted to its South African environment. It is known today not as Chenin Blanc but as Steen (sometimes Stein) and is used in making very good dry wines as well as sherry-type wines.

It may be assumed that time is an ally of the Steen as well as other varieties introduced or relocated comparatively recently. In any case, adaptations of this kind have much to do with the continuing debate among ampelographers and oenologists over the exact identities of certain grapes. Is the Grenache of France still the same grape as Spain's Garnacho (one of Rioja's most important varieties)? Is Italy's Trebbiano, the grape of some of its better-known white wines, still the same as the Ugni Blanc of France? Obviously these ampelographic questions have biogeographical dimensions.

Such ampelogeographical aspects are perhaps best subsumed under the rubric of "regional association." The Pinot Noir of Burgundy, the Cabernet Sauvignon of Bordeaux, the Zinfandel of California, the Gamay of Beaujolais, the Riesling of Germany—these are just a few prominent regional relationships between grape and territory. Except for the Zinfandel, which came to its California home comparatively recently, these are old (in some instances even ancient) regional associations. Early Roman viticulturists described a cultivar of Gaul that is unmistakably the Pinot Noir. The Riesling may have stood in Germany sixteen centuries ago; it certainly was an established cultivar during the twelfth century. Pliny the Elder during the first century A.D. described a grapevine that probably was Bordeaux's Cabernet Sauvignon. But not all successful regional associations have such distant origins, nor do they invariably involve established varieties of *vinifera*. In South Africa, for example, a cross between the Pinot Noir and the Hermitage (the local name for the French grape known as Cinsaut) produced a cultivar called the Pinotage. This cultivar, whose grapes ripen early and have high sugar and acid content, can withstand intense sunlight and high heat; the vine is resistant to diseases and can survive the strong winds that sometimes buffet the vineyards of the Cape, where it was developed during the 1920s. The Pinotage has become one of the Southern Hemisphere's successes, producing very good wines not only in South Africa but markedly so during the comparatively short, cool summers of New Zealand's North Island. Over time, the Pinotage will evolve and adapt further to its particular environments, producing still better wines. Its success is evidence of the potentials of practical ampelography.

Prominent Cultivars of *Vitis Vinifera*

The cultivated varieties of *vinifera* may number about twelve dozen, but the world's great or good wines come from a much smaller group of distinguished cultivars. Some of these varieties, as has been noted, have become identified with the regions where their success has been greatest; others have emerged comparatively recently, and their wines are still gaining recognition.

Any grouping or listing of cultivars is arbitrary and noncomprehensive. Grapes and wines can be categorized on several bases, but no such scheme is completely satisfactory. One obvious grouping divides "red" (and blue, purple, and black) wine grapes from "white" grapes, but white wine is made from both dark- and light-skinned grapes. Another possibility is to group varieties according to distinctive flavors of the wine they generate, but this is a subjective basis that loses much of its validity beyond the sweet-dry differentiation. Geographical (regional) factors also are not useful, because the mosaic of cultivars is so complex that generalization is impractical. Hence the cultivars are grouped here on the most obvious basis: the color of the skins of the mature grapes.*

Red (Dark) Cultivars

Cabernet Sauvignon

Pride of place among red cultivars must be given to the Cabernet Sauvignon, the grape of the great (and lesser) chateaux of the Bordeaux region (Fig. 2.11). This is a relatively small, tough-skinned grape high in sugar and acid content, resistant to damage and disease, late-ripening, and capable of yielding a noble wine that improves with age. The Cabernet Sauvignon still produces at its best in the region of its historic emergence, on the banks of the Gironde River in Southwestern France, but it also does well in other regions of the world. California's Cabernets, notably from the Napa and Sonoma-Alexander valleys, have taken their place among the world's finest. Chilean wines in which the Cabernet is the prime component also have achieved high quality. Some South African Cabernets are superb. In Australia, good years produce magnificent, long-lived vintages, with the Cabernet-Shiraz blend a major achievement. In New Zealand the Cabernet Sauvignon has proved itself capable of good results. And this great grape contributes to viticulture in numerous other countries, including Argentina, Italy, Yugoslavia, Romania, even Bulgaria. In its home region, Bordeaux, the Cabernet Sauvignon is most often blended with other red wines, producing the special flavor and character for which particular chateaux are famed. Elsewhere, however, the wine identified as Cabernet Sauvignon on the label is likely to have been made of 100 percent Cabernet grapes, or very nearly so. Such wines may possess an initial astringency or sharpness that is mellowed by years of aging in wood and bottle.

It should be noted that the noble Cabernet Sauvignon is not only blended with "softer" grapes such as the Merlot, but also has been crossed to produce new and interesting varieties. With the prolific Carignane of France it becomes the Ruby Cabernet, a productive cultivar whose grapes make soft, pleasant wines. A combination of the Cabernet and the Grenache plus the Merlot has produced the Carmine, a variety that has, among its merits, the retention of a strong Cabernet flavor while ripening earlier than its parent

---

*Two dark-skinned varieties, the Thompson Seedless and the Mission, will be discussed in later chapters.

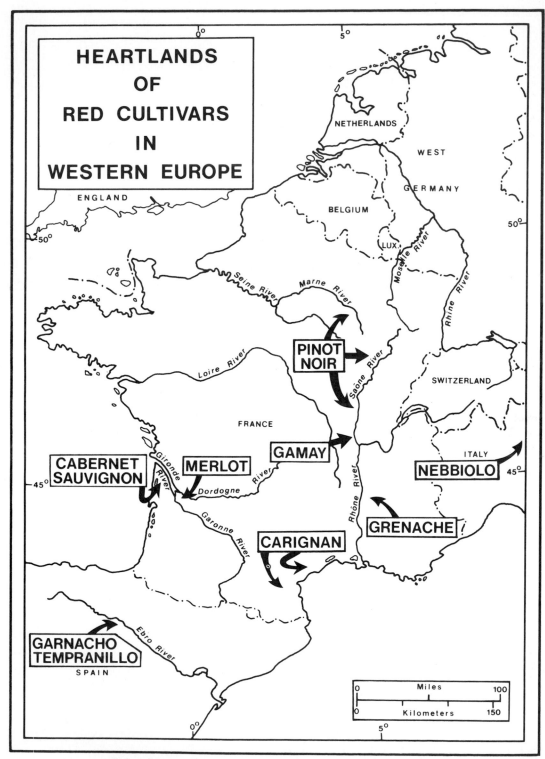

Figure 2.11 Heartlands of Red Cultivars in Western Europe

and showing a stronger resistance to disease. Such experimentation continues, with promising results.

Pinot Noir

Many oenophiles would rank the great red grape of Burgundy, the Pinot Noir, as equivalent—or even superior—to the Cabernet Sauvignon, and its wines, the great Burgundies, as better even than the magnificent Bordeaux. In fact, each wine has its particular character, and such comparisons are matters of personal preference. The Pinot Noir as a cultivar is rather less hardy than the Cabernet, and it matures somewhat earlier. It not only creates the noble Burgundies, but also is used in the making of the world's best champagnes. Cultivating the Pinot Noir is a challenge, because its early ripening demands timely and quick harvesting; the grapes are very susceptible to sunburn if not picked promptly when ripe.

Given the great wines the Pinot Noir produces in Burgundy, it is not surprising that this cultivar has been planted in many other areas of the world, not only in Europe (Germany, Italy, Austria, Switzerland, and farther east), but also in California, Oregon, and Washington, in Chile and Argentina, in South Africa, Australia, and New Zealand. But the sensitive Pinot Noir has not adapted to these distant environments as well as the Cabernet. California's success with the Cabernet Sauvignon has not yet been matched by similar achievements with the Pinot Noir, although such an accomplishment may now be in sight. The diffusion of the cultivar northward into Oregon and Washington is an interesting development, considering Burgundy's northern location in Western Europe (Fig. 2.11). In the Southern Hemisphere, no truly notable wines have come from Pinot Noir plantings. In Australia, only a few dozen hectares stand under Pinot Noir; in New Zealand the Pinot Noir has produced promising wines.

Thus Burgundy's monopoly over quality continues. Unlike Bordeaux wines, the Pinot Noir is the sole ingredient of the great Burgundies, and no blending takes place. The Burgundies reach their full development rather more rapidly than the finest Bordeaux wines, usually within a decade of the vintage and sometimes earlier still.

The quality and character of the Pinot Noir have led to attempts at crossing and hybridization, but the only noteworthy result remains the Pinotage of South Africa, still cultivated successfully only at the Cape and on New Zealand's North Island. It is as though the temperamental Pinot Noir is unwilling to dilute the strength of its historic regional association.

Zinfandel

Surely one of the most remarkable modern viticultural developments (compared to the almost ageless Cabernet and Pinot) is the emergence of the Zinfandel in California. This is a recent story recorded in decades, not centuries. The Zinfandel appeared in California in 1852, when viticulture in that still-remote area was being promoted by several pioneers, among whom the colorful "Count" Agoston Haraszthy was the leader. Haraszthy often is credited with this introduction, and it is possible that he did bring the Zinfandel from his native Hungary or some other European source area.

In any event, Haraszthy recognized the Zinfandel's potential in California very quickly, and as its hectarage expanded, he wrote enthusiastically about its prospects as California's answer to Europe's "clarets." Today, just twelve decades later, no red cultivar in California commands a larger hectarage, and aging Zinfandels rank among California's (and the world's) finest wines.

The origin and diffusion of the Zinfandel is an ampelogeographic problem that has defied solution for a long time, although "final" answers have been announced repeatedly. If Haraszthy brought this vine to California, he left no indication of its European source. Some oenologists have suggested that the Zinfandel possibly came to America from (or via) Spain, with Cortez and his invaders of Mexico; that it was brought to California, along with other *vinifera* varieties, as the missions were established there. Another opinion was that the Zinfandel grew as early as the 1830s in nurseries in New York and several northeastern states, whence it was carried to California. But the Zinfandel, meticulous analysis notwithstanding, did not release its secret; nothing in America or Europe exactly matched its properties. Then, in the late 1960s, a chance observation by a visiting American botanist of a Southern Italian variety, the Primitivo di Gioia, led to its introduction to California for comparative purposes. The Primitivo's leaves, bunches, grapes, and other characteristics appeared so similar to the Zinfandel's that such an experiment was clearly warranted. The results appear to confirm the relationship—but this is not the first time that the ultimate solution to the Zinfandel's riddle has been proclaimed.

The Zinfandel ripens early, and its susceptibility to overripening and sunburn is revealed by the cracked and raisined grapes amid the bunch. Under the optimum conditions of the relatively cool near-coastal valleys of California, and under methods of vinification as careful as those of Bordeaux and Burgundy, the Zinfandel yields magnificent wines of depth and complexity, wines that improve in the bottle for decades. But even under less than ideal conditions, the Zinfandel proves its versatility by producing a wide variety of wines ranging from pleasant rosés to fruity, Beaujolais-style reds, and even acceptable whites.

California's success with the Zinfandel has not been repeated in other regions. No significant cultivation of this variety occurs anywhere in the Southern Hemisphere, although experiments are in progress. And if the Primitivo of Southern Italy is indeed the same grape as the Zinfandel, its wines cannot match those of its California relative. Most wine derived from the Primitivo serves as bulk, blending wine, whose identity is lost long before it is bottled.

Gamay

The principle of regional association is also underscored by the Gamay, the cultivar that yields the unique wines of Beaujolais. The Gamay ripens comparatively early in the season, and its wines can be deep, dark, rich, and early-maturing. Its most popular wines, however, are the lighter, fruity, easy-drinking wines that are consumed as soon as they reach the market. At the southern end of the Burgundy region the Gamay creates wines on its favorite granite hillslopes in a manner it equals nowhere else in the world.

The Gamay, it should be noted, is another complicated cépage that

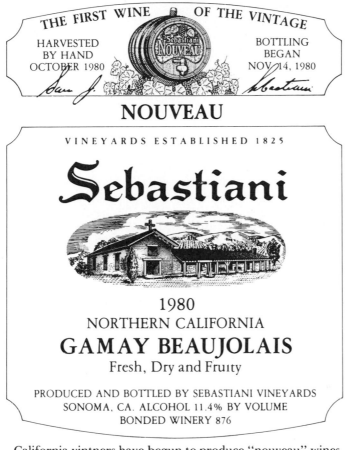

THE FIRST WINE   OF THE VINTAGE

HARVESTED
BY HAND
OCTOBER 1980

BOTTLING
BEGAN
NOV. 14, 1980

NOUVEAU

VINEYARDS ESTABLISHED 1825

Sebastiani

1980
NORTHERN CALIFORNIA
GAMAY BEAUJOLAIS
Fresh, Dry and Fruity

PRODUCED AND BOTTLED BY SEBASTIANI VINEYARDS
SONOMA, CA. ALCOHOL 11.4% BY VOLUME
BONDED WINERY 876

California vintners have begun to produce "nouveau" wines for early consumption, in the manner of Beaujolais. Among leaders in this venture is the winery of Sebastiani, whose Gamay Beaujolais has attracted attention and gained popularity.

includes a host of clones. Differences that are subtle in field and laboratory are beyond doubt when it comes to the Gamay's wines. In the case of Beaujolais, ampelogeography takes an ironic twist. The name of the grapevine that makes the popular young Beaujolais (the *nouveau*, consumed in the very year the grapes are harvested and the wine made), is the Gamay *noir à jus blanc*. But another Gamay, the Gamay *noir à jus coloré*, is prohibited by law from cultivation in Beaujolais, being regarded as inferior. To complicate matters still further, a grape grown widely in Beaujolais and used in the darker, longer-lasting *grand crus* of Beaujolais and in the so-called Beaujolais Villages (see Chapter 8), probably is not a Gamay at all but a member of the Pinot Noir family. This cultivar was transplanted to California, where it was named "Gamay Beaujolais" on wine labels. When the French objected to this name, the issue came under study and it was realized that the nomenclature was indeed proper and that, in this case, the California winemakers were naming their wine after the grape, not the French region. That a member of the Pinot Noir cépage should constitute a major component

of wines made in Gamay-dominated Beaujolais—and that the French themselves had not realized it until the dispute with California brought it to
light—was a source of some embarrassment in France.

Nevertheless, the wines of Beaujolais remain unique, and the Gamay *noir*
makes them so. The cultivars of Beaujolais may grow in California, and
even do well there. But the special character of true Beaujolais retains its
regional identity.

Syrah

A European transplant that has proved itself to be more versatile in overseas
environments is one that also has been given several names: Syrah (or Serine)
in France's Rhône region; Shiraz (or Hermitage) in Australia; and Shiraz
(but *not* Hermitage, which refers to a different grape) in South Africa. In
California a cultivar named Petite Sirah was for some time thought to be
the same variety, but this appears now to be incorrect. The Syrah contributes
a certain pungency to the taste of wines from France's Rhône region, and
in South Africa and Australia it is bottled unblended as a rich, fruity wine
or blended with other wines. Australian winemakers have been especially
successful in combining Shiraz with Cabernet Sauvignon. The Shiraz also
is used in the creation of a port wine in Australia.

Grenache (Garnacho)

Another French cultivar that has been disseminated quite widely is the
Grenache of the Rhône region, a crucial ingredient of Châteauneuf-du-Pape
wines (Fig. 2.11). Actually, the Grenache appears to have spread after the
twelfth century from its original home in Spain into Southern France. In
the Rhône Valley it attained its modern character, and then, during the
nineteenth century, it was reintroduced into Spain. In Spain, the Grenache
has since become an important ingredient of Rioja wines and is known as
the Garnacho (also Garnacha). Here is one of those instances where geographic
relocation has changed the character of the wine and its grapes. The Garnacho
may still be the same as the Grenache in ampelographic terms, but not
viticulturally. It also grows successfully in California, where it yields good
rosés; in Australia, where it figures importantly in red "jug" wines; and, to
a lesser degree, in South Africa, where it is susceptible to the downy mildew
disease and is less popular.

Other Red Cultivars

Among numerous other red cultivars grown in Europe and transplanted to
the New World and beyond are several that thrive in new habitats as well
as source areas. In the Bordeaux region, five cultivars may be blended with
Cabernet Sauvignon. One of these is the Merlot, which matures earlier and
can stand alone as a soft, generous wine. It is the dominant varietal in the
Bordeaux district of Pomerol, and elsewhere in the Bordeaux region the
soft, fruity and nonastringent Merlot contributes importantly to the roundness
of the Cabernet Sauvignon–dominated reds. In Northern Italy, Southern

Switzerland, cooler areas of California, the Stellenbosch area of South Africa, and (recently) in Australia the Merlot is cultivated with good results. The Cabernet Franc ripens somewhat earlier and has a lower sugar content than Cabernet Sauvignon, and it also can produce a high-quality wine; in many respects it is similar to its more famous relative. The Verdot (or Petit Verdot) is one of those unusual cultivars that thrives in a good, deep, fertile soil (see Chapter 4), and it has not been disseminated successfully to other major wine regions. The Malbec can produce a soft, pleasant wine, and it is the principal cultivar of the enormous vineyards of Argentina. The Malbec in Australia is subject to *coulure* (imperfect setting of the fruit, usually because of bad weather during the flowering season), and it has not reached its full potential there or in South Africa. The Carmenère, fifth of the Bordeaux cultivars used for blending, remains a local variety and does not appear in New World or Southern Hemisphere vineyards.

France's most productive and most widely grown cultivar is not the Cabernet Sauvignon or the Pinot Noir, but the Carignan (Carignane in California). This variety does not produce a characterful wine, but it bears heavily and reliably and is much used as a blend. From Southern France (it is the leading grape of the Midi) the Carignan has spread to Spain, to Algeria and its neighbors, to Israel, to California, and, to a very limited extent, to South Africa and Australia. Although the Carignan grape tends to rot in humid weather and is susceptible to oidium and downy mildew, these problems are minimized under the hot, dry summer conditions of Mediterranean regimes. Its limited diffusion to South Africa and Australia is surprising.

Certain European grape varieties contribute crucially to the production of prestigious regional wines but have not established themselves in other world areas. The important grape of Rioja (Spain), the Tempranillo, may contribute 50 percent or more of a Rioja wine. The Tempranillo is a robust wine whose grapes ripen rather early. Alcohol levels, however, are not as high as those of the Garnacho, and neither is acidity as strong. The Tempranillo alone, therefore, would yield a wine that would be rather "soft" and lifeless; the Garnacho (and the Graciano and Mazuelo) confer freshness, flavor, and aroma upon the finished wine. Rather more self-reliant is Italy's Sangiovese, the grape of Tuscany and hence of Chianti wines, also a major ingredient of other prestigious Tuscan wines such as the Montepulcianos. Here is another strong regional association: the Sangiovese is vigorous and productive in Tuscany, the grapes ripen in mid-season, the bunches are of good size and well filled, acid balance is good, flavor is pleasant. But the Sangiovese has not done as well even in Italy beyond Tuscany; although some hectares have been tried in California, the Sangiovese has not become the mainstay of California's "Chiantis." Again, another Italian variety, the Nebbiolo, grows in the Piedmont and in Lombardy, where it is the basis of Barolo, Barbaresco, and some Valtellina wines. The Nebbiolo produces red, full-bodied wines of depth and flavor, and these are among Italy's best. They are known to age splendidly, and Barolos have been favorably compared to France's Northern Rhône wines (including Châteauneuf-du-Pape). And yet the Nebbiolo has not succeeded to any substantial extent beyond its European regional base.

On the other hand, Italy's Barbera, a noteworthy variety that produces a long-lived, dark-purple wine high in acid, has become one of California's more useful cultivars. Although its juice is often used for blending, California

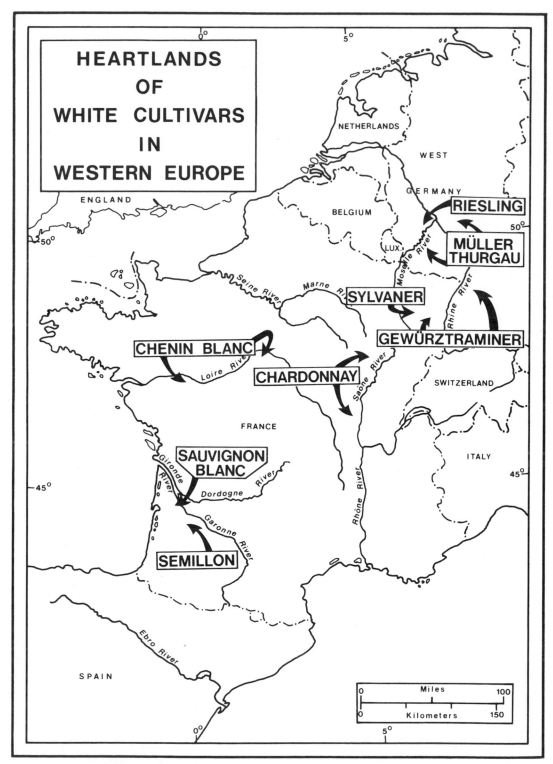

Figure 2.12 Heartlands of White Cultivars in Western Europe

Barbera is bottled also as a varietal wine. The Grignolino, another cultivar from Italy's Northwest, has been introduced in California as well, although in smaller quantity than the Barbera. The Grignolino is known for the special color of its wine, best described as pink-orange, unmistakably different from the usual rosé wine.

Last but not least, among the red cultivars should be mentioned the Muscat grape. This is the descendant of the grapes planted along Mediterranean shores by the ancient Greeks, and it was the basis for the first wine industry not only in Italy and France, but, much later, in South Africa and Australia as well. Sweet wines withstood the times better than dry, and the Muscat always was hardy and disease-resistant. At one time the Constantia estate of South Africa produced a highly valued Muscadel for European markets. Still today, the Muscat grape yields sweet wines from Portugal to Greece and Hungary and from California to Australia. It has dozens of subvarieties ranging in color from dark purple to light yellow, and predictably the many members of this extensive cépage also have numerous names.

White (Light) Cultivars

Just as two dark-skinned grape varieties produce the two noblest of red wines, so two light-skinned cultivars create the greatest of whites. Which of these two should rank at the top of a hierarchy depends, again, upon personal taste and preference: one of the great white grapes makes a magnificent dry wine, the other a series of unparalleled sweet wines.

Chardonnay

The Chardonnay, the premium white grape of Burgundy and California, produces the dry whites for which these regions are famous. In France, the sensitive and modest-bearing Chardonnay stands not only in the Southern Côte d'Or, where it creates the magnificent Montrachets, but also in Champagne, in Chablis, and, south of the Côte d'Or, in the Mâconnais, the Châlonnais, and even in Beaujolais (Fig. 2.12). Again the members of the Chardonnay cépage adjust and adapt to the various environments expressed by these regional names, and their wines range from the flinty, straw-shaded Chablis to the soft, golden, complex Montrachets, and back again to the assertive Pouilly Fuissés.

The Chardonnay is quite susceptible to disease and injury, which, in addition to its habit of low yield, has contributed to the vine's rather slow diffusion from its source area. At present there is just one (other) region where it has achieved noteworthy, even great success: the slopes of the cooler, coastal counties of Northern California. There, the Chardonnay creates wines which, at their best, are comparable to the noblest of white Burgundies. California Chardonnay hectarage is rising steadily, and the region's success with Burgundy's Chardonnay is comparable to its achievements with the Cabernet Sauvignon of Bordeaux.

No other world wine-producing region has matched California's accomplishments with the Chardonnay. Some interesting Chardonnays have been made in New York State, and there are plantings in countries of Eastern Europe, in the Soviet Union, in Chile (where some good wines have been made with it), in Argentina (where its juice is used as a blend), in South Africa and Australia (where it is beginning to develop), and in New Zealand (where the cool North Island environment promises a bright future for this cultivar). Again, the modification that comes with distance and time and new environments should be taken into account. The Chardonnay of Chile or New Zealand may be clones of, but not identical to, the great cultivar of the Côte d'Or.

Riesling

In a class with the Chardonnay is the Riesling of Germany's Rhine region, also called the True Riesling, the Rhine Riesling, the White Riesling, and the Johannisberg Riesling (because it yields the famous wines of Schloss Johannisberg in Germany's Rheingau). The Riesling has grown in its German region of origin since Roman times, and although it has been transplanted all over the world it still produces its best wines at its source (Fig. 2.12). There, the Riesling's most aristocratic wines result from the grape's unique relationship with the *Edelfäule, pourriture noble* or noble rot, a disease (*botrytis cinerea*) that actually enhances the wine. Ripe grapes are left on the vine, and *botrytis* attacks the weakening skins, causing fine cracks to form. Water seeps from the grapes and evaporates; normally the grapes would simply rot away. But under the particular conditions of the Rhine and Mosel valleys the grapes slowly turn into raisinlike berries, rich in sugar. These are carefully, individually harvested and pressed, resulting in a juice that has 35 to 40 percent sugar, about double the sugar content of juice derived from pre-*botrytis* grapes. From this juice is made a rich sweet wine that is widely regarded as the best of its kind made in the world.

Many wines labeled Riesling are not in fact made this way; most are not even made from the True Riesling grape. The White Riesling does grow and make excellent wine in the vineyards of Alsace (adjacent to the Rhine region but in neighboring France), in Switzerland, in Austria, and in Northern Italy, and it has been planted in California and in all the major Southern Hemisphere regions. But nowhere—not even in California—are the grapes affected by the noble rot picked by hand, individually, or the resulting wines graded by sweetness as they are in Germany. California's Johannisberg Riesling, for example, may be a late-harvest Riesling, and it may be dry or pleasingly sweet, but it cannot yet be compared to Germany's best. Again, Chile's "Riesling" often is made from the Sylvaner, a cultivar also called the Franken Riesling but not a Riesling at all; Australia's "Riesling" (on the label) may well be a Sémillon in the bottle.

Not only does the True Riesling have a host of relatives, therefore; it also has a whole crowd of neighbors called Riesling of one kind or another— none of which is in fact a real Riesling. Some of these neighbors do have a claim to partial Riesling ancestry, for example the Emerald Riesling (a cross between the True Riesling and a Muscadel). Others simply capitalize on the True Riesling's reputation, such as the so-called "Italian" Riesling, one of a group of *Wälschrieslings* that goes by various names, which is not a Riesling, and probably came from France, not the Rhine-Moselle region. In recent years official action has been taken by the European Community (EC) to end the use of such misleading designations.

Sylvaner

Among the True Riesling's neighbors—ampelographically as well as geographically—is the Sylvaner (Silvaner in Germany), planted on even larger areas in Germany than the Riesling itself. Not only does the Sylvaner contribute importantly to German wines (it, too, is subject to the noble rot), but it also stands extensively in Alsace, Switzerland, Austria, and Northern Italy, in smaller locales in Eastern Europe, in California (to a limited extent), and in Southern Hemisphere vineyards. It produces its best wines in Germany's Franken (Franconia) region, hence its erroneous name Franken Riesling; in California it bears generously, but the grapes lack Riesling's acidity and distinctive flavor. Perhaps the strongest regional association involves its position in Alsace, where the Sylvaner has been elevated to "noble" status. But Alsatian wines from the Sylvaner are not impressive.

Müller-Thurgau

Given the True Riesling's remarkable qualities it is not surprising that numerous attempts at crossing and hybridization have been made. The best-known among these still is the Müller-Thurgau, one of those cultivars which, while familiar, also pose ampelographic questions. In this case the Müller-Thurgau has long been thought to be one result of numerous experiments carried out by a Swiss viticulturist in the 1880s, producing a cross between the True Riesling and a Sylvaner. Decades later, ampelographers began to doubt the grape's origin, on the basis of its recorded properties and those of its supposed parents. Experiments to recreate the cultivar failed to match the original, and it has been concluded that the Müller-Thurgau is in fact a cross between slightly different members of the Riesling cépage. The source of the cultivar's name is even in doubt. Swiss officials have objected to the use of the name Thurgau (which is the name of a Canton) for the grape, since such regional designations are disapproved under EC rules. But the German response has been that Thurgau was the maiden name of Müller's wife, and that while there is a coincidence, Müller-Thurgau is a perfectly legal name for the variety. Whatever the doubts surrounding the Müller-Thurgau, it has become Germany's most widely planted variety—not because of its breed, but because it contributes hugely to Germany's ordinary table wines, being productive and reliable if somewhat low in acid. A more nearly perfect environment for the Müller-Thurgau may yet be found. In New Zealand it makes light and quite delicate dry wines, and can be vinified into an even better, slightly sweet wine.

Sémillon

If there is a competitor for the True Riesling's great wines it comes from Bordeaux, from the Sauternes district, where the Sémillon grape also is subject to the noble rot. The Sémillon is the grape that produces the famed wines of Château d'Yquem, and here it reaches its zenith; it may have stood in this area twenty centuries ago. Today's great Sauternes are blended wines, with a majority of Sémillon plus some Sauvignon Blanc and a small amount of a Muscadel. In turn, the Sémillon contributes somewhat to the good dry wines of Graves nearby.

The Sémillon has proved to be adaptable and versatile, but by itself it produces rather ordinary wines. When interplanted or blended, however, it contributes significantly to some excellent wines, not only in Bordeaux but also in California, in Chile, in South Africa, and in Australia. In Australia, it has been the basis for many Hunter Valley wines of high reputation.

Sauvignon Blanc

The leading white cultivar of the Bordeaux region, the Sauvignon Blanc, creates the outstanding dry white wines of Graves and contributes to the sweet wines of Sauternes. But the Sauvignon Blanc is no Riesling, nor a Chardonnay; it is a great but not a superb cultivar. This is a strong and productive cultivar, and it has spread into the Loire Valley of France, where it is called the Blanc-Fumé and produces such wines as Pouilly-Fumé and Sancerre. Transplanted to California, the Sauvignon Blanc at first did not do well, but as viticultural and vinicultural technologies improved so did the wines derived from this variety. Today it has come into its own, its wines called Sauvignon Blanc and Fumé Blanc and quite distinctive in character.

Chenin Blanc

The Chenin Blanc is the predominant grape of the Loire Valley (it is sometimes called, improperly, Pineau de la Loire), the white grape of Anjou and Touraine. It makes Vouvray in France and some excellent, intense, fragrant wines in California (where it is also misnamed Pinot Blanc and White Pinot). The Chenin Blanc is an ancient cultivar, like the Riesling, and it was disseminated to distant lands at an early stage of viticulture's world-wide diffusion. In Australia it never took hold to any real extent, but in South Africa it became the leading white grape. At the Cape the Chenin Blanc, over time, adapted to its new environment by becoming, in effect, a different variety—the Steen. It "changed so much that it does most things better than its parent does in France . . . is resistant to most crop hazards, bears well, is a strong grower [and] makes wine high in both sugar and acid [with] a rich flavor and a recognizable flowery bouquet."[9]

Other White Cultivars

The Ugni Blanc, grown extensively in Southwestern and Southern France, is a white cultivar with less character than the Chenin Blanc. In Italy the Ugni Blanc is called the Trebbiano, an ingredient of Soave whites, and in the Cognac area of France it is known as the St. Emilion. Nowhere does the Ugni Blanc achieve distinction, although it does well in Australia (where it is also called the White Hermitage). In Australia as elsewhere, the Ugni Blanc's wines are blended with fruitier wines to produce pleasant if undistinguished whites. This cultivar is grown in California's Livermore Valley, and in South Africa it stands in the irrigated vineyards of the Little Karroo. In France, in addition to its use for table wines, the Ugni Blanc is now the chief ingredient of Cognacs, replacing the long-used Folle Blanche.

In Colombar (also Colombier in France and French Colombard in California), also grown in the Cognac area of France, lies one of the success stories of viticulture's diffusion. The Colombar yields an adequate white wine (its high acidity enables distillation, hence its popularity in Cognac), but it is a versatile cultivar; today it is California's leading white grape by total hectarage under cultivation (about 20,000 hectares in 1983, well above the Zinfandel). Its wine is sold as French Colombard, as "chablis" in jugs, and as an ingredient in mass-produced "champagnes." In South Africa's irrigated vineyards the Colombar produces surprisingly sound wines, but it is not grown in Australia.

The Pinot family of grapes is represented among the whites by Pinot Blanc and the Pinot Gris (or Rülander). Neither cultivar reaches the heights of the Pinot Noir among the reds, but under suitable environmental conditions both can yield good wines. Grown fairly widely in Europe, and (in the case of the Pinot Blanc) transplanted to California, the white Pinots have not succeeded nearly as well as the Chenin Blanc in the New World.

Among distinctive white cultivars is the Gewürztraminer, also called the Traminer, a grape with a checkered history. Its origins may lie in Eastern Europe; it was once Germany's chief cultivar, until the potentials of the Riesling became evident. Then the Gewürztraminer declined in the Rhine region, but it held on in France's Alsace, whence its best wines now come. The Traminer yields an especially spicy, pungent, but sweet wine, distinctive and unmistakable and, at its best, full of character. It loses something of this character in areas beyond Alsace (Tyrol, Eastern Europe, California), but on occasion it suddenly produces a superb vintage. California's Gewürztraminers have tended to be somewhat low in acid, but improvement is occurring; and noteworthy Traminers have recently come from cooler slopes of Oregon and Washington, perhaps a sign of things to come. Chilean Traminers are yet uneven; Australia's production began in the 1960s, and in New Zealand experimentation continues. The future for the Gewürztraminer obviously is bright.

The problem of name identification is perhaps nowhere better exemplified than by the so-called Tokay wines. In the first place, the true Tokay comes not from a Tokay cultivar, but from the Furmint (and Hárslevelü) varieties grown in a small district in northeast Hungary's Carpathian Mountains called Tokaj-Hegyalja. The wine is often described as a sweet, powerful essence; it is unique and, at its best, unparalleled. Nevertheless, "Tokay" wines of doubtful origin are made—in Europe, America, and Australia—allegedly from Hungarian grapes, but not the Furmint. Australia's "Tokay" probably came from Austria.[10] California's "Tokay" is a pink dessert wine consisting of ruby port, California sherry, and angelica (a white sweet wine) in approximately equal amounts.[11]

Of course the Muscat varieties are represented among the white cultivars, notably by the Frontignan, a superior cultivar that yields a golden, sweet wine of great distinction in its native habitat near France's Mediterranean coast. Transplanted to California, it produces an unattractive, rather dry white wine; nowhere else does it reach a quality comparable to the French version. The Palomino, on the other hand, has been disseminated throughout the world, and under numerous different names, often producing very good wines. This is the cultivar that forms the basis for Spain's great sherries, and it makes good "sherries" in California also. In South Africa it was introduced for the same purpose, but it proved to be excellent for the region's quality brandies and even produces some table wines as well. In Australia the Palomino is among the ten leading white varieties and is used for various vinicultural purposes.

Crosses and Hybrids

The sensitivity of many varieties of *vinifera* to environmental extremes in their region of occurrence has quite naturally led to numerous attempts to cross and hybridize vines, thus to produce new cultivars with desired characteristics. Such new cultivars might better be able to withstand late frosts, heat, humidity, winter cold, or other threats to less-tolerant varieties. Literally thousands of combinations have been tried, and many natural métis have been identified and experimentally cultivated for these purposes. Some of them hold promise not only for established vineyard regions, but also for developing viticulture areas in Great Plains states and other frontier zones.

A problem with these emerging varieties is their nomenclature. First, they tend to have unfamiliar names and, second, the origin of the names and numbers with which they are identified is complicated. Many of these varieties are French-American hybrids, some arising naturally in France as a result of the presence of North American species amid the *vinifera*, others the result of experimentation. Those developed in France tend to have French-sounding names, such as the De Chaunac, a hybrid brought to North America by a French viticulturist who recognized its considerable potential in cool (eastern) North American climes. A popular red hybrid in many areas of the world, the Baco Noir, was developed by the French hybridizer Maurice Baco; in North America it is called Baco No. 1. Another French name is Seibel, an enormously successful specialist who developed a large number of French-American hybrids which sometimes have more romantic names in France (such as the Aurore) than in the United States (where the same grape is usually called Seibel 5279!).

Seibel 5279 deserves more than passing attention, because this, the Aurora (its Anglicized name also is used), has become the most widely planted of the French white hybrids in New York State and adjacent areas, and the virtues of other Seibels are increasingly recognized. Another French-American hybrid, Seyve-Villard 5276, more pleasantly known as the Seyval, has been gaining on the Aurora and is bottled as a varietal called Seyval-Blanc; it also is used in the creation of good sparkling wines. The Vidal also has succeeded well in Eastern North America, where it produces a distinctive white wine.

Although the issue is debatable, the white hybrids may be said to have succeeded rather more than the red. The Baco Noir, for all its vigor and disease resistance, makes a quite astringent wine that is useful in blending, but not on its own. The De Chaunac under good conditions can yield a pleasant wine, and the Chambourcin has been vinted quite successfully, but on a very limited scale. If volume is evidence, the whites lead by far; their wines, furthermore, are more consistently agreeable.

Serious research into the potentials of hybrids began in America in the

1930s, and additional successes may be anticipated. The frontier of viticulture keeps expanding, a process that has carried the industry into all states of the U.S.A. except Alaska (and it occurs very near peninsular Alaska in British Columbia), in several other areas of Canada, in the United Kingdom, and in Japan's northernmost large island, Hokkaido. Without the hybrids, no such claims could be made.

Additional Reading

On viticulture, ampelography, classification problems, and numerous related topics:

Amerine, M. A.; Berg, H. W.; Kunkee, R. E.; Ough, C. S.; Singleton, V. L.; and Webb, A. D. *The Technology of Wine Making.* 4th ed. Westport: AVI Publishing, 1980.

Amerine, M. A., and Joslyn, M. A. *Table Wines: The Technology of Their Production.* 2nd ed. Berkeley: University of California Press, 1970.

Amerine, M. A., and Singleton, V. L. *Wine: An Introduction.* 2nd ed. Berkeley: University of California Press, 1977.

Galet, P. *A Practical Ampelography.* Translated by L. T. Morton. Ithaca: Cornell University Press, 1979.

Wagner, P. *A Wine-Grower's Guide.* New York: Alfred A. Knopf, 1980.

Weaver, R. J. *Grape Growing.* New York: John Wiley & Sons, 1976.

Winkler, A. J.; Cook, J. A.; Kliewer, W. M.; and Lider, L. A. *General Viticulture.* Berkeley: University of California Press, 1974.

On terminology, definitions, summaries:

Turner, B., and Roycroft, R. *The Winemaker's Encyclopedia.* Boston: Faber & Faber, 1979.

Wile, J. *Frank Schoonmaker's Encyclopedia of Wine.* 7th ed. New York: Hastings House, 1981.

A decorative volume with magnificent illustrations and insightful text:

Ramey, B. C. *The Great Wine Grapes.* Burlington: Great Wine Grapes, Inc., 1977.

3

An Historical Geography
of Viticulture

Although the beginnings of viticulture remain shrouded, there is early evidence of the systematic production and consumption of wine. The domestication of *Vitis vinifera* appears to have occurred in an area located between the southern flanks of the Caucasus Mountains (now in the Southern Soviet Union between the Black and Caspian seas), the highlands of Eastern Turkey, and the Zagros Mountains in Iran. Eight thousand years ago, when the first planned cultivation of grapes may have occurred, this area of Southwest Asia may have had climatic regimes somewhat different from those of today; in general it probably was cooler and perhaps somewhat more humid. The vine that stood there when human communities began to understand the benefits of organized agriculture was *Vitis vinifera silvestris,* and the cultivar that may have yielded the first grapes destined for winemaking was *Sativa.*[1]

Archeological excavations have yielded grape pits, stems, and other evidence that the grape was among the fruits consumed by our distant ancestors. But this does not prove, of course, that wine was being made from these grapes. Certainly it is likely that the process of natural fermentation of wild grapes, with their own yeasts, was discovered as soon as grapes were stored in containers capable of holding liquids. Undoubtedly the result of the consumption of the "wine" (perhaps in excess) was the same as it is today. It was not unreasonable to ascribe intoxication to godly powers. That connection—which was to sustain viticulture and viniculture for thousands of years to follow—was established early.

Historical geographers conclude that viticulture was learned as early as the end of the fourth millennium B.C. by the Mesopotamians. It is certain that wine was exported from Babylonia to Egypt before 3000 B.C.[2] The

Egyptians themselves were growing grapes and making wine by the beginning
of the third millennium B.C., so (since wild vines did not grow in Egypt)
they had imported the plants and acquired the knowledge necessary to
cultivate them. The intermediaries in this diffusion process were the Phoenicians, interconnectors of the Eastern Mediterranean on sea and land. The
kings of Egypt's First Dynasty had large wine cellars, and wine was a crucial
commodity in temple ceremonies. Ancient Egypt's first viticulture, depicted
on so many wall paintings and vessel decorations, was without question
religious and served priests and royalty. These were not vineyards as we
know them today, but "vinegardens . . . the vines were trained on trellises
supported by rafters fixed to columns of brick or stone often finely carved,
and forming many colonnades . . . the vines thus shaded the soil and
minimized loss of water by evaporation."[3] Protected from intruders by walls,
irrigated by water tanks, and meticulously tended, these vinegardens formed
an important element in ancient Egypt's cultural landscape.

The Egyptians made lasting contributions to viticulture, especially when
grape growing ceased to be a monopoly of the privileged. The growers
experimented with simpler structures for the training of vines, developed
ways to plant and prune vines into self-standing, bushy rows, found methods
to induce the soil to retain more precious moisture, and tested the productivity
of different cultivars under various conditions. Their vinicultural methods
also became more sophisticated as time went on. Grapes were treaded in
large vats, but various kinds of wooden wine presses also were created. Heat
was applied to the must (grape juice ready for fermentation) to concentrate
and sweeten the wine, proving that the Egyptian winemakers also were
experimenters. The wine was filtered through cloth and stored in earthen
vessels that were stoppered and sealed with natural tar. The Egyptians of
old kept careful records of their vintages and declared the quality of each
wine on labels attached to the jars.

While Egyptian viticulture developed, the vineyards of Mesopotamia and
adjacent areas also continued to expand. The diffusion routes shown on
Figure 3.1 represent the most generalized directions of dispersal, and there
is no doubt that "reverse" dissemination occurred as well. Some of the
viticultural and vinicultural innovations of Egypt were carried back to the
Middle East, where the vine had become an essential element of agriculture.
It is recorded that a vineyard near the town of Haran in Northern Mesopotamia, early in the second millennium B.C., consisted of nearly 30,000
vines; when the Assyrian state emerged and rose to regional power, its kings
regarded wine (along with food) a strategic commodity that should be denied
to an enemy whenever possible.[4]

During the third millennium B.C. the practice of wine consumption during
religious events, burials, and festivals reached the island of Crete, as did
viticulture itself. These innovations probably came from both Egypt (with
which Crete had much trade contact) and present-day Turkey (Anatolia),
where the cultivation of the vine was in full flower. Again the Phoenicians
undoubtedly played their connective role. It was during the days of Minoan
Crete that the religious cult which gave rise to the Greek god of wine—
Dionysus or Bacchus—probably had its origins. Contact between the Minoans
of Crete and the Mycenaeans of Greece brought Cretan practices to the
Greek mainland, including religious rites and rituals; during the second
millennium B.C. viticulture and the use of wine diffused throughout the
Greek peninsula. When the Greeks became colonialists and extended their

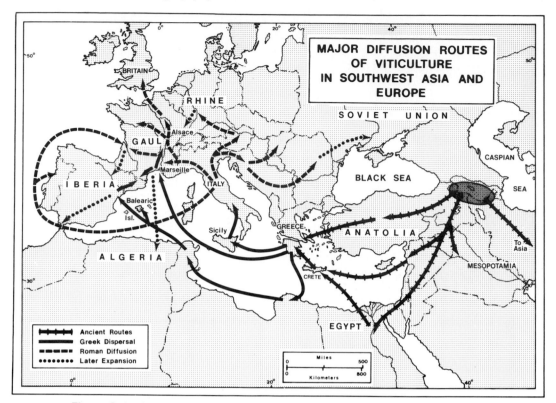

Figure 3.1   Major Diffusion Routes of Viticulture in Southwest Asia and Europe

sphere of influence westward along Mediterranean shores, wine had become an essential ingredient of their culture, and its use spread with them.[5]

The first millennium B.C. witnessed this expansion, as Greek settlements were founded from North Africa to Iberia. During the eighth century B.C. Greek trading posts and (later) towns and agricultural settlements, including Syracuse, were founded on the island of Sicily. The Greeks entered Southern Italy and established their "Magna Graecia"; conflict with the Etruscans of Central Italy led to difficulties with the Phoenicians, who were ensconced in their North African headquarters at Carthage. When the Greeks challenged the Phoenicians in the Western Mediterranean they faced a powerful adversary, but Massilia (modern Marseille) was nevertheless founded at the mouth of the Rhône River about 600 B.C., and the Rhône became an avenue of Greek trade. Greek footholds also succeeded in coastal Eastern Spain and the Balearic Islands, and in North Africa in present-day Libya (at Cyrene, about 632 B.C.).

The Greeks were strong colonizers and merchants, but they were not as effective innovators and teachers as the Romans were to become—at least in fields of agriculture, and notably viticulture. Part of this, undoubtedly, resulted from the comparatively ephemeral character of Greece's western colonies. Massilia remained an important center, but Greek influence along the Rhône trade route declined rather soon. Greek settlements on Iberian shores never became major colonies, although viticulture did begin there about 500 B.C. If there was a challenge to the wine industries of Greece

Oĩνos Ἐρυθρós Ξηρós

Red Dry Wine

ΠΑΡΑΓΩΓΗ - ΕΜΦΙΑΛΩΣΗ: ΕΝΩΣΗ ΠΑΡΑΓΩΓΙΚΩΝ
ΣΥΝΕΤΑΙΡΙΣΜΩΝ ΠΕΖΩΝ ΗΡΑΚΛΕΙΟΥ ΚΡΗΤΗΣ
PRODUCED AND BOTTLED BY: PEZA GROWERS
COOPERATIVES ASS' N. IRAKLION CRETE GREECE
ΑΡΙΘΜΟΣ ΑΔΕΙΑΣ Γ.Χ.Κ 6/1968
ΕΛΛΗΝΙΚΟ ΠΡΟΙΟΝ - PRODUCT OF GREECE
ΠΕΡΙΕΧ. **0,375** L. NET CONT. **12,7** OZ. ALC. **12%** VOL

Wine from an historic heartland of viticulture: the Eastern
Mediterranean. On the island of Crete, viticulture and
viniculture reached new heights as the industry diffused
northward and westward. Archeological sites have yielded
sophisticated wine presses, vessels, and other equipment,
all in use before primacy was yielded to Greece itself.
Modern Cretan wine comes from vineyards some of which
are more than three thousand years old. The motif on this
label relates to the Minoan spectacle of bullfighting, in
which unarmed athletes confronted specially consecrated
bulls, grabbing their horns and somersaulting off their backs
as the animals charged.

itself, it came from the vineyards of Sicily and Magna Graecia, where Greek
occupation reached farthest. Herodotus described Southern Italy under Greek
rule as "Oenotria" (Vineland), and toward the end of Greece's hegemony
in this region the production of wine was indeed prodigious.

During the centuries of Greek supremacy, viticulture in Greece made
significant progress. Reference already has been made to the emergence of
ampelography as a science; in practical fields, the Greeks experimented
widely. They recognized that pruning techniques were the key to wine
quality. They realized that climatic variations had impact on grape as well
as wine. They tried to combine particular environments with specific vines.
Using the resin of Attica's pine trees, they sealed their wine containers,
only to discover that the resin served as a preservative as well; ever since,
Greek wines have been characterized by their resinous taste, still the local
preference. And the best vintages of Thrace and Macedonia were renowned

throughout the realm, high-priced and desired wherever wine was consumed. Even while Roman power grew and Greek influence waned, well into the second century B.C., Greek wines continued to prevail on Mediterranean markets, and knowledgeable Roman consumers preferred Greek wines over their own.

Roman Expansion

The Western European diffusion of viticulture was substantially a Roman achievement, but it was not simply a matter of continuing a course the Greeks had set. The Greeks may have introduced viticulture in Sicily and stimulated its growth in Southern Italy, but viticulture in pre-Roman Italy was indigenous. It has been suggested that the Etruscans, the ancient occupants of Tuscany, learned viticulture from the Greeks, and that the basis of Roman winemaking was thus laid. But the Etruscans knew viticulture and inhabited Tuscany before the Greeks reached Italy, and in view of the prolific wild vines of the peninsula it is (to say the least) highly unlikely that the Etruscans waited for the Greeks to convey the obvious to them. Again the archeological record indicates that the Etruscans made and consumed wine: tell-tale accumulations of pits and stems indicate that grapes were being pressed in volume.

Viticulture in ancient Rome thus had local antecedents, but there was no precedent for what was to happen when Roman viticulture and viniculture evolved as part of the Republic's agricultural base. During Roman times, wine became a mainstay of society, and viticulture a crucial element of farming. Grapes were grown on hundreds of thousands of small farms, wine (ordinary wine, not the expensive Greek vintages) was part of every daily diet, and profits in the emerging industry were high. Quality rose markedly, and during the first century B.C. Roman wines eclipsed their Greek counterparts. But as Rome and other Roman cities and towns grew, demand increased, and so did the concentration of wealth in those urban places. Eventually a process all too familiar to small farmers began: the Roman capitalists bought out the grape growers by the hundreds, consolidated their lands, and created huge wineries that drove remaining private growers out of business. It was the first industrialization of viticulture, and with it began a series of ups and downs that has been experienced in other areas of the world and at other times since. As elsewhere, government intervention ultimately was necessary to save an industry suffering from overproduction, quality decline, diminishing profits, and lack of confidence.

While Rome's domestic wine industry matured, the Roman Empire absorbed most of Western Europe, and viticultural and vinicultural practices diffused as never before. Roman writers chronicled the rise of the industry, and the science of oenology was born. Cato the Elder (234–149 B.C.) produced a treatise on viticulture that includes specifications for the layout of wineries, descriptions of wine presses and other viticultural equipment, and ampelographical notes on grape varieties grown in Roman times. Among Roman viniculture's innovations was the use of wooden barrels for aging wine, a major advancement. Progress also was made in horticultural methods, pest and disease control, and the use of particular cultivars in specific environments. The Roman geographer Pliny, writing in A.D. 70, reported that the Romans

ΡΕΤΣΙΝΑ ΑΤΤΙΚΗΣ

ΟΝΟΜΑΣΙΑ ΚΑΤΑ ΠΑΡΑΔΟΣΗ

1895

ΚΟΥΡΤΑΚΗ

ΠΑΡΑΓΩΓΗ·ΕΜΦΙΑΛΩΣΗ
Δ.ΚΟΥΡΤΑΚΗΣ Α.Ε.
ΜΑΡΚΟΠΟΥΛΟ ΑΤΤΙΚΗΣ
ΑΔ.ΕΜΦ.ΓΧ.Κ.ΠΑΡ ΑΘΗΝΩΝ 10/63
ΕΛΛΗΝΙΚΟ ΠΡΟΪΟΝ

ΑΡ.ΕΛΕΓΧΟΥ ΥΠ.ΓΕΩΡΓΙΑΣ

ΠΕΡ. ΛΙΤΡ. 0,46   **ΑΤ**   **658999**   **ΖΤ**   ΟΙΝ. ΒΑΘ. 12 % VOL.

Although resin is no longer needed either as a sealant
or as a wine preservative, the *retsina* taste continues
to be preferred by many Greek wine consumers,
especially in Southern Greece. Thus the resin flavor
is added to the wine, as this label (*Retsina* from *Attica*)
indicates.

had identified about eighty cultivars, of which two-thirds were then grown
in Italy.[6]

The Romans completed the westward spread of *Vitis vinifera* by establishing
vineyards and organizing viticulture in the Rhône Valley, the Gironde area
(Bordeaux), Burgundy, the Loire Valley, Champagne, and as far north as
the Rhine and Mosel valleys (Fig. 3.1). The introduction of viticulture
followed the Roman legions' military successes, and eventually vineyards
stood even in Roman Britain. It is important that the Romans not only
introduced their vines, but also brought order and organization where vines
already stood. The Roman geographer Strabo described how vines grew all
around the Greek-founded city of Massilia, not on trellises or poles, but
along the ground, uncontrolled. Roman viticulturists changed the cultural
landscape of the Rhône region very quickly. In Spain, too, the Greeks had
brought the first vines about 500 B.C., but it was the Roman intervention
that gave viticulture its first real impetus.

So effective was the Roman diffusion of the vine that Italy became an
importer of wines from the provinces rather than the exporter it had long
been. This, coupled with a growing scarcity of the food staple, wheat, led
the emperor Domitian to issue his infamous "law" of A.D. 92, which prohibited

the expansion of vine hectarage in Italy and ordered the uprooting of half the vineyards in the provinces of the empire. Actually, this decree was not obeyed to the letter. Some vineyards were destroyed in Gaul (France), but the great new wine regions facing the Rhône and the Gironde survived, and those of Burgundy were in fact founded after Domitian's proclamation.

Thus the viticultural map of Europe emerged, the location of the vineyards having been determined by principles of accessibility (hence such river-mouth regions as Rhône and Bordeaux) rather than soil and climate, a rule with but few exceptions. In round numbers, the vineyards of the Rhône existed by the middle of the first century A.D., those of Bordeaux by A.D. 100, Burgundy by A.D. 200, the Rhine and Mosel region very shortly thereafter. In the case of the Rhineland there is evidence that ancient German peoples made and consumed wine from *Silvestris* as long ago as 4000 years, but the practice had ceased to exist by the time the first Romans reached the area and reintroduced it.[7] The vineyards of Champagne were founded about 350, and some ill-fated viticulture facing the Seine River was begun about the same time. In the meantime, vines had been introduced into England, but real development occurred at about the turn of the fourth century. In Portugal, viticulture dates from about 400.

The cultivars introduced by the ancient Romans occasionally proved amazingly durable, even if some of them found more suitable locales than those where they were first planted. Germany's White (True) Riesling, for example, almost certainly is the Romans' Argitis, first cultivated in the Rhône area during the third century A.D. Pliny's description of a grape called Biturigiaca (later Biturica) of the Gironde is very much like the anatomy of the Cabernet Sauvignon. Ancestors of both the Pinot Noir and the Gamay stood in the Rhône-Saône region during the first century. The Roman legacy in European viticulture has been permanent.

Post-Roman Survival

If an early identification with religion promoted viticulture in the ancient world, viticulture's very survival depended on its religious associations during the centuries that followed the fall of the Roman Empire.[8] Europe's Dark Ages might have extinguished viticulture altogether were it not for Christian monasteries, industrious monks, and wealthy patrons who sought salvation by giving the church their vineyards. If wine was a sacramental substance, vineyards must have been the most desirable of properties, so they became the hallmark of royalty and nobility as well. Monasteries and royal houses nurtured some of Europe's greatest vineyards; during this period of stagnation in other pursuits in Europe, the vines thrived under skillful and meticulous attention. They also began to acquire some of the qualities that later thrust them to the forefront of world viticulture as better and more suitable grape varieties were introduced, field methods were improved, and vinicultural techniques were refined.

Indeed, the role of the religious houses in the survival and development of viticulture and viniculture during the Dark Ages cannot be overestimated. With their wealth and in their relative security they alone could afford not only to foster the wine industry, but also to improve the vines and to refine distillation methods. For twelve centuries following the breakdown of Roman order the monks operated Europe's largest and best wineries. In France,

JEAN MORIN *PROPRIÉTAIRE*
du Château de la Tour au Clos-Vougeot

CHATEAU DE LA TOUR

CLOS·VOUGEOT

APPELLATION CLOS-VOUGEOT CONTROLÉE

> The Clos de Vougeot, its vineyards first developed by the Cistercians, remains an honored name in Burgundian winegrowing to this day, although the property is now divided among dozens of owners and the quality of its wines varies.

the largest Burgundian vineyard, Clos de Vougeot, was a property of the Cistercians. In Germany, Schloss Johannisberg lies on a hill overlooking the Rhine River, given to Benedictine monks by the Archbishop of Mainz; in the eleventh century these monks began an era of viticulture on its slopes that eventually carried the name Johannisberg to high repute among wines. In Austria, Switzerland, Italy, Spain, Portugal, and even in England the monks cultivated the vine and made wine of quality. As villages clustered near the abbeys, the monks encouraged viticulture by providing vine shoots to the peasants and by teaching them techniques of cultivation and pruning. As these settlements grew, so did the demand for wine, sacramental as well as unconsecrated. In the ninth century, the vineyards of Saint Germain des Prés produced as much as 400 hectoliters (11,000 gallons) of wine annually.[9]

Thus monasticism contributed to the survival of European viticulture in still another way. By disseminating and diffusing viticulture, the religious houses spread the vineyards so widely that they could survive the renewed dislocation of society, as happened during the ninth and tenth centuries. Invaders destroyed towns, villages, and croplands; they eliminated countless vines and vineyards, demolished wineries, and prevented organized agriculture—but the wine industry was too widely dispersed to be extinguished. When a semblance of stability returned, the abbeys soon recovered their primacy as centers of stability and productivity. Before long the demand for wine exceeded the levels that had been reached before the chaos.

Eventually and inevitably, interregional trade in wine developed as Europe revived. Again the monks fostered and extended this commerce. During the twelfth century the first durable patterns emerged, mainly from Northern France and the Rhine region to England. Within a hundred years the trade had intensified as wines were transported from the Bordeaux area (then under English control) to England, Flanders, and Northern France, from Burgundy to surrounding cities, and from the Rhine and Mosel regions to more northern towns. Wines came to English and Northern European markets not only from these comparatively nearby sources, but also from Portugal, Spain, Sicily, and even Crete and Cyprus.

Europe's river system was a crucial factor in the regional trade, and in the location of many market-oriented vineyards. Wine was transported by river boats in wooden barrels, often by circuitous routes.[10] A monastery located in present-day Belgium, for example, might own vineyards along the Rhine River in Germany. In order to secure its wine, shipment took place down the Rhine to the North Sea, southward along the coast to the mouth of the Scheldt River, and up the Scheldt to a place as near as possible to its destination. Other Rhine-region wineries exported their wines along similarly tortuous routes. Germany's Kloster Eberbach maintained a large fleet of barges specifically for its long-distance wine trade.

It is not surprising that viticulture was tried wherever there was hope that the vine might grow and produce; transport of this kind did little for the quality of the wine and was expensive, yet consumption rose steadily. During the twelfth century many new vineyards sprang up: in Flanders (present-day Belgium) and in Southern England (where the Romans earlier had attempted viticulture, unsuccessfully). It is noteworthy that relative location had the effect of isolating Burgundy, now one of Europe's greatest wine regions, from these early developments. Although Burgundy did have river connections with market areas for its wine, these were comparatively limited, and in any case they lay mostly northward where Rhine and Mosel wines already were popular. Hence Burgundy, relatively landlocked and inadequately linked to the outside world by poor and seasonally impassable roads, continued for a long time in the tradition of the Dark Ages: although remote, its viticulture was nourished by church and nobility and improved steadily.

During the Middle Ages the church continued its role as the chief producer of wines, but the power and influence of Europe's royal houses was on the increase. In the thirteenth and fourteenth centuries the Duchy of Burgundy (centered on Dijon) and the County of Burgundy (mainly east of the Saône River) were major prizes in feudal struggles that repeatedly changed their political affiliations and relationships, and the thriving vineyards were among the chief spoils. In the late 1300s the two Burgundies were united under Philip the Bold, who not only built the great Chartreuse de Champol monastery in Dijon, but who also took viticulture seriously enough to promulgate laws to maintain wine quality. He even sought to eliminate the Gamay variety, which he deemed to be an inferior grape, from his domain.

About a half century later, in 1443, this tradition of royal involvement in viticulture took another turn in Burgundy. Philip the Fair's chancellor for Burgundy, Nicolas Rolin, and his wife Guigone de Salins founded the Hospice de Beaune, a charity hospital for the town's numerous indigents. The now-famous wine center of Beaune in those days was a poor, insolvent place, and the Hospice was a godsend to its many poor and aged; appropriately the hospital became known as the Grande Hôtel Dieu. It was sustained by

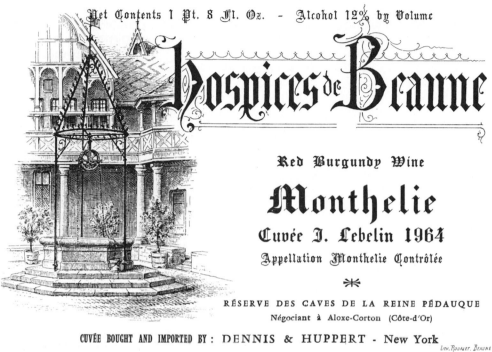

Net Contents 1 Pt. 8 Fl. Oz. - Alcohol 12% by Volume

Hospices de Beaune

Red Burgundy Wine

Monthelie

Cuvée J. Lebelin 1964

Appellation Monthelie Contrôlée

❋

RÉSERVE DES CAVES DE LA REINE PÉDAUQUE

Négociant à Aloxe-Corton (Côte-d'Or)

CUVÉE BOUGHT AND IMPORTED BY : DENNIS & HUPPERT - New York

LITH. ROUALET. BEAUNE

The Hospices de Beaune is prominently identified on this label, signifying its relationship with the Hôtel Dieu and the famous auction. The wine itself was made in Monthelie.

proceeds from vineyards given to the hospital by chancellor Rolin and his wife, and over the centuries that followed the Hôtel Dieu became ever more intimately associated with Burgundian viticulture. Many vineyard owners followed the Rolins' example and donated additional vineyards to the hospital. Originally the wines derived from these vineyards were sold privately, but in 1851 they were, for the first time, auctioned at the Hôtel Dieu. The practice continues to this day: usually the auction, a major event on Burgundy's calendar, occurs on the third Sunday of November. By the early 1980s the hospital owned some 58 hectares (143 acres) of Burgundian vineyards, a huge holding by regional standards, and more than thirty wines carrying the names of the original donors on their labels were sold. The auction is an event of such prestige that it attracts world-wide attention and international attendance. Because of its historic associations, its charitable goals, its attendant publicity, as well as the pride in ownership of Hospice-auctioned wines, prices often far exceed the real values of the wines, but the good cause merits such excess.

Increasing interregional wine trade and competition, as well as intensifying political conflict in Europe, had predictable impact on the wine industry. England took control over Bordeaux and much of the present French Département of Gironde surrounding it, and held this great wine-producing region from 1154 until 1453, the period during which the English taste for "clairet" developed. An English imprint was permanently etched on Bordeaux's cultural landscape during these three centuries, and trade between Bordeaux and the English ports thrived. But the importing of French and Mediterranean wines destroyed the fledgling industry of Southern England and Flanders. Meanwhile, as the popularity of wine diffused eastward, viticulture was attempted in areas remote from convenient water transport routes. Small vineyards serving local markets dotted the landscapes of Czechoslovakia, Poland, and other areas of Eastern Europe; viticulture also spread into the Danube basin from Southern Germany and Austria. The vine also did well in Tyrol, Hungary, and eventually in Romania. In Yugoslavia, where the Romans had established the first viticulture, the wine industry now revived.

In Western Europe, however, tariffs, treaties, and other barriers began to impede the flow of wine from vineyard to market. The Eighty Years' War (1568 to 1648) of the Netherlands against Spanish domination, the Thirty Years' War (1618 to 1648) that pitted the French against the Hapsburg powers, and various associated conflicts during that convulsive period disrupted trade patterns, and viticulture suffered setbacks. During the second half of the seventeenth century the strife abated and old routes of trade and markets reopened, but the recovery was short-lived. Crucial to the historical geography of the wine industry was the decision by the English to support the Hapsburgs in their struggle against the Bourbons for power over Spain, because this led London to seek the allegiance of strategic Portugal. In order to secure Portugal's support, England entered into the Methuen Treaty of 1703, an agreement that strongly favored Portugal's wine industry.[11] By the Methuen Treaty, the English lowered the duty on wine imported from Portugal to only two-thirds of that imposed on wines from France. Since England constituted the major external market for mainland wine (especially for Bordeaux wines, a pattern established during the British administration there), the impact of this agreement was enormous. Imports from now-disadvantaged France declined; the Portuguese wine industry, on the other hand, flourished. British capital flowed to the Portuguese vineyards, and much of Portugal's cultural landscape was transformed as vineyards replaced food crops.

The Methuen Treaty, indirectly, had a vinicultural consequence as well. The quality of Portuguese wines flowing to English markets was much lower than that of the French wines to which English winedrinkers had been accustomed. As the English began to turn to alternatives, the Portuguese developed a wine fortified with brandy, called Port. The introduction of Port in England was such a success that, after 1720, this wine began a steady climb that eventually placed it first on English markets.

Technical Progress

While political upheaval, armed conflict, and economic dislocation afflicted Europe periodically, viticulture and viniculture nevertheless progressed significantly, due not only to continued investment by royalty, nobility, and clergy, but also to several significant technical innovations. One of these involved the storage of wine. The ancient Egyptians and Greeks had introduced containers smeared with pitch to preserve their wines, and sealed them with wax. In the dry world, leather bags also served as wine vessels. The Romans employed wooden casks and floated olive oil on top of the wine to minimize contact with the air; thus it was possible to tap casked wine into earthenware jugs for distribution, without serious deterioration to the reserve. In Europe during the Dark Ages, the wooden barrel came into general use, and barrel making (from oak or Spanish chestnut) improved; but the wines did not travel well over long distances in barges and on wagons. But then, in the fifteenth century, the art of glass blowing and bottle making, dormant since Roman times, revived. This technology came to Western Europe from Byzantine Rome via Venice, and while mass production of bottles still was centuries away, the use of glass for the storage and aging of wine was to be a major development.

The first bottles to come into use as wine containers were quite fragile. The glass was thin and weak, and the bottles were wrapped in a protective wicker cover to reduce breakage (today the wicker cover remains as a decorative feature). Their shape resembled that of a carafe or bell-shaped decanter, and their main function was the same as that of the old Roman earthen jugs: to carry wine from barrel to table. But the obvious advantages of glass led to further experimentation, and eventually this resulted in the production of the first true wine bottles. This was achieved by English glass blowers, probably in the mid-seventeenth century. A thicker, pigmented glass (dark green or brown) could be fashioned into a bottle that initially remained bulb-shaped but was endowed with a strong, slender neck capable of being closed quite tightly.

This English invention gave new value to the cork as a means of closure. The Romans had used wooden bungs to close their larger casks, and they employed cork-bark for this purpose as well. The cork did not become an essential ingredient in the maturing or aging of wine, however, until its new utility as a bottle-stopper was established. The concept of bottle-aging emerged as it became clear that wine benefited from time in a corked bottle. At the beginning of the eighteenth century the wine bottle still was balloon-shaped, but as time went on the side narrowed, then flattened; by the end of the 1700s a rough version of the modern, high-shouldered (Bordeaux) bottle had appeared. In the 1780s the practice of laying down bottled vintages for cellar-aging commenced at Château Lafite.

Associated with these developments was the introduction of a sparkling wine that became known as Champagne. Certainly effervescent wines had been produced, purposefully or accidentally, at least since Roman times. But the technique of champagne making required what was finally achieved in the seventeenth century: a strong bottle and a means of closure to withstand the pressure exerted by sparkling wine. "Champagne" of a kind was un-doubtedly made before the end of the seventeenth century by English winemakers, using the sturdy bottles made in England first, decades before it was invented independently by the man often credited with its discovery, Dom Pérignon, in the French region that gave its name to the wine.

Dom Pérignon (1638–1715) was for 47 years the winemaker at the monastery of Hautvillers, just 5 kilometers (3 miles) from Epernay and not far from Rheims. He directed the excavation of the abbey's enormous cellar, and the wines he cellared there commanded the highest prices of the entire district. More importantly, Dom Pérignon was a brilliant innovator who contributed much to viticulture and to vinicultural technology. It is virtually certain that he developed the particular method of grape pressing, still used in Champagne today, to produce white wine from red grapes.[12] He discovered the efficacy of wine blending, crucial in the creation of the great Champagnes' delicate balance. And, of course, he was preeminent among those who seized the opportunities provided by glass and cork to capture that special sparkling wine marked by a second, in-the-bottle fermentation. He is another example of the connection between church and wine: a Benedictine monk who made Champagne a world standard, an achievement imitated from Catalonia to California—and never equaled.

In quite another context, important technological changes occurred as well. Across the Gironde River from the Médoc, and north of the Bordeaux region, lies the Charente region, presently delimited by two Départements, centered on the town of Cognac. Charente wines were traded as early as the tenth century, and possibly earlier; but they were harsh compared to the better wines from the Loire Valley to the north and from Bordeaux to the south. Scandinavian, English, and Dutch ships nevertheless carried Charente wines home, until—so some historians suggest—the Dutch during the sixteenth century suggested that the wine be concentrated by eliminating its water content, thus reducing the bulkiness of the cargo. Once put ashore in Holland, the water could be added again and the original formula restored. But when the concentrated spirit was tasted, the *brandewijn* ("burned wine") was found to be so agreeable that no one wanted to dilute it with water. The market for brandy (a corruption of the Dutch term) was born, and with it the search for improved distillation techniques, more suitable grapes, and appropriate aging methods. One result of this effort was the introduction of oak aging in barrels made from oak trees found near the town of Limoges (*Limousin* Oak), a practice that greatly refined the brandies.

Economic and historical geographers have proposed some other explanations for the transformation of Charente wines into brandies (the name Cognac came to identify the best, and eventually received French legal sanction). One possibility is that the practice of shipping concentrated wines began as an effort to reduce the weights of wine shipments, and hence the taxes to be paid thereon. Another factor may have been cultural: the vineyards of Charente lay in a district that was severely affected by strife between Catholics and Protestants, so that the vines were repeatedly destroyed. The vintners could not wait, time and again, for the maturation of replacements, so they began to harvest and press grapes from young, immature vines. Only distillation could render the result potable.

The distillation process had remarkable results in Charente, whatever the stimulus; elsewhere it added still another element to the widening range of vinicultural products. In Portugal, brandy was used to fortify local red wines in the creation of Ports. In Spain, grape brandy played a vital role in the making of Sherries destined for export. Although it has been suggested that the Moors were responsible for the discovery of pot-still distillation and thus enabled the fortification of wines of Southern Spain a thousand years ago, it is more likely that the organized and intended process of Sherry production came much later. While records exist to indicate that the first export of wine from Jerez to England occurred soon after the Moors' ouster from Iberia, that wine undoubtedly was not a true Sherry; nor was it in Chaucer's time, nor in Shakespeare's. The real development of the *solera* system of Sherry production came with the intervention of foreign (mainly British) capital and companies, refined distillation methods, and the emergence of the English market. Sherry-wine exports from Spain reached a peak, as a result, during the nineteenth century.

Revolution and Reorganization

The role of relative location in the development of European viticulture and viniculture was pervasive. River and canal connections, coastal exposures, strategic beachheads, and cultural marchlands either favored or suppressed regional wine industries. Geopolitics made some wine industries and broke others. Changing preferences of distant markets transformed local landscapes. Through it all, the setbacks were outstripped by progress and expansion. Permanent reputations were forged. Regions and their estates gained prestige and fame.

France remained at the heart of European viticulture, so that upheaval in France had far-reaching impact on the industry generally. Toward the end of the eighteenth century the familiar French regions—Bordeaux, Burgundy, Champagne, Chablis, the Loire—were clearly circumscribed and internationally respected for their wines. Thus the French Revolution would have serious effect on viniculture. The rising tide of chaos erupted in 1789 into a revolt that was to destroy the old order. Certainly the vineyards were part of the old order, owned as many of them were by the church and the nobility. One of the Revolution's major aims was the redistribution of the means of production.

The French Revolution's impact was especially severe in the vineyards of Burgundy, where church ownership had prevailed. The ecclesiastical properties were taken away and put on the open market; speculators bought them and divided them for later resale. This process produced thousands of tiny parcels of vines owned by peasants who would subdivide them again under French inheritance laws. The coherence of Burgundy's vineyards was lost. Clos de Vougeot, for example, that great vineyard established by the Cistercians about A.D. 1100, covered 50 hectares (125 acres) which ultimately were divided into 60 properties with about 100 owners. At one time the Clos had produced wines that ranked among France's greatest (it was tradition that the French army, marching past, saluted the winery); that dependability was lost as a result of fragmentation. Today, some Clos Vougeot still is excellent, but other properties within the ancient wall produce mediocre wines.

Although some Burgundian vineyards were less affected than others, the overall effect of revolutionary and postrevolutionary events in Burgundy was disruptive. The vineyards owned by the Hôtel Dieu remained intact, since the proceeds therefrom were made available to nonreligious charities, including the Hospice itself. The excessive fragmentation of Burgundy's vineyards was to some extent mitigated by the emergence of a cadre of *négociants* or shippers, merchants who blended wines from the grapes of small vineyards to a high level of quality. But when, in the twentieth century, a national system of wine classification was established, Burgundy's complicated patchwork made its application difficult and its representation on labels confusing.

The situation in Bordeaux was rather different. There the large estates were not predominantly under church control, so that there was less outright confiscation of vineyards. Still there were efforts to divide holdings of châteaux and to make the pieces available for open sale. Some of this occurred, but the original holdings were mainly reestablished, and the pattern of ownership, so radically transformed in Burgundy, remained much the same.

France's politico-geographical reorganization of the Napoleonic period resulted in the framework of Départements, the largest of which, centered on Bordeaux, was Gironde. The wines of this region are not commonly known today as Gironde wines, but in the nineteenth century they certainly were. And during the first half of that century the wines of France gained greatly in reputation and prestige. Enhanced cultivation methods, improved viticultural and vinicultural knowledge and technology, better maturation and aging procedures, careful quality control, and knowledgeable marketing practices had the effect of raising the prices as well as the stature of French wines, and especially those of the Gironde.

These achievements at an early stage led to attempts to establish a ranking of French wines. A French author, A. Julien, published a volume under the title *General Classification of Wines* as early as 1816, and W. Franck, an English oenologist, produced a *Treatise on the Wines of the Médoc* in 1824. Various other efforts of this kind were made before 1850, including a series of articles by L. de Beauvais, a French author. De Beauvais recognized nearly 1200 French wines and deemed 210 of these to be good enough to merit classification.

All this was a prelude to a momentous event in French wine circles, the publication of the 1855 *Classification of the Wines of the Gironde.* This classification, contrary to those of individual observers published earlier, had official sanction; it was the result of recommendations made by the Syndicate of Bordeaux Wine Brokers for use during the great Paris Exhibition of that year. It addressed only the wines of two of Gironde's districts, Médoc and Sauternes (although it also included one famous château of the District of Graves), hence the châteaux of the Districts of Saint Emilion and Pomerol (as well as all but one of Graves) were excluded. This omission spelled considerable disadvantage for these unclassified districts, but such was the domination of the Médoc.

The 1855 Classification identified 60 properties (*domaines*) in the Médoc, plus Château Haut-Brion in Graves, as meriting inclusion in a five-tier ranking (Table 3.1). At the top were four famed *crus* (growths): Châteaux Lafite-Rothschild, Latour, Margaux, and Haut-Brion. Below these First Growths came 15 Second Growths, 14 Third Growths, 10 Fourth Growths, and 18 Fifth Growths. Inclusion in any of these five categories implied a recognition that many of the chateaux recorded on their labels: Cru Classé en 1855 became a prideful announcement. The phrase can be seen on Bordeaux labels to this day.

The 1855 Classification proved to be extremely durable, its shortcomings and arguable rankings notwithstanding. Since 1855 there has been just one official modification: the elevation of Château Mouton-Rothschild from Second Cru to First, in 1973. This is not to suggest that the 1855 Classification remains wholly valid or that it ought not to be modified. Indeed, efforts have been made to initiate a revision, but these have failed to gain official approval. The fact is that not all the domaines classified in 1855 continue to produce; parcels of land have been sold to neighbors; ownership of châteaux has changed; viticultural practices are not as they were in the mid-nineteenth century. These and other considerations did lead, in 1959, to the creation of a committee by the French National Institute of Appellations, charged with the study of the classification of Médoc growths. By 1961 it

Table 3.1 1855 Classification of the Wines of Gironde (Médoc District)

First Growths
  Ch. Lafite-Rothschild (Pauillac)
  Ch. Latour (Pauillac)
  Ch. Margaux (Margaux)
  Ch. Haut-Brion (Pessac-Graves)

Second Growths
  Ch. Mouton-Rothschild (Pauillac) [a] +
  Ch. Rausan-Ségla (Margaux)
  Ch. Rauzan-Gassies (Margaux)
  Ch. Léoville-Las-Cases (St. Julien)
  Ch. Léoville-Poyferré (St. Julien)
  Ch. Léoville-Barton (St. Julien)
  Ch. Durfort-Vivens (Margaux)
  Ch. Lascombes (Margaux)
  Ch. Gruaud-Larose (St. Julien)
  Ch. Brane-Cantenac (Cantenac-Margaux)
  Ch. Pichon-Longueville-Baron (Pauillac)
  Ch. Pichon-Lalande (Pauillac)
  Ch. Ducru-Beaucaillou (St. Julien)
  Ch. Cos d.Estournel (St. Estèphe)
  Ch. Montrose (St. Estèphe)

Third Growths
  Ch. Giscours (Labarde-Margaux)
  Ch. Kirwan (Cantenac-Margaux)
  Ch. d'Issan (Cantenac-Margaux)
  Ch. Lagrange (St. Julien)
  Ch. Langoa-Barton (St. Julien)
  Ch. Malescot-St. Exupéry (Margaux)
  Ch. Cantenac-Brown (Cantenac-Margaux)
  Ch. Palmer (Cantenac-Margaux)
  Ch. La Lagune (Ludon-Haut-Médoc)
  Ch. Desmirail (Margaux) [b] 0
  Ch. Calon-Ségur (St. Estèphe)

Third Growths (cont'd.)
  Ch. Ferrière (Margaux) 0
  Ch. Marquis d'Alesme-Becker (Margaux)
  Ch. Boyd-Cantenac (Cantenac-Margaux) [c] 0

Fourth Growths
  Ch. St. Pierre (St. Julien) −
  Ch. Branaire (St. Julien) +
  Ch. Talbot (St. Julien)
  Ch. Duhart-Milon-Rothschild (Pauillac) +
  Ch. Pouget (Cantenac-Margaux) [c] 0
  Ch. La Tour-Carnet (St. Laurent) 0
  Ch. Lafon-Rochet (St. Estèphe) −
  Ch. Beychevelle (St. Julien) +
  Ch. Prieuré-Lichine (Cantenac-Margaux)
  Ch. Marquis-de-Terme (Margaux) −

Fifth Growths
  Ch. Pontet-Canet (Pauillac) +
  Ch. Batailley (Pauillac) +
  Ch. Grand-Puy-Lacoste (Pauillac)
  Ch. Grand-Puy-Ducasse (Pauillac) +
  Ch. Haut-Batailley (Pauillac)
  Ch. Lynch Bages (Pauillac)
  Ch. Lynch-Moussas (Pauillac) 0
  Ch. Dauzac (Labarde-Margaux) 0
  Ch. Mouton-Baron-Philippe (Pauillac)
  Ch. du Tertre (Arsac-Margaux)
  Ch. Haut-Bages-Libéral (Pauillac) −
  Ch. Pédesclaux (Pauillac) 0
  Ch. Belgrave (St. Laurent) 0
  Ch. de Camensac (St. Laurent) 0
  Ch. Cos Labory (St. Estèphe) 0
  Ch. Clerc-Milon-Rothschild (Pauillac) 0
  Ch. Croizet-Bages (Pauillac) 0
  Ch. Cantemerle (Macau) +

[a] Officially decreed a First Growth in 1973.
[b] No longer in production.
[c] Châteaux Boyd-Cantenac and Pouget adjoin each other and are under one owner, who routinely blends the two wines. Yet Boyd-Cantenac is a Third Growth and Pouget a Fourth Growth. This is but one argument for revision of the 1855 Classification.

Note: Communes in which the châteaux are located are shown in parentheses. Châteaux marked "+" would probably attain a higher ranking upon reclassification. Châteaux marked " " would be demoted. Châteaux marked "0" might be excluded altogether from highest ranks.
  Below the Classified Growths, the 1855 Classification recognized Exceptional Growths (*Crus Exceptionnels*) for seven châteaux: Villegorge, Angludet, Chasse-Spleen, Poujeaux-Theil, la Couronne, Moulin-Riche, and Bel-Air-Marquis d'Aligre. Next followed a large number of *Crus Bourgeois* and, finally, *Crus Artisans*. Several of these low-ranked châteaux would be included among the classified growths if the 1855 Classification were revised today.

CHATEAU
GRAND-PUY DUCASSE

REGIS SEMPER AMICI

CRU CLASSÉ EN 1855

1961
PAUILLAC
APPELLATION PAUILLAC CONTROLÉE

STE CLE DE GRAND-PUY DUCASSE
PROPRIÉTAIRE A PAUILLAC (GDE)

MESTREZAT-PRELLER, ADMINISTRATEURS

MIS EN BOUTEILLE AU CHATEAU

GIP-LIBOURNE

Chateau Grand-Puy Ducasse was classified a Fifth Growth
in 1855, and its label still proclaims its recognition. The
year 1961 was one of the century's best in the Bordeaux
region. Note the statement always to be present on better
Bordeaux labels: *Mis en Bouteille au Château* (Put in the
Bottle at the Chateau).

was obvious that this "Committee of Experts" could indeed recommend a
sweeping revision of the 1855 Classification on very sound bases, but that
the official ratification of such a redesign would not come easily. In fact, it
did not come at all. Unofficial versions of a proposed revision were circulated,
however, and these offer useful insights into the changes that have come
to the Médoc in the past century.[13]

Of course, the 1855 Classification was a precursor to a far more important
system. What was really needed was legislation to maintain and protect the
quality that had been achieved, to avoid dilution and fraud. Laws and
regulations would determine what the label of a château might state. This,
however, was not accomplished until the twentieth century, and not before
the triumph of French winemaking had been followed by disaster.

Global Diffusion

Before returning to viticulture's European stage, it is appropriate to take note of a series of crucial developments that began soon after Columbus arrived in America (Fig. 3.2). Attempts at winemaking were made even before any European vine shoots were brought from overseas, because the *conquistadores* of Hernán Cortés found wild grapes growing in Mexico and tried, rather unsuccessfully, to vinify them. One of Cortés's captains is credited with the planting of America's first vineyard in the highlands near Parras de la Fuente, about 200 kilometers (120 miles) west of Monterrey. Soon after the Spanish Conquest, Cortés instructed all Spanish settlers to plant a minimum of 5000 vines for every hundred Indians living on the lands they had taken. By the middle of the sixteenth century the new transplants (mainly the Criollas or Mission grape) clothed the central highlands of Mexico, and the first vintages of the New World were a success. Colonists and missionaries carried the vine to other Mexican locales, and soon the wines produced by these plantations were sold throughout colonial Spanish America.

Before long, the volume of wine produced in Mexico was large enough to cause concern in Spain itself. Under pressure from local winemakers, who wanted to exploit the potentially lucrative trade to the colonies, King Philip II in 1595 forbade any further planting of vines in the Spanish-American possessions.

The Catholic religious orders were exempted from the royal decree, however, and so the Jesuits, Franciscans, and Dominicans became keepers of the industry in America. Their large wineries produced sacramental wine, and undoubtedly some excess as well. The friars (as in the Old World) sustained and fostered the industry, and promoted its diffusion. As has been the case so often in the history of viticulture, an individual pioneer did much to encourage the industry. In Mexico, Father Juan Ugarte, retired professor at the Spanish College in Mexico City, was a skilled gardener and knowledgeable viticulturist. He came to Baja California and is believed to have planted the first vineyard facing the Pacific, near the Loredo Mission, probably in 1701. From there, viticulture spread steadily northward.

Viticulture in Mexico's Baja California developed slowly around the missions. Not long after the vineyards at the Loredo Mission were planted, the vineyards at the Mission of Santo Tomás de Aquino came into production. But social problems in the area soon were reflected at the missions: disease decimated the Indian population, the missions' role declined, and so did the mission settlements themselves. By the early 1800s their fate was obvious. When the mission at Santo Tomás closed in 1848, only a few monks were tending a small vineyard. Viticulture in Baja California might have been extinguished altogether were it not for a few hardy settler families who continued to cultivate some vines until, in the 1880s, European immigrants arrived who revived the old Santo Tomás vineyard. They were followed in 1905 by a group of Russian settlers, who saw the opportunities of the Valley of Guadalupe and the adjacent Calafia Valley and began viticulture there. Today these valleys contain the largest wine-producing district of modern Mexico.

Spain's major colonizing thrust in the Americas was westward and south-

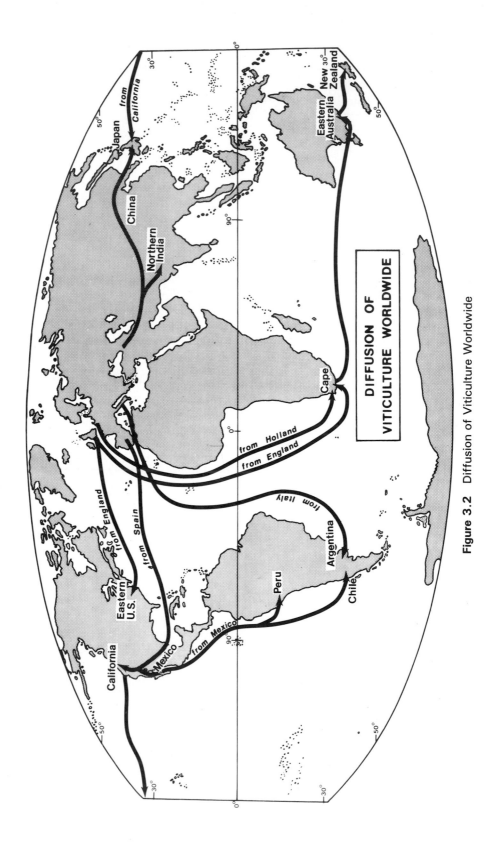

Figure 3.2 Diffusion of Viticulture Worldwide

ward at first, across the Middle American peninsula and along South America's west coast. Even before Philip's edict, vines had been planted in Peru and Chile, perhaps as early as the 1530s, certainly by the 1550s and 1560s. The first *vinifera* plantings in Peru were made near Cuzco, probably by the same missionary who established the vine near Lima and, later, near Santiago in Chile: A. Carabantes. A Jesuit priest named Cedron was the first to plant a vineyard in what is today Argentina, in 1556. Within a year, settlers at Santiago de Estero, also in Argentina, followed Cedron's example.

These were timid beginnings, and no substantial wine industry arose from the missionary plantings of the sixteenth century in Middle and South America. Chile (today the producer of South America's quality wines) and Argentina (now the fourth largest wine-producing country in the world) received the crucial stimulus much later—not from Spain or Mexico, but from France and Italy respectively. In the early 1850s Silvestre Ochagavia, a Chilean scholar, recognized what others had failed for centuries to see: the middle part of Chile's elongated territory, between the deserts of the north and the forested fiordlands of the south, contained areas of prevailing climate and soil that are ideally suited to the cultivation of *Vitis vinifera*. Assisted by French specialists, Ochagavia laid out new vineyards and stocked them with seedlings brought from France. It was the auspicious beginning of what was to become a thriving industry.

Argentina's potential was realized by Italian immigrant farmers who irrigated the dry lands along the eastern foot of the Andes Mountains and transformed desert into vineyard. Beginning in the 1850s (following national unification), Argentina's Italian settlers supplemented the still-prevalent Criollas grape with other varieties from France and Italy, and laid the foundations for an industry that now ranks among the world's largest. In this effort they were aided by Miguel Pouget, who introduced many *vinifera* cultivars to the Province of Mendoza, today the heartland of Argentinian viticulture, and by Justo Castro, who planted *vinifera* varieties in San Juan Province.

California

Thus viticulture spread southward in the Americas; it also diffused to the north. One route, logically, led from the Franciscan missions of Mexico northward along the West Coast: from Baja California (where viticulture existed in the early eighteenth century) to the mission at San Diego (where the Mission grape was first planted in 1769) and beyond to Northern California. This northward progression was completed by 1823, when most of the twenty-one missions of Upper (Alta) California had plantings of the vine (Fig. 3.3). Again, however, these mission vineyards did not directly generate a wine industry. The real development of California's viticulture came after the secularization of the missions by the Mexican government (1830) and the planting of private vineyards. The missions' vineyards did prove, nevertheless, that California's environment was suitable for *vinifera* vines.

The decline of the missions did not take place without destruction and disruption. The older southern missions, in general, produced the largest amounts of wine. Some mission property, including wine presses and other vinicultural equipment, was destroyed by friars angered by the secularization acts; at San Luis Obispo and San Miguel, the padres even pulled out most

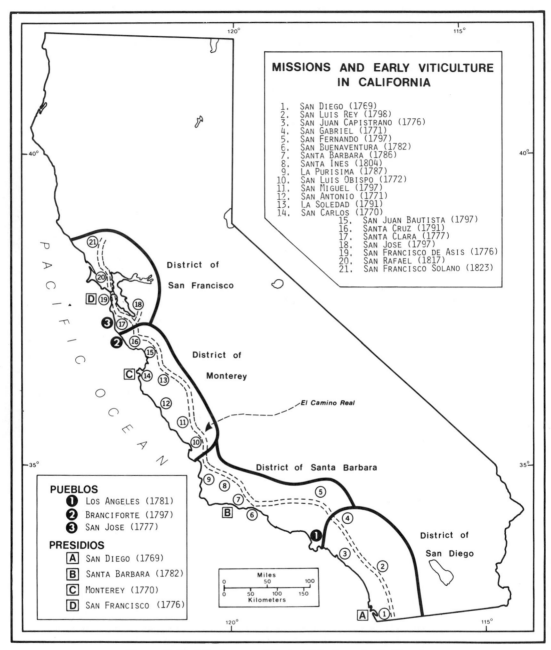

Figure 3.3 Missions and Early Viticulture in California

Note: Dates indicate year of establishment of Missions, Pueblos, and Presidios.

of the vines. Elsewhere, local peasants tore up the abandoned vines for firewood. Irrigation canals lay neglected. Broken fences went unrepaired and livestock roamed the dying mission vineyards.

But the mission vineyards were not the only stands of the vine in California of the 1830s. Well before the decline of the missions began, vineyards had been planted and maintained by ordinary settlers, *rancheros* and others, in Southern California. For these, the Pueblo of Los Angeles was the main focus (Fig. 3.3). As early as 1818, there were more than 50,000 nonmission vines around the town. In 1824, Joseph Chapman settled in the area and planted a vineyard containing about 4000 vines; his may have been the first commercial vineyard in California. Chapman abandoned viticulture fairly soon in favor of other pursuits, but he was followed in 1831 by a settler who could better perceive the possibilities of the area. This was Louis Vignes, who came from Bordeaux, and who brought to California the first nonmission grape varieties for experimentation.

Vignes's El Aliso vineyard thrived even as the missions' vines withered. Vignes was a talented vintner, and as he planted European cultivars, he fashioned his own barrels from local oak trees, created a large cellar, and began a local wine trade. By midcentury his vineyard contained 40,000 vines, and his wines and brandies enjoyed high repute.

Another pioneer viticulturist of the Los Angeles area was William Wolfskill, whose vineyard, begun in the 1830s, was even larger than Vignes's El Aliso. By about 1850 Wolfskill owned 60,000 vines, and he shipped some of his wines north to the growing town of San Francisco. There, the gold rush was causing rapid expansion of the market, and soon that market stimulated local viticulture. The Sonoma and Napa valleys witnessed viticulture's rebirth; among vineyards that rose to prominence was that of George Yount, from timid beginnings in the 1830s. Yount's name is commemorated on the Napa Valley map in Yountville.

During the 1850s California viticulture grew rapidly, a prelude to even more explosive growth to come. New areas were opened; millions of vines were planted. The Los Angeles area remained in the forefront, but other countrysides turned green under the vine in Santa Clara County, Sonoma and Napa counties, El Dorado and Sonora counties in the Sierra Nevada foothills, Sacramento and Tuolumne counties, and in scattered locales elsewhere. German, French, Italian, Spanish, and English settlers tended the vines, and a regional geography evolved. The Los Angeles area, oldest among the regions, concentrated on Port-style wines and sweet wines, and brandies; the North Coast (Sonoma and Napa areas) produced mainly dry red and white wines, but also some Sherry-style wines and "Sauternes" mainly from Sonoma; in the Sierra Nevada foothills, fortified wines prevailed. Shippers and cooperatives made their appearance; the trade flourished. When the 1850s ended with a bad harvest and the 1860s opened under the same conditions, the industry could easily withstand such setbacks. But future tests would be more severe.

While California viticulture thrived in the 1850s a figure appeared on the scene who would permanently etch his name on the industry. A reputed "count" and "colonel," politician and pioneer, colorful man of many professions, Hungarian-born Agoston Haraszthy arrived from Wisconsin at San Diego in the last weeks of 1849. There, and later near San Francisco (where he moved in 1852), he experimented with European vines. Among his first batch of 165 European cultivars there was one that was to emerge as California's own regional associate: the Zinfandel.

During the 1850s Haraszthy became ever more deeply involved in viti-culture. In 1858 he acquired the Buena Vista farm in the Sonoma Valley, and began its expansion into the largest vineyard of California. Haraszthy was a vocal, articulate, and persuasive promoter of the California wine industry, and constantly urged that thousands, not just a few hundred, of European varieties should be tested in California environments. In 1861 Governor Downey sent Haraszthy to Europe on a viticultural mission, to arrange for the shipment of as many vine shoots as he could secure. Haraszthy arranged for the transportation of 100,000 vines representing 1400 European varieties, and 95 percent of the shipment arrived in California in good condition. With tragic results, the California legislature failed to capitalize on Haraszthy's work and refused to organize the planting, maintenance, or distribution of the treasure. Haraszthy personally tried to salvage the situation, but he could not do so indefinitely. Confusion set in at his nursery, where name tags were lost and grape identities became muddled. Some vines died out; others were sold at random.[14] Nevertheless, the impact of Haraszthy's mass importation was significant. California viticulture was enormously di-versified, and many of the new varieties, even some of uncertain origin, brought success to their owners.

Haraszthy not only introduced new vines; he also published numerous articles and a book, *Grape Culture, Wines, and Wine-Making* (1862), thus assisting local and newly arrived viticulturists in their selections of land and grape varieties.[15] He organized the Buena Vista Viticultural Society and endowed it with his Sonoma Valley vineyard; he was not afraid to encourage competition. Appropriately, he became known as the father of the California wine industry.

Haraszthy's life ended in characteristically dramatic style. He emigrated to Nicaragua in 1868 and opened a sugar mill there. About a year later he disappeared on a certain afternoon, but his last movements were traced to a waterside tree on his plantation. A broken tree limb rested in the crocodile-infested lake water. Haraszthy's body never was found.

In two decades Haraszthy almost singlehandedly achieved a diffusion of *vinifera* more comprehensive than had occurred during hundreds of years previously. In the wake of his innovations the California wine industry experienced a series of ups and downs that continued for more than a century. Large areas were planted with vines, and the search for suitable environments intensified. During the decade of the 1860s the size of the vineyards tripled (to 26.5 million vines), and wine production in 1870 was more than 75,000 hectoliters (2 million gallons). In 1860 there were 11 wineries; in 1870, the number was 139.[16] California wine went to world markets from England and Germany to Australia and China. By ship it reached markets in the Eastern United States. But with the end of the gold rush came the first major decline, and by the late 1860s wine sold for a fraction of its gold-rush price. Another boom was in the offing, however, because the completion of the first transcontinental rail link (1869) brought the lucrative eastern markets, long the virtual monopoly of eastern wineries, within California's reach.

As California wines sold in volume in New York and other eastern centers, disputes arose between winemakers from East and West over viniculture methods—specifically, the use of sugar. The practice of adding sugar during fermentation was common in the East and opposed by California winemakers. But soon California's attentions were diverted by the coming of *phylloxera,* which ravaged Western vineyards during the mid-1870s and may have reached the state on some of Haraszthy's vine shoots. Set back once again, California viticulture began another upward trend after adopting the grafting methods developed in France. The period from about 1885 to 1915 saw the industry thrive as never before; California wines won prizes at international exhibitions and competed successfully on world as well as domestic markets. But another disaster lay ahead: the Prohibition law was passed (1920) and many promising wineries closed or lay abandoned. Production declined precipitously; the industry survived only because wine could be legally produced for "medicinal" and "sacramental" purposes, and exports continued. When Prohibition was repealed in 1933, however, California viticulture was merely a skeleton of its turn-of-the-century prosperity. The past fifty years have constituted a half century of recovery—but the impact of Prohibition has never been fully overcome.

Eastern North America

In America north of the Rio Grande, Eastern viticulture actually predates that of California and the West. The first wines were made by French Huguenot settlers in the vicinity of present-day Jacksonville, Florida, in the 1560s. These early efforts at viniculture, however, were not successful. North American species of *Vitis* grew in profusion, but wine made from *rotundifolia* (the "Scuppernong" grape) was unattractive. In the early 1600s Lord Delaware began the introduction of *vinifera* varieties in Virginia; later Lord Baltimore tried it in Maryland, and near the century's end William Penn experimented with French vines in Eastern Pennsylvania. None of these efforts succeeded, because the European vines could not withstand the diseases afflicting them in their new environment; the extreme winter cold also was a factor. The answer appeared to be that an indigenous North American vine should be domesticated and, possibly, crossed with a *vinifera.* This was achieved by James Alexander, a gardener in the employ of William Penn's family. The grape was a *Labrusca;* whether the cross was accidental or not is open to debate. In any case, extensive vineyards planted with the hardy Alexander (as the variety became known) were established, first in Pennsylvania in the 1790s and later in many other Eastern states. The Alexander example encouraged growers to develop other native varieties. During the first half of the nineteenth century the Catawba, Isabella, Concord, and Elvira made their appearance, and the vineyards of the East spread into the Midwest.

In the 1850s the Ohio River, east and west of Cincinnati, came to be called the "Rhine of America." The vineyards of German settlers on steep slopes overlooking the Ohio River created a cultural landscape reminiscent of the Rhineland itself. Optimistic predictions for the state's viticulture appeared confirmed when, late in the decade, Ohio led the United States in wine production. From Ohio's vineyards in 1859 came 21,600 hectoliters (570,000 gallons) of wine, twice as much as California produced and, indeed, more than a third of the entire country's output.[17] The Kentucky side of the river gave the viticultural region still greater dimensions.

But California's productivity was rapidly rising, and quite another threat

North Carolina

SCUPPERNONG
Sweet
1980

*The Scuppernong - America's first cultivated wine
grape-produces this native North Carolina wine. It has an
exceptional fruity flavor and bouquet. Sweet Table Wine.
Serve chilled. Alcohol 12.5% by Volume.*

DUPLIN WINE CELLARS
Varietal North Carolina Wines

*Produced and Bottled by
Duplin Wine Cellars, Rose Hill, N.C. 28458*

The Scuppernong grape may not enjoy wide popularity,
but it continues to be vinted in eastern wineries.

arose as well: disease. Black rot attacked Ohio's vines, and, more seriously,
the powdery mildew *oidium*. Entire vineyards died off, and there was no
technology to stop the attack. The supply of healthy grapes dwindled.
Winemakers left the Ohio River country and moved to the lake-shore country
of the northern part of the state, where the water-cooled breezes provided
protection for the vines. The heart of the Ohio wine industry had withered,
however, and California's rising production surpassed it. Then, in 1866,
Ohio was eclipsed even by Missouri, briefly the country's second-largest
winegrowing state.

The entire eastern industry soon faced not just one, but two dangers:
disease and growing support for Prohibition. Long before national Prohibition
closed the wineries in 1920, whole states had gone "dry": Kansas in 1880,
Iowa, Georgia, Oklahoma, Mississippi, North Carolina, Tennessee, the Vir-
ginias thereafter. Wineries closed. Vineyards not ravaged by disease were
abandoned to die.

Thus the modern map of eastern wineries (Fig. 3.4) represents the revival
of viticulture during the past half century, the post-Prohibition era. New
York State now ranks a distant second to California, its wine-grape hectarage
about 8 percent of California's. Another western state, Washington, out-

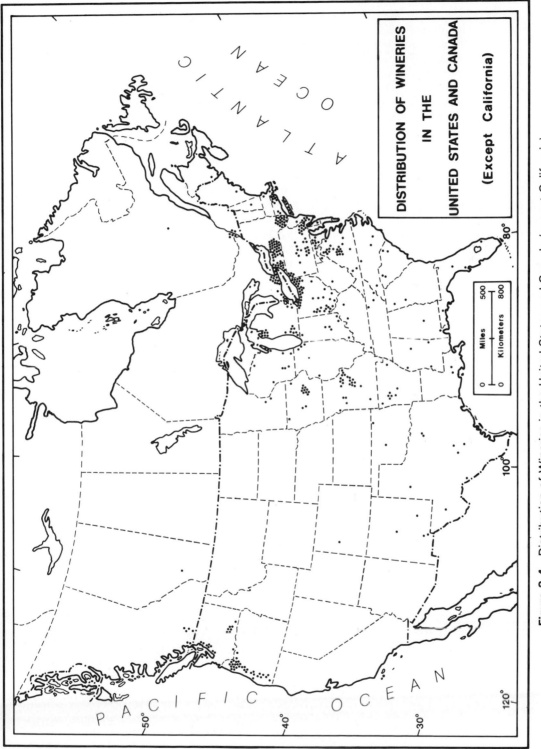

Figure 3.4 Distribution of Wineries in the United States and Canada (except California)

produces New York in some years; the dimensions of the eastern industry remain modest. But what it lacks in size, the eastern states' viticulture and viniculture industry makes up in variety. Cultivars range from the old American *Labruscas* to French *vinifera* varieties, and include a growing range of promising hybrids. Wines of huge diversity are produced, including "Champagnes," Port- and Sherry-style wines, and dry whites and reds. Wines and/or wine grapes are produced in every state of the Union except Alaska, and the renaissance of eastern viticulture still is under way.

Disease and Disaster

While France debated the merits of the 1855 Classification and the diffusion of viticulture proceeded in both hemispheres, the seeds of disaster were being sown in the very heartland of viticulture itself. The dreadful sequence of events actually began before the Paris Exhibition. In the 1840s a fungus disease, affecting vines and grapes, made its appearance in England. It had the form of a powdery mildew, which covered the leaves and berries with a white or gray powder. Slimy to the touch and with a moldy odor, this fungus inhibited the growth of young stalks and leaves, shriveled mature leaves, broke the skins of grapes, and drained them dry. By the early 1850s it had spread through Northern France and into the southern vineyards. In 1852 it was found throughout Southern and Eastern Europe, in North Africa, and even in Madeira. Grape yields declined, and wine production plummeted. Vineyards stood gray and bleak.

The fungus *oidium* also attacked *vinifera* vineyards in America, where it was the death of the Ohio River vines. But it also was known that certain North American varieties, such as the Catawba, were somewhat resistant to it. This induced viticulturists to bring shoots of the resistant North American vines to Europe, to replace the mildew-affected *vinifera* there. This was not to be the cure: in France, experts developed a method of "sulphur-dusting" that eventually saved the vines. By the time this treatment became generally available, shortly after 1860, many thousands of American vines had already crossed the Atlantic.

This transoceanic mission constituted a terrible irony, because those same American vine shoots that were supposed to defeat *oidium* carried the vector of a far more severe affliction of the vine: *phylloxera*. Again the first alarm was raised in England, where it was noticed on a vine in a botanical garden in 1863. Before the year was out, farmers in France were reporting that a strange affliction was killing vines along the Rhône River. (Scattered reports of unexplained deaths had been reported since 1858, but the outbreak on the Rhône's banks left no doubt.) The problem would begin with the yellowing and reddening of the leaves of the vine, often in the middle of a healthy vineyard. Before long the leaves fell off, and the whole vine dried out. If it survived, it would barely carry leaves—and no flowers—the following years. In that year, several other vines near the original sick one would be affected, and soon an ugly patch of dead and dying vines would scar the vineyard. The disease continued to spread, and in a few years the whole vineyard was destroyed. This was something far worse than *oidium*, which could be defeated by dusting the vine with a sulphur powder; in any case, *oidium* did not kill the vine itself. But the new disease did; when the dead vines were dug up, their roots were found to be black and rotting, and they simply fell apart to the touch.

Phylloxera was identified for what it was in 1868: the work of an aphid, a tiny insect. A French researcher, M. Planchon, was the first to note that all the dug-up, dead and dying vines had small yellow insects on their roots. On some the insects were so numerous that the roots appeared to be varnished yellow.[18] This was the vine louse, *Phylloxera vastatrix*. What the researchers did not know, in 1868, was that *phylloxera*, like *oidium*, had come to Europe from its source area, America, on the roots of the very vines imported to defeat the powdery mildew.

Now began a period of painful mistakes and costly delays as the biologists tried, first, to persuade wine producers and the French public at large that *phylloxera* was indeed the cause of the death of whole vineyards and, second, to find a cure for it (which required the cooperation of the public as well as the winegrowers). Among the first remedies tried was the flooding of vineyards over extended periods, thus drowning the *phylloxera* or driving them elsewhere. It is a technique that had some small success in France, but it proved far more suited to the flat, irrigated vineyards of areas such as Argentina; many French vineyards lie on hillslopes and cannot be kept inundated. Another experiment involved the use of chemicals and insecticides, after the success of such methods against *oidium*. Convinced that such remedies would work, the French government sent "treatment teams" into the villages and the vineyards, where they were resisted, sometimes violently, by local winegrowers. Years were lost to prove that the insect could withstand these treatments. In the meantime, *phylloxera* continued to spread. By 1880 the Bordeaux region was ravaged; Burgundy was being invaded from the south and was severely affected; the Rhône region lay destroyed; the Midi and Provence were being consumed (Fig. 3.5). Only the Loire Valley, Chablis, and Champagne still remained substantially beyond *phylloxera*'s deathly reach although, as Figure 3.5 shows, the Loire Valley had just become affected.

The social dislocation resulting from the impact of *phylloxera* was far-reaching. Vineyards were abandoned by their bankrupt owners. Attempts were made to stretch the dwindling supply of wine, and scandals broke out. From the devastated Midi region, families by the thousands emigrated to Algeria where, far from the scourge, they started new vineyards and exported their wine to France. In 1873 Algeria produced a mere 221,000 hectoliters (5,830,000 gallons) of wine; thirty years later, its production had risen to 8 million hl. (211 million g.).[19] *Phylloxera* changed the cultural map of North Africa.

While the disease and its devastation mushroomed, a solution was found. It had been noted that some vines escaped *phylloxera*'s effects, specifically those American vines that had been brought to France earlier in the effort to defeat *oidium*. The idea that French vine shoots might be grafted onto healthy and disease-resistant American rootstocks emerged even before 1870, but the "Americanists" were outflanked by the "chemists," who appealed to French emotions to keep the vineyards "pure" and who asserted that insecticides combined with better fertilization and improved vineyard care would defeat *phylloxera*.[20] As *phylloxera*'s inexorable march continued, the tide swung in favor of the "Americanists," their case strengthened by the evidence from several healthy vineyards where the grafting method had been applied.

The "Americanists" eventually prevailed, and studies were made to determine which American varieties were most resistant to *phylloxera*. *Vitis rotundifolia*, *V. rupestris*, *V. riparia*, *V. Berlandieri*, and *V. cinerea* were identified as having strong resistance, but reconstituting the French vineyards was not

Figure 3.5   France: *Phylloxera,* 1880

Source: Modified from G. Ordish, *The Great Wine Blight* (New York: Scribner's, 1972).

simply a matter of importing all these rootstocks and planting them. Some of the American varieties did not do well in French soils; the cultivars of some American species were more resistant than others. Grafting proved easier on certain of the American rootstocks than on others. And of course the task was an enormous one, even when the suitable rootstock for a particular vineyard region had been identified. In 1880 France had more than 2.2 million hectares (5.4 million acres) of vineyards with an average of 5000 vines per hectare. Thus there stood 11 billion vines, virtually all of them requiring replacement. This almost unimaginably vast undertaking would involve the transoceanic importation of the needed rootstocks. And still there were domestic obstacles: the introduction of American vines to Burgundy had been forbidden in 1874, and this decree was not repealed until 1887, by which time the map looked far worse than Figure 3.5. Some observers continued to voice their opposition to "Americanization" and urged winegrowers to resist it.

Ultimately these obstructions disappeared, and French nurseries were crowded with American rootstocks being prepared for grafting and transplanting. Healthy vineyards once again began to occupy the best of France's wine regions; large harvests (too large, some complained, at the expense of quality) were again recorded. Henceforth almost all French wine would result from an American-French collaboration brought on by the transatlantic diffusion of a tiny vine louse.

World-Wide Threat

It is natural that the main arena for the battle against *phylloxera* would be in France. The reputation and value of French wines rendered the invasion of the disease especially serious there; the resources to combat it were greatest in France itself. But *phylloxera* knew no political or physical boundaries; and its diffusion through Europe (and to the susceptible *vinifera* vines of America) was swift.

Phylloxera had a major impact in neighboring Spain, where it was first detected near Malaga in 1876 and spread throughout the country in just a dozen years. Its rapid destruction of the vineyards induced thousands of winegrowers to leave for the Americas, many of them to Argentina where they contributed strongly to viticulture. In Portugal, *phylloxera* afflicted the northern vineyards most severely, beginning in 1868 in Douro and spreading without letup until the entire country was affected by about 1895. In Italy, *phylloxera* diffused throughout the decade of the 1870s, although the first official identification was not made until 1879 at Valmadrera in Como. Germany's vineyards first felt the impact of *phylloxera* in the late 1870s; in Switzerland the most meticulous efforts to stop the disease failed after *phylloxera* was first found near Geneva in 1874. As the disease spread through Yugoslavia, Austria-Hungary, Romania, and Bulgaria, it left a wake of destruction that reached Greece in the late 1890s. Even Algeria, where the winegrowers of the Midi had fled, was not safe. *Phylloxera* was first seen in 1885 on the coast, and by 1894 only the area around the capital, Algiers, remained unaffected.[21] In Tunisia, another refuge of European growers, *phylloxera* appeared late (1906) at Souk-el-Khemis, and continued to spread for thirty years.

In all these areas the solution first found in France—the planting of American rootstocks in the afflicted vineyards—was necessary. Such was the demand for American vines that the viticulture industry in the United States acquired a whole new dimension: the sale of nursery-raised rootstocks to the winegrowers of foreign countries. In the Eastern United States, where growing competition from California, creeping Prohibition, and problems with other diseases were threatening the industry, this alternative was a welcome aid to survival.

Other Hemispheres

The diffusion of viticulture into the Southern Hemisphere (where wild grapevines never stood) and into the Eastern Hemisphere (where vines and

CONSTANTIA WYN VAN OORSPRONG
SUPERIEUR

Produk van Suid Afrika

Produce of South Africa

GROOT CONSTANTIA
LANDGOEDWYN   ESTATE WINE
PINOTAGE

GROWN, MADE AND BOTTLED ON THE GOVERNMENT ESTATE GROOT CONSTANTIA, CONSTANTIA, CAPE
GEKWEEK, BEREI EN GEBOTTEL OP DIE STAATSLANDGOED GROOT CONSTANTIA, CONSTANTIA, KAAP

C.T.P. LTD.

Groot Constantia is South Africa's most historic wine estate, and it
continues, after more than three centuries, to produce excellent wines.
As the seal on the neck of the bottle confirms, this Pinotage merits
the *Superieur* designation. Groot Constantia also produces very good
Cabernet Sauvignons.

viticulture have ancient roots) did not protect the distant vines from *phylloxera*.
Only Chile remained *phylloxera*-free, and the scourge was kept under control
in Argentina; but elsewhere *phylloxera* struck, sometimes with devastating
consequences.

The diffusion of *vinifera* to Africa, Australia, and New Zealand began
when Dutch settlers carried seedlings to South Africa's Cape in 1652 (Fig.
3.2). Unlike Chile and Argentina, where the initial plantings did not generate
a real industry until centuries later, South African viticulture took commercial
root almost immediately. In South Africa, vines were planted under the
aegis of the Dutch East India Company, not missionaries; the purpose was
commerce, not ceremony. The Company's captain Jan van Riebeeck planted
the first vineyard near the site of present-day Cape Town, and before the
end of the decade the first wine was made at the Cape. In 1654 a new set
of European seedlings arrived, increasing the range of varieties tested in
the South African environment, and Governor Simon van der Stel in 1679
laid plans for the establishment of an estate that was to become the country's
most famous vineyard: Groot Constantia. Van der Stel was the colony's
foremost winemaker and merchant, and Groot Constantia served as an
example to other farmers. In a valley east of Cape Town he founded the
town of Stellenbosch, and encouraged newly arrived settlers to develop
vineyards in that area. The diffusion of *vinifera* at the Cape was followed

fortuitously by the arrival of a large number of French Huguenot refugees, who emigrated to South Africa by way of Holland. Many of these new settlers, whose arrival began in 1688, were farmers whose knowledge of viticulture gave a boost to the industry. By the early 1700s South African wines were being shipped to European markets, where they had a reputation for excellence that made Constantia a prestige name ranking with famed French châteaux.[22]

The English took the Cape from the Dutch in 1806, an event that stimulated the wine industry still further. The French Revolution and its aftermath had denied English consumers their favorite clarets, and South African wines were excellent substitutes. Thus the English established preferential tariffs for Cape wines, and Cape viticulture thrived as never before.

But political circumstances change; English relationships with France improved in the post-Napoleonic period and, in South Africa itself, disharmony between Briton and Boer worsened. In 1861 the British government abolished the preferential tariffs long enjoyed by Cape winemakers, and the lucrative English market was lost. Many vineyards were uprooted in favor of other crops; viticulture everywhere suffered a decline.

Some Cape viticulturists persisted, however, convinced that economic conditions would once again improve. Their vineyards, surviving on the limited local market, were attacked by *phylloxera* in 1885. Virtually every vine was destroyed, and not until two decades later did extensive replanting of *vinifera* scions grafted onto *phylloxera*-resistant American rootstocks begin.

The post-*phylloxera* period at the Cape witnessed the reestablishment of many vineyards and the revival of viniculture, to the extent that, without adequate overseas markets and limited home consumption, there was overproduction and minimal financial return for the grower. The situation was especially critical during the years of World War I, which isolated South Africa altogether. During this period a movement developed that was to save the industry and guide its twentieth-century reemergence: the Cape Winegrowers' Cooperative (KWV). With official government status, this organization has played a central role in returning South African viticulture to its present, healthy condition.

Dionysus Downunder

Viticulture was first attempted in Australia in 1788, the year the first group of settlers arrived from England.[23] Captain Arthur Phillip's flotilla of eleven small boats sailed to Australia's east coast via Cape Town, and in South Africa he collected vine cuttings and grape seeds for planting at journey's end. Among items brought from England also were grape seeds, probably of the Cabernet Sauvignon. Shortly after the settlers arrived at Sydney Harbor, Phillip planted seeds and seedlings near the present location of Sydney's Botanical Gardens. Unlike South Africa's Cape, however, the environment at Sydney Harbor was not favorable for viticulture. Diseases developed almost immediately as the heat and humidity of the site promoted fungus growth, and Phillip was forced to seek a better locale. He tried the banks of the Parramatta River (which flows into Sydney Harbor), but was unable to see the project through when ill health forced him to return to England in 1792. Nevertheless, the foundation of Australian viticulture had been laid. Following Phillip's example, farmers experimented with vines on

The Seppelt name lives on in Australia, where Joseph Seppelt planted vineyards five generations ago. In the Barossa Valley, the Seppeltsfield winery with its characteristic German style continues to produce quality wines.

the farms surrounding the settlement. As the colony's area expanded, new environments came into view—including the Hunter Valley, about 150 kilometers north of Sydney. The first vines were planted in the Hunter Valley in the 1820s, and James Busby, William Kelman, and George Wyndham were among the first to recognize the Hunter's potential. Viticulture in the Hunter Valley expanded during the 1830s and 1840s, with the Cabernet Sauvignon producing red wines (a brandied red was sent to London, where it received a silver medal during a wine exhibition), and the Riesling and Sémillon producing whites. Although the Hunter Valley experienced periods of prosperity as well as serious decline, it has remained one of Australia's leading wine-producing regions, capable of yielding world-class wines.

The diffusion of viticulture within Australia proceeded with the spread of settlement. In Victoria the first vines were planted in 1834, the first wine production recorded in 1845. South Australia's first vineyards may have been planted by John Reynell and Richard Hamilton in 1838, but the really important South Australian wine region, the Barossa Valley about 50 kilometers (30 miles) north-northeast of Adelaide, was opened to viticulture a decade later. Johan Gramp established a vineyard in the valley in 1847, and Joseph Seppelt (still a leading name in Australian viniculture) followed suit in 1851. The Grenache, Shiraz, Mataro, Pedro, and Riesling varieties did well in this region, which shares pride of place with the Hunter Valley in Australian viticulture.

Numerous other areas in Australia proved suitable for the cultivation of the vine, including the far west in the hinterland of Perth, and after the middle of the nineteenth century the wine industry made considerable progress both spatially and quantitatively. Then *phylloxera* made its appearance in 1877 at Geelong in Victoria, near the coast southwest of Melbourne. Although the Barossa Valley was spared, *phylloxera*'s impact on Australian viticulture was serious; destructive outbreaks continued until the end of the century. Recovery was impeded by the collapse of prices during the glut of the period after 1914, which led to government intervention in support of the industry. Just as overseas markets were contributing to the wine industry's revival, World War II again isolated Australia, and viticulture experienced renewed decline. Since 1947, its resurgence has been marked by further expansion and diversification. In recent years an Australia-California connection has emerged, and cooperative ventures between these New-World regions lie ahead.

The most remote locale to which *vinifera* diffused from its European source area is New Zealand. Chronologically, it arrived late: Samuel Marsden's vineyard, planted in 1819, was the first. James Busby, who had played a leading role in Australian viticulture, came to New Zealand in 1831, saw the potential, and returned in 1833 with shoots of French and Spanish vines. He developed a vineyard at Waitangi on North Island and vinted the first New Zealand wine in 1840. His field work and his writings gave him the permanent status of pioneer of New Zealand viticulture.

Busby was followed by a group of French immigrants, who settled near Christchurch on South Island and began viticulture there; in 1860 a religious order, the Marist Brothers, proved the possibilities for viticulture at Hawkes Bay, North Island. Still another milestone in New Zealand viticulture was the visit by an Italian specialist, Romeo Bragatto, who studied local environments and pronounced Blenheim (at the northern end of South Island) and Te Kauwhata (south of Auckland on North Island) as especially favorable for viticulture.

New Zealand's environments, as Busby had written many years earlier, are quite suitable for the cultivation of *vinifera* varieties. The early winegrowers tried a number of these, including the Riesling, Sylvaner, Pinot Noir, Shiraz, and Cabernet Sauvignon. But even New Zealand did not lie sufficiently remote from *phylloxera*. The disease arrived late—in the 1890s—and dealt the fledgling industry a severe blow, forcing some New Zealand viticulturists out of business. Those who could afford it tried to plant American varieties of *Labrusca*. But the industry weakened, and in 1923 there were only 45 hectares (112 acres) of vineyards in the country, about half devoted to the production of table grapes.[24] By 1938 there still were only 75 hectares (185 acres) of wine grapes.

Development in recent decades, however, has been rapid. In 1980 the hectarage under vines in New Zealand was approaching 5000 (more than 12,000 acres), with 400 hectares being planted annually over the six previous years. While North Island has the most varied viticulture, extending from the Henderson Valley near Auckland and Hawkes Bay on the east coast to the coastal zone between Wanganui and Wellington in the south, the largest single vineyard block lies on South Island, near Blenheim.

East Asian Viticulture

The introduction of cultivated grapes into China came via Central Asia (Fig. 3.2). It dates from the Han Dynasty, and wine was made in China more

Chinese wine produced for home consumption tends to be sweet and
Sherry-like, but Chinese winemakers are aware of foreign preferences.
This wine, available to foreigners in China and exported as well,
proclaims its "dry"ness.

than two thousand years ago. The modern Chinese wine industry has more
recent origins, however. Christian missionaries during the nineteenth century
planted *vinifera* grapes in various parts of China. Later (1892) the first
commercial grape winery was established on the north coast of the Shandong
Peninsula. This winery has been in nearly continuous operation for more
than ninety years, and its viticulturists have experimented with hundreds of
imported cultivars from Europe and America.[25]

The main Chinese grape-producing area remains in the far west, in
Xinjiang (Sinkiang), but most of the harvest there is destined for the table
or for raisin production. Wine-grape cultivation occurs in widely scattered,
small areas in North and Northwest China, near Beijing (Peking), adjacent
to the Great Wall, and in provinces that share the catchment of the Chang
Jiang (Yangtze River). At least seven distinct viticulture regions can be
identified: (1) Xinjiang; (2) the Zhangjiakou Prefecture and Changli County
of Hebei Province near Beijing; (3) the Shangdong Peninsula; (4) the Great
Wall region; (5) Kiangsu; (6) the area centered on the ancient city of Xian;
and (7) the Liaoning Peninsula. As recently as 1980, it was estimated that
China had just 30,000 hectares (74,100 acres) under vine, including vineyards
devoted to table-grape and raisin production; the wine industry is therefore
in its infancy. But China is making vigorous efforts to develop its wine
industry, and Chinese wines have begun to make their appearance on Western
markets.

Viticulture's beginnings in Japan remain uncertain, but there is evidence that winemaking and wine consumption were practiced as early as the Nara period (710–784). It may be surmised that the eastward diffusion of Buddhism played a crucial role in the process, just as the Christian churches sustained and disseminated viticulture in Europe. In Japan, viniculture remained a small and confined industry even when the capital was moved to Kyoto and cultural-national integration accelerated.

Viticulture reached its modern focus, the Kofu Basin, toward the end of the twelfth century (Fig. 3.6). Grape hectarage expanded during the centuries that followed, as viniculture was stimulated by examples of foreign wines introduced from abroad by missionaries and traders. During the Sengoku jidai (fourteenth to seventeenth centuries) viticulture reached Yamagata (1630) and spread toward Edo.

Japan's closure to outsiders and, more importantly, the choice of Edo (Tokyo) by the Tokugawa Ieyasu as his administrative headquarters (1600) brought a new era to viticulture. The growing city created an expanding market, especially for table grapes, and in time the consumption of wine, still a very local practice, diffused to other parts (especially the growing urban centers) of Japan. The well-located Kofu Basin thrived, and when the Meiji Restoration came, there already was a sufficient shift in eating and drinking habits to encourage the idea of a national wine industry as part of the great modernization.

Before the end of the nineteenth century, viniculture was practiced as far north as Hokkaido and as far south as Shiga Prefecture. European and American cultivars were introduced, but the European varieties failed to withstand Japan's summer environments; those that did survive were devastated by *phylloxera* (1907). North American varieties proved stronger and became the mainstays of Japan's twentieth-century wine industry, along with the domestic Koshu grape. Today, five grape varieties occupy about 90 percent of Japan's wine-grape hectarage: the Delaware (a cultivar of *Vitis Labrusca*), Campbell's Early (a hybrid of *Labrusca*), two Muscat varieties (Neo-Muscat, also used as a table grape, and Muscat Bayley A, another *Labrusca* cultivar), and the Koshu. The remaining 10 percent support small vineyards of European varieties, most of them introduced after about 1960: Cabernet Sauvignon and Merlot among the reds and Sémillon, Riesling, and Chardonnay among the whites. These European varieties produce Japan's most distinguished wines, and their hectarage is expanding; diversification also continues, especially in Yamanashi Prefecture. Small hectarages of local varieties such as the Ryugan grape in the environs of Nagano City add still further to a complex viticultural mosaic.

Japan's war effort of the late 1930s relegated viniculture to "nonessential" status—until, during World War II, the need for tartaric acid (which can be extracted from wine and which also forms on the corks of bottled wines) in radar technology created an unexpected revival. Much poor-quality wine was made, but when the available supply of sake decreased because of the pressure on staple grains, this inferior wine enjoyed a ready market. As a result, the years 1940 to 1944 recorded the highest annual volumes of wine hitherto produced in the country: 1944 yielded a then-unprecedented 116,150 hectoliters (3,328,000 gallons).[26]

The end of the war and the early postwar period brought disruption and decline. In 1939 there had been nearly 3000 winemakers in Yamanashi Prefecture; ten years later there were only 164. Government intervention and the emergence of large companies, however, again saved the industry

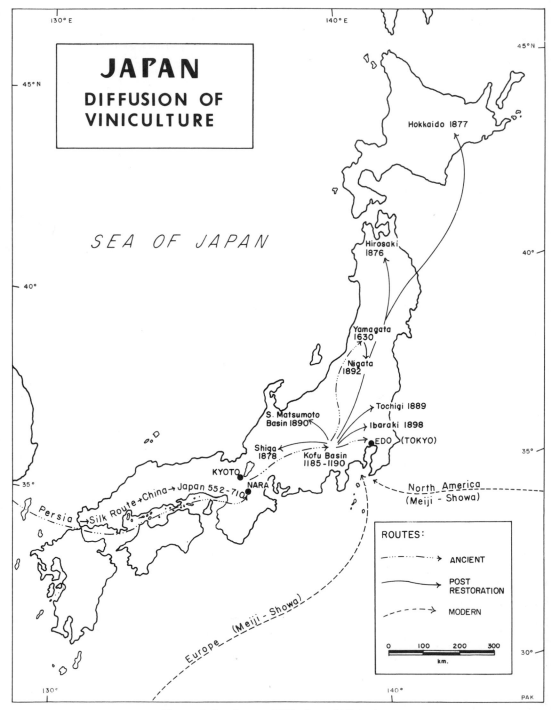

Figure 3.6 Japan: Diffusion of Viniculture

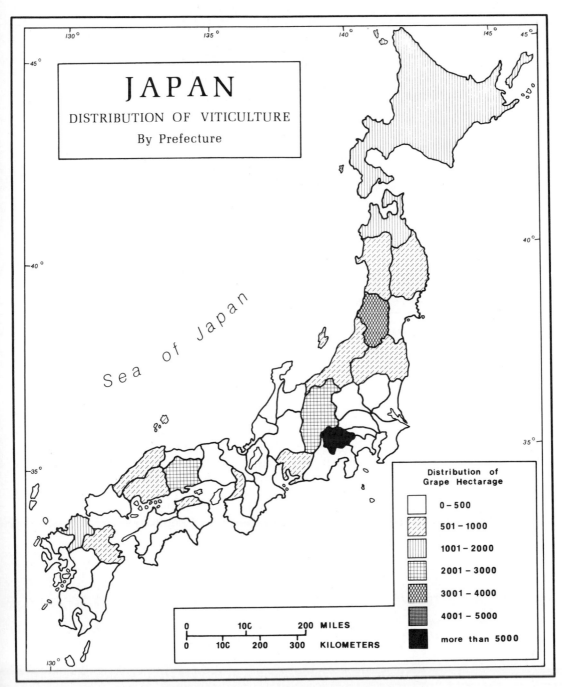

Figure 3.7   Japan: Distribution of Viticulture

Many Japanese wine labels imitate those of Bordeaux, but Manns simply announces that this wine is made from Cabernet Sauvignon grapes. The only regional information provided is that the wine was bottled at Katsunuma.

and generated a boom that has now been sustained for more than two decades.

Thus the world-wide diffusion of viticulture and viniculture still continues as new lands are opened to viniculture in the New World as well as the Old. Some of the world's noblest wines now are made in regions where viticulture was just taking root two centuries ago, and even more recently. National preferences are changing; technologies continue to improve. The sequence of events that began in Southwest Asia thousands of years ago is far from ended.

Additional Reading

On viticulture in ancient times:

Hyams, E. S. *Dionysus: A Social History of the Wine Vine.* New York: Macmillan Co., 1965.

Lutz, H. F. *Viticulture and Brewing in the Ancient Orient.* New York: Macmillan Co., 1922.

Perold, A. I. *A Treatise on Viticulture.* London: Macmillan & Co., 1927.

Seltman, C. *Wine in the Ancient World.* London: Routledge & Kegan Paul, 1957.

On the development of European viticulture:

Dallas, P. *Italian Wines.* London: Faber & Faber, 1981.

Faith, N. *The Winemasters.* New York: Harper & Row, 1978.

Fletcher, W. *Port: An Introduction to Its History and Delights.* London: Sotheby Parke Bernet, 1978.

Forbes, P. *Champagne: The Wine, the Land and the People.* London: Victor Gollancz, 1979.

Hallgarten, S. F. *German Wines.* London: Publivin, 1981.

Penning-Rowsell, E. *The Wines of Bordeaux.* 4th ed. New York: 1981.

Ray, C. *Cognac.* New York: Stein & Day, 1974.

Read, J. *The Wines of Spain and Portugal.* London: Faber & Faber, 1973.

Seward, D. *Monks and Wine.* New York: Crown, 1979.

Yoxall, H. W. *The Wines of Burgundy.* New York: Stein & Day, 1978.

On the global diffusion of viticulture:

Adams, L. D. *The Wines of America.* 2nd ed. New York: McGraw-Hill, 1978.

Carosso, V. P. *The California Wine Industry, 1830–1895.* Berkeley: University of California Press, 1961.

Haraszthy, A. *Grape Culture, Wines, and Wine Making.* New York: Harper & Brothers, 1862.

James, W. *Wine in Australia.* Melbourne: Sun Books, 1978.

Knox, G. *Estate Wines of South Africa.* Cape Town: David Philip, 1976.

Sutcliffe, S. *André Simon's Wines of the World.* New York: McGraw-Hill, 1981.

On other topics addressed in Chapter 3:

Ordish, G. *The Great Wine Blight.* New York: Charles Scribner's Sons, 1972.

Pounds, N.J.G. *An Historical Geography of Europe 450 B.C.–A.D. 1330.* Cambridge: Cambridge University Press, 1973.

4

Wine and Physical Geography: Of Sun and Soil

Vitis vinifera is an adaptable, versatile species whose grape varieties grow well in a considerable range of natural environments. Figure 2.1 indicates *vinifera*'s climatic preferences, but the vine's range is expanding in both the Northern and Southern Hemispheres. Wine is being made from grapes grown in Canada and Florida, Peru and Zimbabwe. Where elevation moderates low-latitude temperatures, and where soil and moisture suffice, the hardy vine will produce—even in Tanzania and Hawaii. And constantly the search goes on, in laboratories from California to South Africa, for hybrids better able to withstand the rigors of excess cold and withering heat, wilting humidity and searing drought.

The physical geography of viticulture is a complicated business. Physical geographers study climate and weather, soil and slope—precisely those aspects of the environment most directly responsible for the health of the grapevine. What, then, are the ideal conditions for the production of great wine? If it is known that the best wines come from Bordeaux and Burgundy, from California's North Coast counties and Germany's Rheingau, is it not possible to establish an environmental formula for viticultural success, and to use this in the search for analogous locales?

If only such a procedure were feasible! Unfortunately the generalized environmental maps of viticultural regions, such as Rioja or Chianti, conceal incredibly intricate mosaics of soil depth, composition, structure, texture, and moisture; of temperature variations and precipitation patterns; of slope angles and orientations; of wind directions and velocities; and more. No two locales are exactly identical physiographically (that is, in terms of their overall, total physical geography). An apparently suitable environment is no guarantee of viticultural success.

Climate and Viticulture

Climate, soil, and slope are the key physiographic factors in viticulture.[1] Of these, climate is in many ways the crucial one. The vine manages to sustain itself in soils that would defy almost any other form of agriculture. But a severe winter cold spell can doom established vines; excessive cold during a spring can do years of damage. Too much summer heat, especially when combined with high humidity, can wither the vine and promote deathly fungus growths. Ill-timed drought also affects the well-being of unirrigated vineyards. A prolonged period of summer dryness ensures good maturing of the grapes, but like all plants, the vine requires moisture at certain times during its annual growth cycle.

The world-wide diffusion of *Vitis vinifera* from its ancient Southwest Asian source area to Mediterranean and Western Europe, the Americas, Southern Africa, and Australia was initially a process of natural dissemination in which human intervention later became the dominant factor. Farmers noted where the vine grew healthily; as settlers in new lands they sought similar conditions to raise new vineyards. But as exact sciences, climatology and meteorology are relatively young, and for centuries the spread of *vinifera* and its hybrids was a sequence of trial and error—as well as trial and success.

Classification and Regionalization

During the twentieth century the elements of climate and weather have been measured and recorded in increasing detail, and climatic regimes as well as weather systems are becoming better known and understood.[2] One geographical dimension of this research has involved the classification and regionalization of global and local climate and weather. Two systems, devised for different purposes and based on dissimilar data, have relevance in the context of viticulture. The regional framework first established by Vladimir Köppen and later modified by Rudolf Geiger was based on observed global vegetation distribution, the synthesis of climatic parameters, and recorded temperature and precipitation data. Among the advantages of the resulting map (Fig. 4.1) are its simplicity and clarity; one disadvantage lies in its lack of practical applicability. The Köppen system is a global generalization, not a device for viticultural (or other agricultural) planning.

The Köppen map also reveals little about the quantity of moisture actually available for plant growth. This was remedied by the work of Charles W. Thornthwaite, who produced a regionalization of climate based on four factors: annual moisture expressed as water need, temperature efficiency, seasonality of moisture, and seasonality of temperature. Unlike the Köppen system, Thornthwaite's spatial scheme can be applied in relatively small areas and used as a predictive device in calculating the availability of moisture for plant growth during the growing season. By measuring the amount of moisture received by a plant in a particular locale, and by comparing this to the amount lost by the plant to the air (through evapotranspiration), it is possible to derive an overall water balance (annual surplus or deficit) and a seasonal moisture budget. Thus it can be determined whether and when a vine will need irrigation or whether, under average climatic conditions,

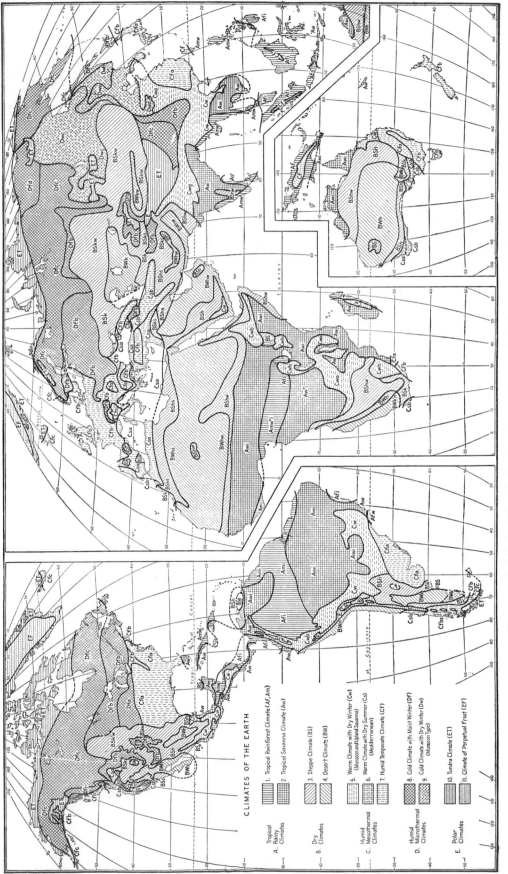

Figure 4.1 World Climatic Regions (according to the Köppen system)

Source: From G. T. Trewartha, *Introduction to Climate* (New York: McGraw-Hill, 1954). Courtesy of McGraw-Hill.

CLIMATES OF THE EARTH

A. Tropical Rainy Climates
 1. Tropical Rainforest Climate (Af, Am)
 2. Tropical Savanna Climate (Aw)

B. Dry Climates
 3. Steppe Climate (BS)
 4. Desert Climate (BW)

C. Humid Mesothermal Climates
 5. Warm Climate with Dry Winter (Cw) (Monsoon and Upland Savanna)
 6. Warm Climate with Dry Summer (Cs) (Mediterranean)
 7. Humid Temperate Climate (Cf)

D. Humid Microthermal Climates
 8. Cold Climate with Moist Winter (Df)
 9. Cold Climate with Dry Winter (Dw) (Monsoon Type)

E. Polar Climates
 10. Tundra Climate (ET)
 11. Climate of Perpetual Frost (EF)

it can grow without such support. Again, it may be determined that artificial watering is needed only as an emergency measure, under abnormally dry conditions.

At the global level of generalization, the Köppen map adequately indicates viticulture's preferred environments. Between 30° and 50° north latitude and 30° and 40° south latitude, the approximate latitudinal zones where *vinifera* prevails, the most extensive climatic zones are the C (temperate, moderate, "mesothermal") and the B (dry) climes. Without irrigation the vine will not grow or, if it survives, yield adequately under arid conditions, so that the crucial climates for viticulture under natural conditions are the C climates, the humid temperate or humid mesothermal climates. Although subsumed under this single category, the C climates are actually quite diverse. Unified by moderate temperatures (no month of the year records a subfreezing average), they display widely varying precipitation regimes. In most of Northwestern Europe, including Northern and Western France and England, precipitation comes throughout the year, every month recording moisture with some increase during the summer period (Cf). Fringing the Mediterranean Sea is a climatic region in which most of the limited rainfall comes during the winter months, and the summer is normally quite dry and, often, hot (Cs). This regime, which prevails over the vineyards of much of Italy, Greece, Israel, Spain, Portugal, and Algeria, is known as the *Mediterranean* climate. As Figure 4.1 shows, it occurs not only in Southern Europe and North Africa but also in western sectors of North America (California), South America (Chile), South Africa (the Cape), and Australia.

The moderate temperatures of C climates prevail in middle latitudes; they also occur where tropical heat is tempered by elevation. Areas that would lie beyond the range of *vinifera*—in Mexico, Bolivia, Brazil, Peru, Kenya, and elsewhere—have proved capable of sustaining the vine in their comparatively cool highlands. Although none of these countries today is a major wine producer (and Mexico's superior wines come from its Baja California vineyards, not the plateau), the potential for the further diffusion of adaptable varieties of *vinifera* is underscored by the map.

Vital to the grape-producing vine is the pattern of temperature distribution during the growing season and the rainfall regime between the first buds of spring and the harvest of autumn. The summer drought of Mediterranean regimes becomes less pronounced toward the margins of Cs regions, and eventually yields to the moister conditions of the Cf climate. The transition zone brings an extension of winter rains into the early spring, a summer with occasional rain and some cloudiness, and a warm, sunny period of a month to six weeks just before the harvest in the early fall. Figure 4.1 indicates that both Burgundy and Bordeaux are located in the southern zone of the Cf climate, not far from the transition of Cs; Bordeaux lies adjacent to the sea and, therefore, experiences maritime influences (a somewhat warmer, cloudier summer) than Burgundy, where summers often are quite cool. Summer warmth and modest rainfall, thus, are crucial. The vine must have moisture, but too much summer rain weakens the crop. In Bordeaux the harvests of 1963, 1965, 1968, to a lesser extent, 1969, 1972, 1973, 1974, and 1977 were affected by inopportune rains. In the early 1970s the pattern was for a good summer to be followed by late rains, some at harvest time, which diluted the vintage and dashed hopes for greatness. In California, ill-timed rains damaged the vintages of 1963, 1972, 1975, 1978, and 1982 in the North Coast counties.

The distribution of temperature also is vital to the crop.[3] Again it is a matter of moderation: excessive cold as well as heat can damage the harvest. Sunny summers mature the grapes and produce the desired balance between acid and sugar, but ideal conditions seldom prevail. In cooler viticulture areas, growers need as many ripening days as possible; they delay the harvest, sometimes several weeks into the fall, because the last sunny days of the ripening period can make the difference between good and great wines. But by delaying they risk the possibility that rains will come just before or even during harvest time, damaging the vintage. In warmer areas, on the other hand, the risk of heat is a constant concern. A heat wave will shrivel and burn the leaves, expose and dry out the grapes; it also may be accompanied by outbreaks of fungus growth. In Bordeaux, untimely rain is a greater problem than excess heat (1976 was a recent year when a heat wave did affect the grapes); but in areas where rainfall and cloud cover during the summer are generally less, for example in marginal Mediterranean zones, the heat threat is greater. Unirrigated vineyards in California, South Africa, and Australia are among those facing the threat of too much summer heat; in California, heat waves afflicted the vines in 1972 and 1976.

Certain varieties of *Vitis*, *vinifera* as well as non-*vinifera*, grow under colder conditions than those of the C climates. Figure 4.1 shows that the vineyards of Michigan, Ontario, part of Germany, the U.S.S.R., Northern China and Hokkaido (Japan) lie under conditions classified as D climates. The third letter of the index (a, b or c) indicates the comparative intensity of summer warmth, the Dfa climate having a warmer summer than Dfb. The annual temperature range of the D climates is greater than that prevailing under the C climates, so that winters often are very frosty, putting the vines at risk. The map indicates that large vineyard areas exist under Dfb conditions in North America as well as Eurasia. The situation does not occur in the Southern Hemisphere, where only the narrow landmass of South America reaches latitudes comparable to those of the German wine country.

These climatic regionalizations should, of course, be viewed in the context of the cultivars grown under the widely varying conditions represented on the map. Where growing seasons are short, cultivars that ripen early are planted. Where winters are exceptionally cold, varieties or hybrids are grown that can withstand a severe cold spell. In very hot areas, grapes that have a high acid content are needed. The most cold-hardy species of the genus *Vitis* is *V. amurensis*, native to China, which is believed to survive winter temperatures of −40° to −50°C. (−40° to −60°F.). *Amurensis* is not a suitable wine cultivar, but it has nevertheless been crossed with several *vinifera* varieties by Chinese viticulturists, to impart the resulting hybrids with its cold-resistant qualities. In North America, *Vitis Labrusca* has varieties with a strong cold resistance, being able to withstand winter cold of −15° to −20° C. (5° to −4°F.), and *Vitis riparia* also is able to survive severe cold. In a very general sense, cultivars of *vinifera* tend to withstand excessive heat better than extreme cold; on the other hand, the heat resistance of *Labrusca* varieties and of *riparia* is only fair.

Such realities lie at the root of the regional associations discussed in Chapter 2. The Pinot Noir thrives in the comparatively cool summers of Burgundy, and is harvested in mid-September or shortly thereafter in good years, and as much as a month later if conditions have been unfavorable. The Cabernet Sauvignon likes the slightly warmer summers of Bordeaux, yet is also harvested (in most years) in September, very rarely in the last days of August, and occasionally in the first half of October. The Pinot

Noir in Bordeaux (even if it adjusted to the Gironde's soils) would suffer from excess heat and sunburn. In Germany, where it has indeed been planted, the Pinot Noir fails to ripen properly and makes thin, incomplete wines.

Heat Summation

Temperature is only one element of climate, but a critical one. It is evident that the vine, between its first stirring in the spring and its return to winter dormancy in the fall, must receive a certain amount of energy from the sun in order to complete its fruiting cycle. The amount normally available—measured as temperature—varies enormously from vineyard to vineyard. This is so *within* winegrowing regions and countries. There is no such thing as "California" climate for viticulture, or a favorable "French" environment.

A comparison of the temperature conditions of viticulture regions around the world yields valuable insights into the varied environments of *vinifera*. In 1938 two scholars of viticulture, Albert Winkler and Maynard Amerine, first classified the climates of California vineyards into five regionally expressed categories, based on their average daily temperatures during the growing season from April to October.[4] Their methodology involved the concept of the "degree-day." This index was measured by recording the average daily temperature and counting the number of degrees that average exceeded 50° Fahrenheit, regarded as the level of dormancy. If, on a given day, the recorded temperature averaged 75°F., that day measured 25 degree-days. The result was a five-level classification (Table 4.1) that reveals the enormous environmental range in California viticulture; when California viticulture regions are compared to those of other areas of the world some remarkable patterns emerge. The coolest parts of the Napa Valley, with fewer than 2500 degree-days during the growing season, rank with Beaune in Burgundy; most of Napa and Sonoma (2501 to 3000 degree-days) are similar to Bordeaux and the Piedmont of Italy. Region V in California (more than 4000 degree-days) resembles Southern Italy and Sicily and the Sherry country of Spain.

The heat summation abstracted in Table 4.1 is represented cartographically on Figure 4.2. Region I, coolest of the five zones, has 2500 or fewer degree-days. In California, the segments of this region are grouped in three areas: (a) north of San Francisco Bay in Mendocino, Napa, and Sonoma counties; (b) facing Monterey Bay in Santa Clara, San Benito, and Monterey counties; and (c) north of Santa Barbara in Santa Barbara and San Luis Obispo counties. Under the cool conditions prevailing in these viticultural areas, premium-quality dry wines are produced from early-maturing grapes, including many of California's superb whites.[5]

Region II also appears on the map as a region of comparatively small fragments, but its spatial pattern belies its great importance in California viticulture. This is the smallest of the five regions spatially, and as Figure 4.2 indicates, the fragments tend to adjoin those of Region I. With 2501 to 3000 degree-days, Region II includes such prominent locations as Napa and Santa Rosa in North Coast counties, three locales on the landward side of Region I around Monterey Bay (including Santa Clara in Santa Clara County), and an area north of Santa Barbara. Many of California's greatest wines come from parts of the Napa Valley, the Alexander Valley, and the Santa Clara area falling within this regional category.

Region III, with 3001 to 3500 degree-days, may be described as moderately

Table 4.1. Degree-Days of Selected Locations

	America	Europe	World
REGION I 2500-	Salinas 2144 Oakville 2300 Sonoma 2360	Geisenheim 1709 Trier 1730 Rheingau 1745 Beaune 2400 Champagne 2449	Coonawarra 2175 Hawkes Bay 2470
REGION II 2501-3000	San Luis Ob. 2555 Santa Rosa 2610 Sta. Barbara 2830 St. Helena 2900	Bordeaux 2519 Douro 2765 Asti 2980	Barossa 2838
REGION III 3001-3500	Livermore 3260 Calistoga 3360		Seymour 3050 Clare 3231 Adelaide 3458
REGION IV 3501-4000	Pomona 3676 Stockton 3715 Sacramento 3788 Sonora 3927	Florence 3530	Great Western 3505 Rutherglen 3654 Benalla 3715 Berri 3840
REGION V 4001+	Riverside 4032 Davis 4057 San Bernard. 4126 Fresno 4680	Naples 4010 Palermo 4140 Jerez Front. 4194	Swan Valley 4079 Griffith 4170 Pokolbin 4538 Algiers 5200

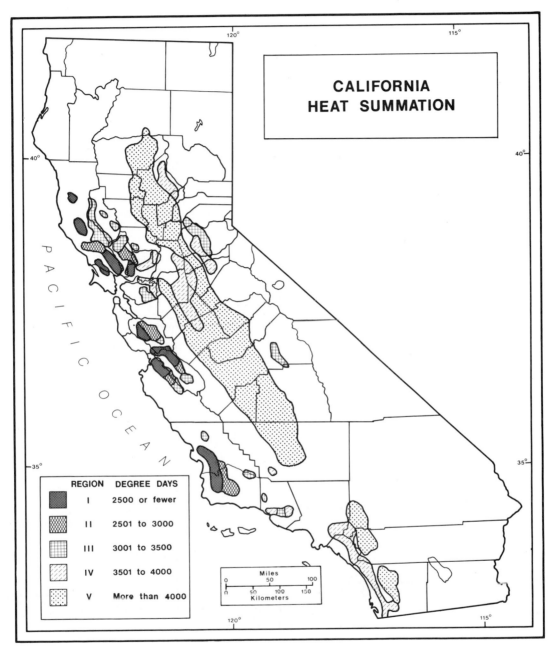

Figure 4.2 California: Heat Summation

warm. In a sense this is a transitional region, in which late-maturing red grapes can produce excellent wines, but good sugar content in the grapes is sometimes unmatched by adequate acid. Very good natural sweet wines can be made, including some of California's popular "Ports," and good white and red wines generally. On the map, Region III extends inland from Region II north of San Francisco Bay and behind Monterey Bay, but in the south it consists of several isolated pockets; also important is its representation in the Sierra Nevada foothills in Eldorado and Amador counties.

Regions IV and V lie adjacent to each other as do Regions I and II. These are the warm and hot interior regions respectively, where irrigation prevails and the emphasis is on large production. Region IV, with 3501 to 4000 degree-days, extends from a northernmost location in eastern Butte County to Southern California in near-coastal San Diego County. Small areas occur in Ventura County. This is a region of sweet-wine production, but low acid in the grapes is a problem for white as well as red table-wine producers. Thus the use of cultivars that yield grapes high in acid prevails.

Region V, hottest of the five, also is the most contiguous and the largest in area. This region, where more than 4000 degree-days are recorded, includes the Sacramento Valley from near Sacramento to Redding and the San Joaquin Valley from Merced to Arvin.[6] Two analogous regions lie in Southern California, in Western San Bernardino and Riverside counties. Here, high-acid varieties are irrigated to produce an enormous volume of wine every year, the mainstay of the production of bulk wines.

The regions delimited on Figure 4.2 are defined by arbitrary criteria, and real boundaries do not, of course, exist in nature. While transition zones rather than sharp divisions separate the regions, the overall framework that emerges has validity. It is especially interesting to compare the California regions with analogous locales elsewhere in the world. As noted earlier, the heat summation of Region V matches that of Southern Italy and Southern Spain; it also coincides with Perth, Australia; Beijing (Peking), China; and Algiers, Algeria. The coolest region (I) has conditions similar to those in Trier, Germany; Reims in the Champagne country of France; Coonawarra, Australia; Geneva, New York; and Beaune, Burgundy. The high-quality, premium-wine–producing region II is paralleled by Auckland, New Zealand; Bordeaux (city), France; Santiago, Chile; Melbourne, Australia; and Budapest in Hungary.

The heat summation provides insights into climatic conditions in widely dispersed viticulture regions, but it, too, remains a generalization. A region in category I, II, or III does not automatically or necessarily produce high-quality wines because excellent wines come from other districts in these cooler regions; the higher heat of Regions IV and V does not preclude the production of good wines there. The schema should be viewed in the context of moisture supply, soil conditions, and other elements of the environment, as well as the talents and skills of the winemakers. Further, it should not be assumed that environmental conditions—even only those relating to temperature—are identical or even substantially similar throughout the delimited regions. Quite apart from annual fluctuations in temperature (and the regions are defined on the bases of long-term averages), regions mapped on Figure 4.1 display considerable internal diversity. The map cannot reveal this, and to the winegrower the heat summation constitutes a beginning, an initial narrowing of options.

The range of environments expressed in Table 4.1 underscores one of the fundamental realities of viticulture: success depends in large measure

Only in South Africa and in New Zealand has the Pinotage produced notable wines. Here, a vineyard planted with this *métis* stands at Groot Constantia at South Africa's Cape.

upon matching particular grape varieties with specific environments. The Gamay makes ordinary, even substandard wine in many parts of the world, but in Beaujolais (as has been noted in Chapter 2) it achieves greatness. The Pinotage produces good wines in several regions of the Southern Hemisphere, but it excels only at South Africa's Cape and on New Zealand's North Island. Pinot Noir is the grape of Burgundy, Riesling of Germany, Cabernet Sauvignon of Bordeaux. Such regional-varietal associations, entrenched by time, spell continuity and dependability. Certainly all have been successfully introduced elsewhere: Cabernet Sauvignon still more successfully than Pinot Noir in California, Riesling in Chile, South Africa, and Australia; Gamay in Yugoslavia. But certain varieties may prove to grow nowhere better than in vineyards of California, Chile, or New Zealand. The Zinfandel probably is in that position in California (it is being introduced with some success in South Africa), and perhaps the Merlot as well; renamed the Steen, the Chenin Blanc by some accounts does better in South Africa than it does in its heartland, France. In research laboratories where climate and soil are dissected, and in nurseries where varieties are grafted and crossed, lies the future.

Microclimates

Climatological generalizations such as the heat summation just described have a useful purpose. They provide a first assessment of the possibilities and limitations of viticultural regions about to be opened, suggest the range of varieties probably best adapted to the prevailing conditions, and indicate what kind of support the vines will need (irrigation for example) in certain zones. In short, they provide precedent, which helps obviate much of the trial and error of earlier years; and without doubt the degree-day concept has constituted a valuable, globally applicable system to evaluate and compare climatic conditions in viticultural areas from China to Chile.

To interpret the range in wine quality and wine styles within important producing regions such as the Napa Valley or Burgundy's Côte d'Or, however, more information is needed than is provided by a heat summation. In California's Napa County, a region only 30 kilometers (20 miles) in length and less than 10 kilometers (6 miles) wide, three distinct climates for viticulture can be identified (Fig. 4.2).[7] Even this level of detail obscures the fact that viticultural conditions change from hillside to valley bottom, from north- to south-facing slope. As two observers of German viticulture write, "the microclimate of a vineyard depends on several factors: whether it faces south or west; the gradient of its incline; the intensity of the sun's reflection from the surface of the river; the proximity of sheltering forest or mountain peak; altitude; and soil humidity . . . separated by a distance of only a few hundred meters, wine of world fame may grow—or nothing more than gorse bushes."[8]

Thus the microclimates embedded in the world map (Fig. 4.1) are crucial in the evaluation of a vineyard location within a viticultural region. In the high-latitude, far-northern viticulture regions of Germany, the best vineyards lie on slopes that face west, benefiting from the maximum insolation of the afternoon sun; next best are the southwest- and south-facing slopes. The greatest wines of Burgundy's Côte d'Or come from vineyards that face east, nourished by the warmth of the rising sun, the soil warming gradually and, toward evening, cooling gently in the shadow of the hillslopes. Soil exposed to the sunset cools more abruptly, to the disadvantage of the Burgundian vine.[9] And environmental contrast occurs even within a single vineyard. The fragmentation of ancient Clos Vougeot into many properties produced a number of wines that are labeled Clos Vougeot; those derived from the vines nearest the road fronting the vineyard are considered to be of lesser quality than those from deeper into the original property, just a few meters away.

Microclimates cannot be easily codified and mapped at such scales. Based on records kept at wineries and in villages it is possible to draw maps showing zones of frost danger, the incidence of high winds, the hours of sunshine received, fog incidence, and other environmental conditions. In conjunction with soil maps and in the general context of latitude, elevation, and exposure, such microclimatic information obviously has great value. But not many viticulture regions have the necessary data for detailed mapping of this kind, crucial though the information may be. When the vineyards at Hamlet Hill in Connecticut were planted on top of a 100-meter (330-foot) high drumlin, the vines were found to benefit from a 9.5°C. (17°F.) temperature differential between top and base of the hill, a vital advantage in these cool environs.

In a few special cases the microclimate is responsible for the development of the condition known as *Edelfäule* or *Pourriture Noble*—the noble rot that affects late-harvested grapes in certain German, French (and a very few other) vineyard districts. In September and October, when the days are warm and the nights cool, the morning dew is heavy and fog comes often, the grapes begin to shrink and shrivel as their skins develop tiny cracks and the water in their juice evaporates. Eventually an unsightly, webby mold envelops whole bunches, and yet these grapes yield the noblest of sweet wines. Only the most delicate combination of microclimatic conditions makes it possible in a very few favored locales.

Soil and Viticulture

If the regional climatology of viticulture provides only partial answers to questions concerning *vinifera*'s adaptation and diffusion, the study of soils (pedology) produces even more uncertainties. It is not a matter of identifying the most fertile, the most mature, or the deepest soils: the vines often thrive in "poor" soils but fail to produce satisfactorily in soils that carry other crops well. Vines grow on steep, rocky slopes above the city of Sondrio in Lombardy; elsewhere in the Valtellina Hills they thrive on terrain so treacherous that the pickers must be mountain climbers to reach the harvest. In Portugal's Douro region, holes are blasted with dynamite in rocky slopes so that the vine may be planted—and yet it thrives. In the Bordeaux region, a district is named after the chief characteristic of its soil—*Graves* (gravel), not the most encouraging appellation for a productive soil. And yet those rocky slopes and gravelly soils produce excellent wines from grapes that mature fully and well. To predict how a vine will grow and yield in a particular soil is even more difficult than to forecast its success under certain climatic conditions.

Hence micropedological studies are more relevant and useful in viticulture than global classification systems, although the latter provide a necessary framework. Soil classification has occupied geographers and other scholars for many years, and various systems were devised in the Soviet Union, Europe, and the United States. In 1960 a major development occurred when the United States Department of Agriculture's Soil Conservation Service published its Comprehensive Soil Classification System (CSCS). This system took into account all previous work and every preceding scheme, and it became known as the "Seventh Approximation" because it was the seventh revision of a system first devised in the 1950s. The Seventh Approximation divides the world's soils into 10 Orders, 47 Suborders, 185 Great Groups, 5000 Families, and 10,000 Series. At global levels of detail, only the Orders can be mapped, and as Figure 4.3 shows, most of the major viticulture regions lie in zones of Alfisols (an extension of a soil class formerly called the Pedalfers): Udalfs in France, New York State, and Southern Australia; Xeralfs in Spain, Italy, South Africa, and parts of California and Chile. In Eastern Europe, the Southern Soviet Union, Uruguay, and parts of the United States Midwest vines are grown in Mollisols; in Australia and Argentina they also thrive in irrigated dry soils (Aridisols) and in "Highland" soils. Vines probably can be found growing in the soils of each of the ten Orders (although the Oxisols of Equatorial latitudes support few cultivated plants for long periods). What is more important is the texture of the soil (whatever its Order or Suborder), and the nutrients available in it.

Soil texture is expressed as gravel, sand, silt, and clay, in descending order of coarseness of its particles. A loam consists of a mixture of approximately equal amounts of sand, silt, and clay; a sandy loam has more sand than either silt or clay. Soil texture is critical, because it indicates the quantity of water the soil can hold, the effectiveness of internally circulating

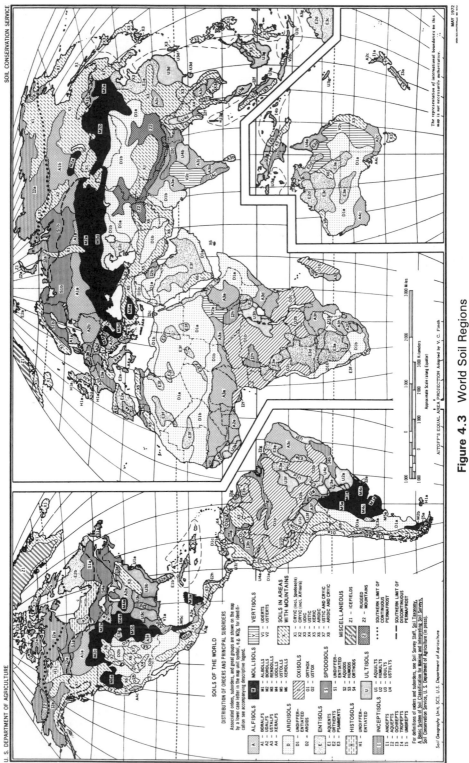

SOILS OF THE WORLD

DISTRIBUTION OF ORDERS AND PRINCIPAL SUBORDERS

Associated orders, suborders, and great groups are shown on the map by a lower case letter in the map unit symbol, e.g. M2b, for identification see accompanying descriptive legend.

ALFISOLS

A
A1 — BORALFS
A2 — UDALFS
A3 — USTALFS
A4 — XERALFS

ARIDISOLS

D
D1 — INDIFFER-ENTIATED
D2 — ARGIDS

ENTISOLS

E
E1 — AQUENTS
E2 — ORTHENTS
E3 — PSAMMENTS

HISTOSOLS

H
H1 — INDIFFER-ENTIATED

INCEPTISOLS

I
I1 — ANDEPTS
I2 — AQUEPTS
I3 — OCHREPTS
I4 — TROPEPTS
I5 — UMBREPTS

MOLLISOLS

M
M1 — ALBOLLS
M2 — BOROLLS
M3 — RENDOLLS
M4 — UDOLLS
M5 — USTOLLS
M6 — XEROLLS

OXISOLS

O
O1 — ORTHOX
O2 — USTOX

SPODOSOLS

S
S1 — UNDIFFER-ENTIATED
S2 — AQUODS
S3 — HUMODS
S4 — ORTHODS

ULTISOLS

U
U1 — AQUULTS
U2 — HUMULTS
U3 — UDULTS
U4 — USTULTS

VERTISOLS

V
V1 — UDERTS
V2 — USTERTS

SOILS IN AREAS WITH MOUNTAINS

X
X1 — CRYIC (incl. Spodosols)
X2 — CRYIC (incl. Alfisols)
X3 — UDIC
X4 — USTIC
X5 — XERIC
X6 — ARIDIC
X7 — USTIC AND CRYIC
X8 — ARIDIC AND CRYIC

MISCELLANEOUS

Z1 — ICEFIELDS
Z2 — RUGGED MOUNTAINS

•••• — SOUTHERN LIMIT OF CONTINUOUS PERMAFROST

— — — SOUTHERN LIMIT OF DISCONTINUOUS PERMAFROST

For definitions of orders and suborders, see Soil Survey Staff, Soil Taxonomy, A Basic System of Soil Classification for Making and Interpreting Soil Surveys, Soil Conservation Service, U. S. Department of Agriculture (in press).

Soil Geography Unit, SCS, U. S. Department of Agriculture.

AITOFF'S EQUAL AREA PROJECTION Adapted by V. C. Finch

Approximate Scale along Equator

The representation of international boundaries on this map is not necessarily authoritative.

MAY 1972

Figure 4.3 World Soil Regions

solutions that carry nutrients to plant roots, and its capacity to contain air and, therefore, retain warmth. Effective drainage, vital to the vine's growth, also is related to texture. Loam drains better than clay or silt, given similar terrain conditions. In the Napa Valley, the soils of the valley bottom are mainly clays, whereas those of the hillsides tend to be sandy to gravelly loams. The vines do better in the loams than they do in the clays, and a major reason is the loams' superior drainage.

As the vines grow older, their root systems penetrate ever more deeply into the solum and beyond, even to the regolith. This accounts for the capacity of the vine to stand, leafy and verdant, amid a gray-dry countryside. The vine's roots search for moisture where others cannot reach, and its efficiency increases with age.[10] And as the root system spreads, the absorption of mineral nutrients is enhanced. These minerals and other nutrients in solution give the grape its particular character and the wines their distinctive taste and individual aroma. There are those experienced tasters who proclaim that they can recognize the contribution of the soil in the taste of the wine; in any case, a combination of suitable texture and a varied nutrient complex is more important to the character of the grape than a humus-rich, fertile soil. Certainly vines grow luxuriantly in fertile soils, but they then produce an abundance of foliage and a huge quantity of indifferent fruit, not an exceptional harvest of quality wine grapes.

Thus a certain soil poverty is not undesirable in viticulture, although varieties of *vinifera* do have soil preferences. The soils of Burgundy are sandy, lime-rich loams in the Côte d'Or, where they are derived from a limestone-supported plateau that has been eroded by glacial action as well as stream water. Downslope, the soils take on the character of calcareous clays. No such generalization is possible in Bordeaux, where soils are enormously varied in composition as well as texture. Two qualities seem to prevail in the best areas: depth (as much as 4 meters and more) and coarse texture (gravelly soils dominate in the Médoc as well as Graves). In South Africa the fine Cabernet Sauvignon and Pinotage of Groot Constantia come from vines that grow in sandy soil derived from a thick stratum of sandstone; but around Paarl and Stellenbosch good wines are produced from vines that stand in granitic and shaly soils. In Australia the best wines are drawn from grapes grown in soils that have a limestone or calcareous content, either as subsoil (as under the volcanic soils in the Hunter Valley) or as part of the upper solum (in the Barossa Valley). But the vine's preferred pedological habitat defies generalization. In many areas of the world the vine is, quite literally, the only cultivated plant that would grow in the harsh ground.

Geology of Wine

The relationship between the vine and the ground in which it stands has even been studied in the context of the underlying geology itself, a step beyond the pedology.[11] This effort has not been very successful: while it is true that Northern Portugal's wines come from ancient Precambrian granites and metamorphics (including schists so hard that individual holes are blasted to permit the planting of vines), Upper Loire vines stand on Hercynian rocks, and the Rhine region is mostly Devonian slates, the relationship between wine and bedrock is not consistent. Rather, it is clear that good wines are yielded by vines standing on virtually any geologic base, whether

Tertiary-Quaternary (Bordeaux), Cretacious-Tertiary (Rioja), or Jurassic (Burgundy). This generalization is neither productive nor new: it applies equally, and more appropriately, to the overlying soil.

The vine is an extraordinary plant, one that can be grown successfully where almost every other crop would fail. Adaptable and versatile, the vine does have its preferences. It generally does least well in heavy clays, very shallow soils that are poorly drained or overlie some impervious layer (such as a hardpan), soils with high concentrations of alkali salts and, naturally, soils that are in some way toxic. Great wines are produced from sand, gravel, loam, even clays; they come from comparatively shallow as well as deep soils. Yet the soil does impart a certain quality—often an important contribution—to the special flavor of the grape and hence the wine.

It is therefore evident that climate, grape variety, and soil are the three cornerstones of viticulture, and that soil ranks last in importance among these three. Climate is the dominant soil-forming factor, and climate controls the life cycle of the vine. The vine is far more sensitive to climatic limits than it is to soil conditions.

Vineyard and Slope

There can be no doubt that sloping ground—often just slightly sloping ground—has a favorable effect on the vine. Many of the world's greatest vineyards stand on hillsides in the Bordeaux region, in the Napa Valley, in Germany, and elsewhere. Even the vineyard's position on the slope has significance: too high may mean excessive exposure to the winds; too low may risk the effect of excessive winter cold resulting from air drainage (see below).

It is important that sloping soil usually means well-drained soil. The internal drainage of a soil is improved when it does not lie flat, as it does in a valley bottom or on a horizontal bedrock surface, where waterlogging may occur.

In several viticultural regions of France, the role of sloping ground under vineyards is reflected on the map. The Burgundy region, for example, is geographically divided into several subregions of which a number are named *Côte* (slope): the Côte d'Or (Slope of Gold, for the color of the vine leaves in the autumn), which in turn is divided into the Côte de Nuits and the Côte de Beaune; and the Côte Chalonnaise to the south. Still farther southward lie the Côtes du Rhône, the slopes of the Rhône River, including the famed Côte Rôtie, signifying a climatic quality, its roasting summer heat. The prefix *Côte* appears in the Bordeaux region as well, for example in the Côtes-de-Fronsac, and at the other end of the country in the Côtes de Toul (Lorraine).

Only in France is the actual term "slope" so entrenched in the nomenclature of regional viticulture, but implications of a similar nature appear in Germany (note the frequent suffix *berg* or mountain[side] on the map) and, of course, in English-speaking countries in valley names.

Environmental Hazards

Cultivars associated with particular regions have proven, by their durability, that they are able to survive even the climatological extremes of centuries.

Specialized trellis to keep the vines and grapes well off the ground, affording protection against high surface heat and creating shade for the bunches; the "gable" is high enough to permit mechanical dusting and other treatment.

They have become a part of regional ecologies. In areas where such near-permanent regional associations have not yet developed, viticulturists plant vines (sometimes hybrids of complex parentage) that are expected to withstand the rigors of the prevailing environment.

Yet the vicissitudes of climate and weather can severely damage vine and harvest. Figure 4.1 is based on averages accrued over many years of weather recording, but any given year may present an unprecedented combination of conditions, far beyond the normal ranges that should, with high probability, characterize the regions. Among these hazards are temperature extremes, insufficient or excessive and ill-timed precipitation, hailstorms, and destructive winds.

The most serious threat to the vine is frost, especially late-winter or spring frost. In a short period of unusually low temperature during the vine's budding or flowering stage, damage can be done from which that year's vintage cannot recover, no matter how favorable the conditions of summer that follows. In California's Napa Valley, damaging frosts affected the vineyards in 1961, 1964, 1970 (when half the potential crop was destroyed), 1971, and 1972 (when the frost was followed by excessive heat and then damaging rains at harvest time). In Bordeaux, growers still talk of the winter of 1956, the century's worst. Cold weather continued into the spring, and in the lower-lying parts of the region (always the most seriously threatened) almost the entire crop was eliminated. Château Cheval-Blanc, one of Saint Emilion's leading estates, lost more than 95 percent of its 1956 harvest, a situation that was representative of other châteaux, especially in low-lying zones of Saint Emilion and Pomerol. And the frost

ROSÉ WINE

DRUMLIN ROSE

alcohol 12% by volume

produced and bottled by **Hamlet Hill Vineyards**
POMFRET, CONNECTICUT 06258

This label of Hamlet Hill Vineyards near Pomfret, Connecticut, acknowledges the significance of a physiographic landform, the glacial drumlin, in the ripening of the wine's main cultivar, the Pinot Noir. The hill, 90 meters (300 feet) high, extends the growing season by about three weeks compared to the area around its base—a crucial advantage in this viticultural frontier.

killed all but the roots and lower trunks of the vines, so that there was no marketable vintage in 1957 or 1958; not until the 1960s did Château Cheval-Blanc return to its pre-1956 production levels. By some estimates it never has recovered its old excellence. A comparatively brief but severe frost can have a long-term impact.

Even an unusually severe early- or mid-winter cold spell can damage or kill vines. This problem is especially serious in more "continental" (Fig. 4.1) regions and in Northern Hemisphere high-latitude regions generally, where annual temperature ranges (and hence risks) increase. The worst possible scenario occurs when a severe frost follows an unusually warm period. Such a sequence of events took place during the fall and winter of 1980 in New York State. November had been a relatively warm month, slowing the vines' normal progress toward winter dormancy. Even by mid-December, sap still was flowing in the vines, and buds were moist. At midday on Christmas eve, the thermometer stood at 1°C. (34°F.). That night the temperature dropped to −33°C. (−28°F.). Temperature declines of 30°C. (54°F.) were common in the Finger Lakes country and in the Hudson Valley. This froze the sap in the vines and crystalized the buds, and destroyed all but the lower trunks of the vines. It was, indeed, the Christmas Eve Massacre. All kinds of vines were affected: *vinifera*, native American species, and hybrids. No amount of cold-resistance could withstand the ravages of so severe and so sudden a frost.

Where the risk of extreme winter cold is great, winegrowers have taken measures to protect the vines during dormancy. This involves pruning back the vine almost to ground level, and burial under a mound of earth sometimes mixed with leaves or straw. The practice occurs in Eastern Europe and in the Soviet Union, and in places in Canada.

Late frosts (those of early spring) endanger the crop in another way. In the past, winegrowers would light smudgepots or set small, smoky fires in the vineyards, but more modern control of the effects of spring frosts is by sprinkling. The irrigation systems seen in the Napa Valley serve primarily as frost protection and are less often used to supplement natural water supply. By coating the vines and buds with a protective ice layer whose temperature will remain near 0°C. (32°F.), the sprinkler system protects against the penetration of even lower temperatures as the early morning cold deepens.

In this context the topographical position of the vineyards is significant. In the spring and fall, when sun angles are comparatively low and daytime heating is only moderate, heat loss from the ground during the night can carry ground temperatures below freezing. As a result a layer of air adjacent to the surface also cools below frost level, and this cold, heavy air proceeds to slide downslope to settle in valleys and basins. This process of *katabatic* air flow (or, more simply, cold-air drainage) creates "lakes" of nighttime cold air in such low-lying areas, and in these places further radiation loss combined with the inflow of frigid air can create serious frost danger. In 1956 katabatic air flow worsened the situation for Château Cheval-Blanc; the other leading château of Saint Emilion, Ausone, situated near the top of a hillslope, escaped the severest nighttime cold. Frost is a hazard especially in high-latitude and high-altitude vineyards, but within those areas it threatens certain locales more than others.

Hail

Another threat to the harvest is hail. It is advantageous to record some summer rain in maturing vineyards, but summer convection can become severe and precipitation may come in the form of hail (the passage of fronts in cyclonic storms also can generate hail). The damage from hailstorms is all too obvious: leaves and branches are stripped off the plant, and if the hail comes during the late summer, it will batter the grape bunches and can destroy the harvest altogether. For unexplained reasons some areas within viticulture regions, and even some specific vineyards, seem to lie in the path of hailstorms more often than others. The harvest in Sauternes was wiped out by hail no less than three times in the past thirty-five years (1951, 1952, 1973). Hail damaged the crop at harvest time in Mendocino County, California, in 1982.

The localized nature of hailstorms is a reality that is reflected on the viticultural map, because it leads growers to acquire and maintain patches of vines in scattered areas. A compact vineyard can be completely destroyed; some dispersal of the property provides insurance against such a disaster. Of course, dispersal also brings with it greater vulnerability, a disadvantage many growers feel is nevertheless outweighed by the protection it provides.

Wind

Hailstorms, of course, are associated with the passage of weather fronts. These fronts also bring with them another hazard to vineyard and grape: high winds. Often localized but very destructive, such winds can rip off the branches, leaves, and the grapes themselves. This is one of the environmental aspects that give a particular vineyard location an advantage over others. In all vineyard regions, strong and potentially damaging winds tend to come from a certain direction or quadrant more frequently than from others. Where there is the opportunity, the vines are best served by a location that puts a natural barrier, such as a hill or ridge, in that path. When such protection is not available, winegrowers may create it themselves by conserving strips of forest or by planting rows of trees or hedges to serve as windbreaks.[12]

Even gentler winds may bring hazards to the vines. It is generally agreed that Burgundy's east-facing vineyards are favored not only because of their orientation to daily solar paths, but also because they thus "turn their backs" to the sometimes moisture-laden air coming from the west. Another risk involves the invasion of salt-laden air from the ocean. The same salt that coats automobiles and patio furniture many kilometers from the ocean also settles on the leaves of the vine—with negative consequences for the vintage, and potential disaster if a salt-air invasion occurs during the harvest. In the Bordeaux area, "salt dew" has been found on the vines as far as 80 kilometers (50 miles) inland from the Bay of Biscay. Perhaps no other viticulture area experiences this problem to the same degree, but salt-carrying breezes do reach exposed vineyards in California, South Africa, Australia, and other viticulture regions situated near coastlines, especially coastlines facing west.

Smoke and Fire

The bushfires have now swept down off the mountain where they started days ago. The district and volunteer brigades and the army have no chance of holding them, fanned by a hot wind overhead to extraordinary activity. The fire storm jumps from treetop to treetop, exploding the drought-dry, oil-filled leaves of the head, leaving in its wake palisades of black boles standing stark. The holocaust jumpt hundreds of feet at a time, depending on the quirks of air currents and eddies from depressions in the ground, contouring the hot stream above. Down go the vineyard fenceposts. Elliots, Tyrrells, Draytons suffer. Vines at the edges of the vineyards are most severely burnt but all the vineyards' greenness, while probably stopping the spread of flames penetrating too deeply, seems to become suddenly dull from the cloud of heat above. Finally, the fire burns itself out, and all is cool and black. The men are exhausted, burnt, suffocated, too many heroes to name individually. Disaster seems universal as the fading smoke pall has dulled the senses.

This entry, dated 19 November 1968, is from *Hunter Winemakers* by Max Lake, and it describes dramatically what happened in that Australian viticulture region when the 1968 vintage approached ripeness. Heat and smoke damage not only the margins of vineyards but can affect the entire harvest. Wherever vineyards stand in dry-zone irrigated regions or in close proximity to fire-prone natural vegetation, the risk exists; the dry summer that ripens the grapes also dries out the vegetation. This was dramatically underscored by the raging fire on Mount St. Helena near Calistoga, California, in September 1982. Whipped by winds of up to 100 kph (60 mph), this huge fire swept along the northern margins of the Napa Valley and into upper Sonoma County. It burned to the edges of several Calistoga vineyards and came within feet of famed Chateau Montelena. Obviously, the probability of fire and smoke is far less in moister and cooler regions such as Burgundy, Germany, and New Zealand: Figure 4.1 suggests where the dry-summer intensity is greatest.

Smog

As urban populations near viticulture areas have increased in size, city smog has begun to affect the vineyards downwind as well. This phenomenon was first observed in the 1950s in Southern California, and air pollution now is a recognized (if not natural) environmental threat. The ozone in the smog does most of the damage, causing a dark "stipple" on the vine leaves. These spots become larger as the summer progresses, resulting in a substantial loss of chlorophyll and of photosynthesis capacity. This in turn reduces the growth of canes, limits the weight of the grapes, and inhibits the sugar content of the grapes.[13] Damage of this kind is not confined to California. It also has been found affecting grapevines in Northern New York State, and it is obvious that vineyards near any smog-producing city are at risk.

Other Hazards

Some environmental hazards to the vineyards are not climate-related, at least not directly. A whole host of insects attacks the vine's flower, fruit, cane, and even the trunk. Birds, rabbits, and deer also inflict damage to vineyards. Birds are especially damaging when the grapes are ripe and sweet, just before the harvest. A large flock can strip a substantial part of a vineyard bare in minutes, and viticulturists use several methods, including elaborate and expensive netting, to discourage birds throughout the ripening period. Against deer, it is necessary to fence the entire vineyard area, although taste repellents also are used.[14] Gophers and rabbits (the latter a problem especially in Australia) are combated by trapping and fencing respectively.

This incomplete enumeration of hazards facing the winegrower underscores the truism that an optimal climate, a well-matched variety or hybrid of *vinifera*, and a suitable soil by no means guarantee a good harvest at summer's end.

Water and Wine

In Chapter 3 the relationship between early market viticulture and river transport routes in Europe was underscored. Not only in Europe, but all over the world there is a close association between rivers and vineyards— even when the rivers never had a transport function. There is a French saying that "the vines should overlook the river," and certain wines are actually named after particular rivers: "Rhine," "Mosel," and "Rhône" wines for example. Some viticulture regions are named after the rivers that form their physiographic arteries: the Napa, Russian, Hunter, and Henderson (River) valleys are cases in point. Other wine-producing regions, though not named after rivers, in fact constitute the valleys or basins of major water-courses: Bordeaux lies at the confluence of the Garonne and Dordogne rivers, and the Médoc faces the Gironde; Spain's Rioja is a segment of the Rio Ebro valley. From France's Loire to Portugal's Douro and Chile's Aconcagua, rivers and river valleys are viticulture's loci.

It is not the rivers themselves that make river valleys desirable viticulture areas, although sun reflection from the water surface does play a significant role in the microclimate of some vineyards, especially in cool regions. In many instances the rivers are only streams of modest size and limited volume; neither the Napa nor the North Para (in the Barossa Valley), for example, is a major watercourse. But the rivers, over many millennia, have fashioned the valleys in which they lie, eroding valley sides, accumulating alluvium, building and redissecting floodplains. Slope and soil mark the record of longtime weathering and erosion, droughts and floods, weakness and vigor. Tributaries have undercut their own valley sides and generated mass movements (rockfalls, landslides) that eventually lowered slope angles and facilitated soil development. The river valley and basin is a summation of the river system's lengthy work, although the river today may be a mere remnant of its more powerful predecessors.

Thus river valleys usually have complex terrain, varied soils, microclimatic variations, and diverse environments among which there will be those suitable for viticulture. Near the river, the water moderates weather extremes; water supply underground is likely to be more dependable.

But not all viticulture regions "overlook the river." Burgundy, at its best in the Côte d'Or, lies 10 to 20 kilometers (6 to 12 miles) from the Saône River. Burgundy adjoins the river only in Mâconnais and in Beaujolais, that is, in its southern half. Countless vineyards in Italy thrive far from rivers and streams. And then there are the great expanses of irrigated vineyards, nourished not by precipitation or attainable water table, but artificially. The water may be drawn from underground sources; if a river provides it, as the Murray does in a large Australian viticulture region, its waters are raised by dams and channeled to the vines through artificial canals many kilometers long. In California and Mendoza the water comes from mountain streams and melting snow as well as boreholes, transforming desert and steppe into islands of green.

Viticulture under irrigation produces grapes and wines, but not at the same level of quality expected in the regions where the vines grow under natural conditions. In the very search for moisture and nutrients that compels the vine to extend its roots deeply into the soil and subsoil lies the character

Irrigated vineyards extend to the horizon (and toward the Murray River) in the Mildura area, Australia.

of the grape and the complexity of the wine. Irrigation ensures the provision of water, but it limits initiative.[15] Certainly good wines are produced (and in enormous volume) in Argentina and in Australia's Murray basin, and some of the South African sherries and brandies produced in the irrigated vinelands of the Little Karroo are of very good quality. What has been achieved in California's Central Valley in terms of volume combined with sustained quality has attracted world-wide attention. But no irrigated vineyard has yet produced wines comparable to the best from unirrigated zones of natural growth.

If the Central Valley cannot compare to Napa, or the Little Karroo to the Cape, or the Murray area to Barossa and the Hunter, it should nevertheless be noted that modern methods of viticulture in unirrigated areas do involve systems of augmented water supply in case of severe drought or other climatic adversity. As noted earlier, these (usually sprinkling-type) systems have multiple purposes. They provide water in times of unusual drought, cooling during periods of excessive heat, and security against frost. Thus human intervention modifies physical environments in "unirrigated" as well as irrigated areas, though less dramatically. The capacity of the vine to grow and thrive under existing, even adverse physical-geographic conditions is the essence of its character and quality.

Reconstructing Past Environments

One dimension of physical geography involves the study of climatic conditions of the distant past, centuries before weather data were recorded by meteorological instruments. This is a fascinating kind of detective work in which every fragment of information is useful and valuable. It also has practical relevance, because the results of this research indicate the timing of cooling and warming phases during the current interglacial period, and suggest the extremes that may occur.

In this connection the records kept by winegrowers, centuries ago, are especially enlightening. The French scholar E. Ladurie pointed out that the date when the grape harvest begins is much affected by a small change in seasonal temperature, a situation that may be extrapolated to the Middle Ages. A 1°C. (1.8°F.) summer-period increase makes a ten-day difference in the timing of the harvest.[16] R. A. Bryson and T. J. Murray, in their book *Climates of Hunger,* compare Ladurie's report on harvest dates with other information about weather during the sixteenth and seventeenth centuries. Two notable series of late harvests occurred in 1591–1602 and 1639–1643. These correspond directly to known glacial cooling about 1600 and again in 1643–1644.[17] J. R. Bray developed a highly significant correlation between French wine harvest dates and central England summer temperature from 1659 to 1879 on the one hand, and Swiss alpine glacial advances based on tree-ring data on the other.[18] One danger inherent in such correlations lies in the winegrower's ability to change cultivars in response to sustained cooling trends, so that the earlier harvest may result from the ripening of varieties adapted to shorter growing seasons. Without evidence that such a change was not made by the grower (evidence that is not always part of the record), the harvest-date method must be used with care.

Going back even further, H. H. Lamb in his book *The Changing Climate* describes William the Conqueror's census of all landowners and their possessions in his newly pacified English kingdom. The Domesday Book of 1085 records that there were thirty-eight vineyards in England, in addition to the king's own; some were as large as 4 hectares (10 acres), and five had existed for a century or more.[19] Lamb mapped the locations of these vineyards, and compared the present-day climate prevailing in the now-extinct English viticultural areas to that of current frontier areas in Germany and elsewhere. In all cases, he found, the May or July temperatures, or both, today fall short of what viticulture needs. He adds that it is true "that individual enthusiasm has succeeded in operating isolated vineyards in specifically favorable sites in the south of England in most centuries since the Middle Ages, but these have never continued long after the retirement or death of the [wine] enthusiast."[20]

Change has come to the viticultural scene in England, even in the two decades since Lamb drew those conclusions. In part this is due to the development of cold-resistant hybrids that push viticulture's frontier northward; in part it may be a response to a period of milder conditions that may end at any time. In 1982 there were more than two hundred wineries in England, nearly thirty making wine commercially—not only in the south, but as far north as Derby and the Midlands. The grapes with which this is being achieved, not surprisingly, tend to be German, the Müller-Thurgau leading among these. But several hybrids also successfully cultivated in New York State are important contributors to viticulture's English revival.

Did viticulture decline in England of the Middle Ages because the climate cooled, or was there, as some historical geographers suggest, another reason? Did the increasing difference in quality between imported French wines and the local product—and the accessibility of mainland wines as Britain's political tentacles and commerce expanded—simply extinguish the domestic industry? The answer may always be in doubt. Climatologists point to their reconstructions and argue that the coincidence between the "Little Ice Age" (as the cooling trend beginning in the thirteenth century is called) and the end of Roman-English viticulture is simply too strong. Economic geographers probably would suggest that the two causes—climate and commerce—worked in concert. As the debate goes on, so does the research.

Additional Reading

On spatial aspects of climate, the heat summation, and soils:

Amerine, M. A., and Singleton, V. L. *Wine: An Introduction.* 2nd ed. Berkeley: University of California Press, 1977.

Holtgrieve, D. G., and Trevors, J. D. *The California Wine Atlas.* Hayward: Ecumene, 1978.

Johnson, H. *World Atlas of Wine.* New York: Simon & Schuster, 1977.

Weaver, R. A. *Grape Growing.* New York: John Wiley & Sons, 1976.

Winkler, A. J., et al. *General Viticulture.* Berkeley: University of California Press, 1974.

General reference on terminology:

Debuigne, G. *Larousse Dictionary of Wines of the World.* London: The Hamlyn Publishing Group, 1976.

On ancient climates:

Bryson, R. A., and Murray, T. J. *Climates of Hunger.* Madison: University of Wisconsin Press, 1977.

Lamb, H. H. *The Changing Climate.* London: Methuen, 1966.

On some aspects of physical geography:

Strahler, A. N., and Strahler, A. H. *Modern Physical Geography.* New York: John Wiley & Sons, 1981.

5

Political Geography of Viticulture: From Wine Laws to Wine Wars

Wine has been the object of competition and conflict almost from the day it was first made. In the time of the ancient Assyrians wine was considered to be a strategic commodity, and the kings decreed that every military effort should be made to stop wine supplies from reaching actual as well as potential enemies. In Roman times the production of wine in the provinces became an issue in Roman Italy itself, and to protect the local industry against competition from Gaul, Emperor Domitian ordered Burgundian vines (and vines elsewhere in the empire) uprooted. Much later the decree of King Philip II of Spain, that the commercial wine industry of Spanish Mexico should be terminated, had a similar objective: the protection of the domestic industry against competition from the colonies. By preferential tariff and favorable treaty, by punitive taxation and ideological prohibition, the world's vineyards have alternately thrived and suffered.

In the nineteenth century a new kind of arena for viticultural politics was opened. This was presaged by the events that led up to the establishment of the famous 1855 Classification of Gironde wines, and reflected a rising awareness, felt most strongly in France at first, that legislation would be needed to confirm and maintain the several recognized levels of wine quality. Had the spread of *oidium* and *phylloxera*, and the massive task of vineyard reconstruction, not interrupted this process, the wine laws that eventually developed would have been established much earlier. As it is, the codification of wine quality—in France as well as in other major wine-producing countries—has been a twentieth-century phenomenon. French regulations were in place by the 1930s after three decades of negotiations. After midcentury, Germany and South Africa moved to establish tight legal controls over wine production

Alcohol 11% by vol.   Contents 24 oz.

RED FRENCH WINE

PRODUCT OF FRANCE

HAUT~POINTE

LE GRAND VIN ROUGE

1972   ✳

BON-VIN, INC, NÉGOCIANT A LA GRAVE D'AMBARÈS (GIRONDE)
SOLE WORLD AGENTS: BON-VIN, INC, HOUSTON, TEXAS.
GIP-LIBOURNE

Nothing on this label indicates the relationship of the wine to the
French classification system. There is no guarantee of any kind for
the consumer.

and labeling. In Italy and the United States, regulations came about in
stages, and are the subject of continuing modification.

Political geographers study the spatial context and impact of such events.
Economists are interested in the terms of tariffs and trade; political scientists
consider the contents of treaties and conventions. But political geographers
are concerned with the impact of these issues on the political, economic,
and cultural landscapes of the communities and societies they affect. Take,
for example, the Methuen Treaty to which reference was made in Chapter
3. The section of the treaty that gave Portuguese wine preferential status
on English markets was only one, comparatively minor, part of the overall
alliance it established. But behind this clause lay a far-reaching consequence
for the farmers of Portugal. The new economic order brought British firms
and capital to Portugal. Land that had been devoted to foodcrops was bought
out and given over to the vine. The entire economic and cultural landscape
of Northern Portugal was changed, and with it the economic geography of
Portugal as a whole.

Other aspects of wine legislation are similarly imprinted on the map.
When France established its complex *Appellation Contrôlée* system, this involved
delimitation of viticultural areas within which a certain wine quality was
assured, and outside of which no such claim could be made. Thus the system
created a viticultural map that enormously favored certain French winegrowers—and disadvantaged others. In Italy, the concept of the *Classico*

zone has a similar connotation, because only wines derived from vines grown in the original heartland of cultivation (and officially delimited) may be so labeled. Thus the wine laws require the drawing of boundaries, and while the resulting maps may not have political elements (states, provinces, counties), they are very much the result of political negotiation and compromise. Wine and politics are inextricably enmeshed.

The *Appellation d'Origine Contrôlée* Laws

The most comprehensive and effective wine laws yet established are those of France. It is true that other countries also have well-conceived wine legislation, notably West Germany and South Africa, but the French achievement should be seen in context of the dimensions and complexity of its wine industry, the range of its products, and the diversity of its interests.

The term *Appellation d'Origine Contrôlée* literally means "controlled place of origin." This constitutes a guarantee that the wine carrying an *Appellation* on its label was made in a locale and under conditions that have the strength of the law behind them. It does not mean that a French winegrower cannot make wine unless his or her vineyard lies within such a locale. As a field trip to a wine shop quickly confirms, not all French wine is "*AOC*" wine. It does establish a broad ranking of French wines, so that the consumer may, at a glance, make a choice between an *AOC* and a non-*AOC* wine.

The *Appellation Contrôlée* system (to use a customary abbreviation) is essentially geographic, and its geography is reflected on the bottle's label. Figure 5.1 is a hypothetical illustration of these fundamentals. The controlled viticultural region lies centered on an imaginary city named Celliers. Its boundary is represented by the solid line on the map. Wine made anywhere within this boundary may carry on its label the words *Appellation Celliers Contrôlée*, even wine made by shippers from grapes purchased in several parts of the region and vinted in a cellar in the city itself. Wine made outside the boundary—as at Château Cider—may be sold behind an impressive-looking label containing a picture of an elaborate château and such words as "grand vin superieur," but it is not entitled to *AOC* status.

Among wines made within the *Appellation Celliers Contrôlée* boundary, there is a clearly defined, geographic hierarchy. As Figure 5.1 shows, the Celliers region is divided into six districts. One of these districts is Carafe; it does not have its own *AOC* status, and wines made there are sold as *Appellation Celliers Contrôlée*, the "lowest," most general *AOC* rank. Another district, Bouchon, does have its own approved *Appellation*, and wines made there, in the vicinity of the town of Chai, have a rank one step higher: *Appellation Bouchon Contrôlée*. Still another district, Charnu, is divided into smaller units centered on villages, one of which, Cave, is named on the map. These smaller areas are called communes, and in the case of the district of Charnu (but *not* in Bouchon) these communes have their own individual *Appellation*. Thus wine labeled *Appellation Cave Contrôlée* ranks above *AC* Bouchon and *AC* Celliers, because the terrain and environment in the commune is deemed to be even finer, and the requirements for production are even stricter, than in the district. And there is an even higher rank, the highest France can bestow: an *Appellation* given to a single vineyard, such as Chalon-Collage on Figure 5.1.

In ascending order of quality, therefore, the *AC* will show region, district,

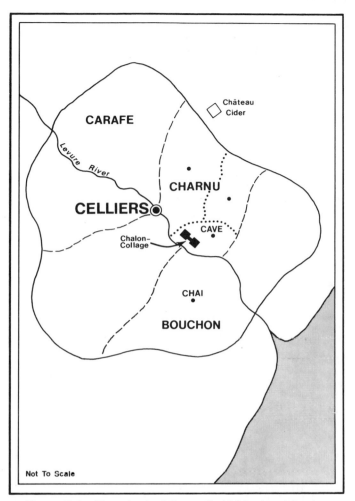

Figure 5.1 Hypothetical Controlled Viticultural Region

commune, and vineyard. Inspection of several familiar Bordeaux labels illustrates its practical application (Fig. 5.2). The first label contains the statement *Appellation Bordeaux Contrôlée*, lowest of the Bordeaux ranks. The next label, with *Appellation Haut-Médoc Contrôlée*, represents the district level *AC*. The highest-ranking Bordeaux label shown comes from the commune of Pauillac, and proudly states *Appellation Pauillac Contrôlée*. To find a label representing a single vineyard it is necessary to select an example from Burgundy, since none exists in Bordeaux. La Romanée, considered by many to be France's finest vineyard, has a separate *Appellation* for its area of less than one hectare (about 2.1 acres).

With viticultural regions as diverse as Champagne and the Loire, Provence and Alsace, it was not a simple matter to apply the principles outlined above to all of France. Indeed, French oenologists themselves admit that short-comings remain. But the system that took three decades to develop and install has contributed enormously to the maintenance of quality—and to French leadership in the world of wine.

Figure 5.2 Three Labels

The effort began in the first years of the century, when the French wine industry was beginning to recover from the *phylloxera* disaster. Many deleterious practices had become routine: the introduction of hybrids into the very heartlands of *vinifera* cultivars (see Chapter 2); overproduction of grapes at the expense of wine quality; the addition of water to "stretch" the wine; the mixing of sugar and water and leftover *marc* to produce more "wine." It was clear that legislation would be needed to bring order to the chaos from which French viticulture was emerging. First in 1905, and then in 1908, important legal steps were taken. By 1908, for example, the geographic boundaries of a number of eventual *Appellations*—Bordeaux, Cognac, and Armagnac among them—were established. That this was no small accomplishment is evinced by the effect of regional delimitation of Champagne. There, the winegrowers disagreed with the official decisions, riots erupted, and the army had to be called out to maintain order while the government reconsidered.

World War I interrupted the proceedings, but in 1919 a new law was promulgated. The shortcomings of that law illustrate the special difficulties in the way of wine legislation. To refer again to Figure 5.1, imagine that the district of Bouchon achieves its own *Appellation* on the basis of excellent wines coming from the vicinity of Chai. In the clayey lowlands of the Levure River grow vines of lesser quality from which mediocre wines (at best) are made; the grapes also are sold to shippers for blending into *AC* Celliers wine. No one ever attached the name Bouchon to these inferior products, but now, the whole district having been awarded an *Appellation,* the growers of the cheap bottomland wines are entitled to use it on their labels. Inferior Bouchon wines begin to appear on the market. Bouchon's traditionally good wines become suspect. Prices decline as large-scale buyers report market resistance. The law has failed to protect quality.

Actual events of this kind led to revision of the 1919 law, first in 1927 when, for the first time, stipulations were added regarding the cultivars that might be grown (hybrids were prohibited), and again in 1935 when the law as it exists today came into effect. Now the law contains a set of stipulations that severely constrain all aspects of viticulture in an *AOC* region. These include specifications regarding (a) the terrain on which *AOC* wines may and may not be produced; (b) the cultivars permitted under certain environmental conditions; (c) viticultural practices that must be followed, including pruning methods and limitations on harvests; (d) the minimum alcoholic content of grape, must, and wine; (e) vinicultural practices, the result of long traditions now codified and inspected by officials and tasters; and (f) distillation procedures and practices for Cognac, Armagnac, and other spirits made in France.

Among the important results of this drive toward wine legislation in France has been the recognition of regions and their particular products. The same restrictions that preclude Château Cider (Fig. 5.1) from stating an *Appellation* on its label also prohibit the use of such terms as "Champagne," "Cognac," or "Beaujolais" for wines or spirits not made within the boundaries of those regions and by methods prescribed by law. That restriction, now in force throughout the European Economic Community countries, unfortunately did not apply to the rest of the wine-producing world. This led to the anomalous situation that winegrowers just outside the very boundaries of the Champagne District, making sparkling wines in accordance with the Champagne method, may not label their wine "Champagne," while winegrowers in California can and do use the term with impunity. So it is with Chablis and Burgundy, as winegrowers outside France capitalize on the reputations of such French regions and their wines to market inferior bulk products.

Actions of this kind underlie conflicts between winegrowing countries. During the development of the French *Appellation* legislation, an international conference was convened to draw up a treaty that would control labeling and descriptive practices, and a convention among European countries was in fact achieved. Since the United States was going through the Prohibition period at that time, it was not a signatory to the convention. In the 1950s the European Economic Community (E.E.C., sometimes simply E.C. for Economic Community) began negotiations to tighten Common Market regulations still further, but the United States was not a party to these discussions, either. Thus California continues to produce "Rhine" wine and "Chablis," "Sherry" and "Madeira" (but, notably, no "Rhône" or "Rioja").

In Europe, the E.E.C. negotiations have established protective rules for the names of regions and their wines, and not only at the highest levels of wine classification, such as the *AOC* system and its equivalents elsewhere. In France and in all member countries, all wines, from the most ordinary to the most prestigious, are subject to a broad classification system that is still undergoing modification toward international compatibility. In France, the *AOC* system is only part of its broader categorization of wines, in which the lowest level is that for *Vins de Consommation Courante* (Wines for Early Consumption). These are nondescript wines with little merit. Above this is the more important category of *Vins de Pays* (Country Wines), wines of comparatively low alcoholic content, made to be consumed young and, generally, destined for drinking in the region of production. These wines are produced under certain officially specified conditions, and the *pays* of origin are specified on their labels. Above these country wines rank the *Vins Délimités de Qualité Supérieure,* Designated Wines of Superior Quality. The conditions governing the production of these wines are much more stringent than those for country wines, and V.D.Q.S. wines often are quite good, if not up to *AOC* quality. Without the *AOC* ranking, they command lower prices; and since some of them come from owner-estates, they can be of more than passing interest. But in the international arena, the *Appellation* system remains France's strongest ally.

German Wine Laws

The evolution of Germany's wine laws illustrates the problems that arise when the viticultural and vinicultural practices of a highly specialized region must be integrated into a wider legal system. Wine legislation in Germany actually began centuries ago (before there was a united German state), and consisted of a set of vinicultural rules. The rule against watering wine was strict: in 1706 it is recorded that a vintner was executed by hanging for stretching his wine this way.[1] The first actual wine law in Germany was promulgated in 1879, to be revised in 1892 and again in 1901; a central issue in this early legislation involved the difference between "natural" and "sweetened" (sugared) wine. The practice of sugaring the must occurs in regions where cool weather may inhibit the development of adequate sugar in the grapes. In France it is called *Chaptalization* after the official who authorized it in Napoleon's time; in Germany the term is *Gallization* in honor of the man who developed the appropriate technology for it. Adding sugar to the must has the effect of raising the alcohol content of the finished wine following fermentation, but it is a procedure that is subject to misuse. In France it is controlled by the *Appellation* laws, but it does have legal sanction and prevails in regions such as Northern Alsace, Burgundy, and occasionally even in Bordeaux. In the United States the question became a major dispute in the nineteenth century between California and eastern winemakers (sugaring the must at any stage of vinification remains illegal in California). In Germany, with its cold-climate viticulture regions, sugaring made vinification possible, but German officials wanted wine labels to reflect whether a wine was sweetened or produced under totally "natural" (that is, unsugared) conditions.

In 1930 Germany arrived at a wine law that established this distinction and, furthermore, proscribed the use of hybrids. All existing hybrids had to be uprooted; henceforth only European varieties, grafted onto *phylloxera-resistant* American rootstocks, were tolerated. Throughout the 1930s there were revisions of the 1930 law, but in outline this remained the basis of German wine legislation.

Then World War II intervened, and after the war the resurgence of the German wine industry brought with it the need for more comprehensive legislation. Again the 1930 law underwent modification, but by the mid-1950s the new laws were so complex that they had lost much of their utility. As many as 30,000 vineyards produced wines under their own names; labeling practices were so confusing that the situation could only be described as chaotic. The Germans were determined to produce wine legislation to cope with these problems, and in 1969 a new law was promulgated that appeared to solve many of them. But in the meantime the Common Market countries, led by France, were working on wine legislation that, if adopted, would have had the effect of voiding much of Germany's 1969 law. The German law was formulated in recognition of the special environmental situation of Germany's high-latitude vineyards; "European" law had different priorities. Thus the Germans set about seeking a compromise with the E.E.C. lawmakers, while simultaneously revising their own 1969 law to bring it (as much as possible) into line with Common Market legislation. This effort produced the 1971 law, which has been the basis for German winemaking since.

Germany's viticultural and vinicultural problems in a European framework relate directly to its geographical location and the environments under which wine is produced. German wines, especially its lower-ranking wines, never had alcohol contents comparable to the wines of warmer climes; grapes that do not ripen fully do not have the sugar content to achieve this. Then the E.E.C., in its Regulation No. 337/79 concerning wines, declared that wines identified as table wines should not have an alcohol content of less than 8.5 percent, "obtained without any enrichment and no longer containing any residual sugar."[2] Since German table wines often attained only about 5 percent natural alcohol before sugaring, that wine would have been illegal under Common Market regulations. Obviously, what was appropriate for France or Italy could not apply to Germany without adjustment. German wine interests united in the face of the Common Market threat and extracted concessions that would permit Germany's federal states to determine critical points of viticultural law based on regional environmental circumstances.

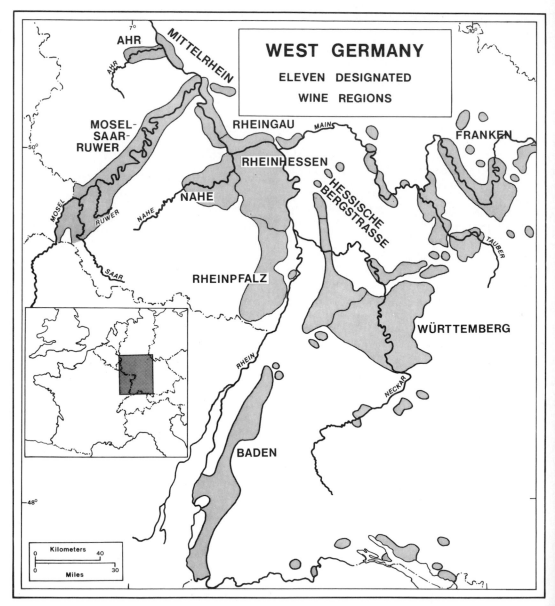

Figure 5.3 West Germany: Eleven Designated Wine Regions

The 1971 (New) Law

German wines are the only wines in the world that are classified not only by geographic origin and by vineyard, but also by degree of ripeness of the grape at the time of picking.[3] Between 80 and 90 percent of the wine made in Germany (and all the truly noble wines) are the wines of white grapes, harvested at various degrees of ripeness. Thus the German label reveals not only the geographic source of the wine, but also, at higher-quality levels, the degree of sweetness of the grapes at the time they were harvested.

The geographic basis of the 1971 law is a hierarchy of regions. Germany has eleven Designated Regions such as, for example, Mosel-Saar-Ruwer and Rheingau (Fig. 5.3). These are similar to France's Bordeaux and Alsace regions, and thus constitute the broadest reference to the origin of a wine. The German term for this kind of region is *Bestimmtes Anbaugebiet* or "specific cultivated area." Next comes what is best described as a subregion or district of a Designated Region. The basis for such a district is the clustering or geographic proximity of similar producing areas and their viticulture and viniculture, and thus in the wines produced. This is what the Germans call a *Bereich*, perhaps a somewhat unfortunate term. If a district is identified by name on the label, that name must be preceded by "Bereich," so that there is no doubt regarding its identity. Among Germany's eleven major wine regions, the number of districts or *Bereiche* varies from only one (in Rheingau and Ahr) to as many as seven (Baden). There are thirty-one such districts in total.

Below the district level are the communities. On the label, this is the name of a village that will provide a more detailed clue to the source of the wine, but it still remains a general reference. In German it is the *Gemeinde*, which translates as small municipality.

Now the reference becomes much more specific and significant. The actual vineyards where the wines are made are referred to as sites or *Lage* and, depending on the size of the vineyard area (always officially and exactly defined), these are large or "general" sites (*Grosslage*) or smaller individual sites (*Einzellage*). Obviously the official recognition of an individual site confers upon it an honor that carries the highest expectation of quality.

This five-level regional hierarchy may not convey the simplicity that was intended, and certainly the German wine label requires some careful inspection. As in Bordeaux and Burgundy, once the label conveys the ultimate in wine quality, familiarity and preference are the consumer's guide. The 1971 law constitutes a major refinement of the situation that preceded it, and the task has certainly been made easier. Before the 1971 law took effect, there were about 30,000 registered and approved vineyard names, including tiny patches of vines. The law decreed that a site (*Lage*) must cover at least 5 hectares (12.5 acres) of vines, effecting a major consolidation (and, admittedly, erasing some old and respected names in the process). This produced approximately 130 *Grosslage* and some 2600 *Einzellage*—a reduction by nearly 90 percent of the number of names in use.

The regional hierarchy thus established is linked to a qualitative classification that places all German wines in four major categories, and here the degree of ripeness of the grapes plays its crucial role. The lowest rank is represented by Table Wine (*Tafelwein*), which may bear the name of one of the German wine regions and that of a community (*Gemeinde*), but never a vineyard name (*Lage*). Stringent government quality tests that apply to higher-ranked wines are not required for *Tafelwein*.

Somewhat superior to the ordinary Table Wine of Germany is the German equivalent to France's *Vin de Pays:* a category called *Landwein* (Country Wine). Until the *Landwein* rank was established, there were only three levels of wine quality in Germany, but the integration of German winemaking into the larger Common Market framework revealed the need for a category between the lowest and middle ranks of Germany's three-tier system. Such wines are identified by a general regional name followed by the term *Landwein*, as in *Ahrtaler* (Ahr Valley) *Landwein* and *Südbadischer* (South Baden) *Landwein.* In most of the designations the name of one of the eleven German wine regions will be evident, but not always, as in *Starkenburger Landwein* from the Hessische Bergstrasse.

The next higher rank of German wines has the complicated name *Qualitätswein bestimmter Anbaugebiete*, abbreviated as *QbA*. Literally, this means Quality Wine from a Designated Region. These wines may be sugared during fermentation. They may carry the name of a specific vineyard (*Lage*) if 85 percent or more of the grapes have come from that vineyard.

The highest-quality German wines are those identified as *Qualitätswein mit Prädikat,* or *QmP*. The translation into Quality Wine with Affirmation is perhaps the most appropriate: behind the details on the label lies a series of inspections and controls that is without parallel in the world of viniculture. The winegrower may produce one or more of five kinds of *QmP* wines, depending on the condition of the grapes, the nature of the ripening season, and the timing of the harvest. The lowest designation among the *QmP* wines is the *Kabinett*, made from grapes that are just barely ripe and have the lowest amount of sugar. Like all *QmP* wines, the *Kabinett* must be made without any sugaring during fermentation and without any addition of concentrate.

The winegrower would prefer, if conditions permit, to make a more prestigious and refined wine. This can be done only when the grapes can be allowed to ripen further, gaining in sugar as the fall progresses. If the decision is made to create the next-higher quality wine, the *Spätlese* (literally: late-picked), the winegrower must inform the authorities of this intention. The grapes will be examined in the vineyard, and later the must will be examined in the winery, and vinification is subject to inspection throughout. As with all the *Qualitäts* wines, there is a certain must-weight that must be achieved before *Spätlese* may be made. (The must-weight index compares the weight of one liter of the must with that of one liter of distilled water and specifies how much heavier the must should be.) Obviously *Spätlese* can only be made from fully ripe grapes harvested comparatively late.

Still the winegrower may wait, just a week or two longer, to be able to achieve an even sweeter, more complex wine from grapes harvested as late as the end of November or even early December. The risk grows, but the rewards of such a wine, an *Auslese* (selective harvest), are enormous. All unripe, diseased, damaged, or otherwise unsuitable grapes are removed by hand, and inspection, tasting, and even chemical analyses confirm the quality of this silky-soft, scented wine.

If the natural conditions of the late fall are exceptionally favorable it is possible to harvest individual grapes that have become affected by *Edelfäule* or "Noble Rot" (see Chapters 2 and 4). These grapes are so ripe that they are close to becoming raisins; the *Edelfäule* has cracked the skins of the berries and water has evaporated, leaving concentrated sugar levels in the juice. Such grapes produce the scarce *Beerenauslese* ("berries picked selectively"), an accurate name. This is among the noblest of German wines, whose price reflects the attention it has received from harvest to bottling.

The ultimate in German wines is the rare *Trockenbeerenauslese:* "dry berries picked selectively." Here the term "dry" does not refer to the character of the wine, but the nearly dry, raisiny grapes from which it has been extracted. This wine is made virtually drop by drop from grapes that yield very little juice; the result is a concentrated sweet wine so memorable that it is deemed to rank among the greatest of vinicultural achievements.

The winegrower always faces the prospect that the grapes still in the vineyard late in the fall may be struck by sudden frost. When this happens, the grapes are quickly harvested and wine is pressed from them. The water in the grapes has turned into ice crystals, causing a concentration of sugar and acid, and in the winemaking process the ice is separated, yielding a must of extraordinary concentration. The result is an *Eiswein* (Ice Wine), a rare and valuable wine that adds still greater luster to German viniculture.

Behind this summary of German wine classification lies an immensely complicated system of vinicultural regulations. Not only must-weights but also alcohol levels, grape varieties used, vinicultural practices, and other conditions must be met, and the rules become more stringent as the ladder of quality is ascended. Nor can the winegrower expect to produce any class of wine desired. Frequently the summer and fall conditions are such that the winegrower can hope to make only *QbA* wines and perhaps some *Kabinett*, but nothing ranking higher. Only the best of years yield the greatest of German wines (see Chapter 8). The highly specialized German wine industry also is a high-risk venture.

Mediterranean Legislation

Germany's lead in wine legislation has been followed by Switzerland and Austria; wine laws in Italy, Spain, and Portugal have instead followed the French model. In none of these countries, however, is wine legislation as well developed as it is in Germany or France. Indeed, viticulture in these Mediterranean countries takes a very different form from that of more northern areas of Europe. Unlike the well-demarcated vineyard areas of the Rhineland, the vine in Italy and Iberia stands almost everywhere, and to pass from an unrecognized area into an officially designated wine region is to experience a transition, not a threshold.

Comprehensive wine legislation in Italy, in many years the world's largest producer of wine, did not emerge until the Common Market conferences of the 1950s and 1960s. Even then it was external pressure that had the greatest effect. Italian governments never did establish legislation to protect Italy's highest-quality wine regions and their products, but the real issue in the Common Market was the huge production of cheap Italian wines. France, especially, feared that the Common Market accords, which lowered tariff barriers among E.E.C. countries, would lead to the invasion of its domestic market by a flood of cheap Italian wine. Italian wine legislation, it was felt, should help stem this tide by imposing limitations on production.

At the same time, quality-conscious Italian winegrowers themselves agitated for legal recognition. In the 1950s and 1960s French premium wines

Figure 5.4   Italy: Designated D.O.C. Areas

dominated export markets, and Italian winegrowers could observe the advantages of France's *Appellation d'Origine Contrôlée* system at all quality levels.

This combination of circumstances led to the promulgation of Italy's first comprehensive wine legislation, in 1963. The law, under the title *Denominazione di Origine Controllata* (Controlled Denomination of Origin), states that "A place-of-origin name is given to wines made with grapes deriving from grapevines traditionally grown in corresponding districts of production, and processed according to local techniques, fair and constant, of that district." In practical terms, the law requires evidence that *D.O.C.* wines are derived from grapes traditionally grown in heartland (*classico*) regions, and that no hybrids are used. It further provides for vinicultural specification, inspection, certification, and labeling. Thus a *D.O.C.* Barolo wine is certified to be derived from the traditional grape of the Barolo-producing region, the Nebbiolo. Where a wine is made from two or more kinds of grapes (Tuscany's Chianti, for example), the *D.O.C.* regulations so stipulate.

Since the Italian wine law's creation in 1963, numerous changes have occurred, and modifications are still in progress. The process of establishing the *D.O.C.* designations (the first, Vernaccia di San Gimignano, dates from 1966) continued into the 1980s, and in 1983 their number approached 220, spatially covering much (some observers suggest too much) of Italy (Fig. 5.4). In the meantime, the system was elaborated to encompass five quality levels. From the lowest to the highest, these are (a) *Vini da Tavola* or Table Wines, representing about 70 percent of Italian production in an average year; (b) *Vini da Tavola con Indicazione Geografica* or Table Wines with Geographical Indication, permitting the use of specific grape varieties with a geographical reference and constituting some 15 percent of national output; (c) *Vini Tipici* or Typical Wines, a category that facilitates the integration of Italian wines into the supranational E.E.C. framework; (d) the *D.O.C.* wines, comprising 10 to 12 percent of Italian production; and (e) a new, highest-quality designation called *Denominazione di Origine Controllata e Garantita,* now in formative stages, with five famous Italian wines to be the first recipients: Barolo, Barbaresco, Brunello di Montalcino, and Vino Nobile di Montepulciano the initial four, with Chianti to follow (Fig. 5.5).

Italy's wine laws undoubtedly will undergo further change. Unlike France's rules, the Italian legislation is of recent vintage and adjustments have been required as implementation took place. The emerging *D.O.C.G.* legislation, for example, has raised questions about variable vintages. What happens when, in a poor year, a *D.O.C.G.* wine cannot reach its *Garantita* standards? Might it then be bottled as a *D.O.C.* wine or, failing even those tests, as a *Vino Tipico?* In another context, should the *Vini Tipici* and the *Vini di Tavola con Indicazione Geografica* be combined in a single category? Major questions such as these still remain under consideration.

Nevertheless, the Italian achievement of the past two decades is a substantial one. Out of a chaotic situation a good deal of order has been created, and while there has been criticism of the *D.O.C.* designations, they certainly constitute an improvement over the earlier vinicultural map, which conveyed little more than that a wine originated in one of Italy's provinces.

Wine laws in Spain have early antecedents, much earlier than those of Italy, but systematic legislation also developed here during the twentieth century. Winegrowers in Rioja, one of Spain's premier winegrowing regions, point to a written and legal definition of their wines, by King Sancho of

Figure 5.5 Italy: Regions of D.O.C. Wines

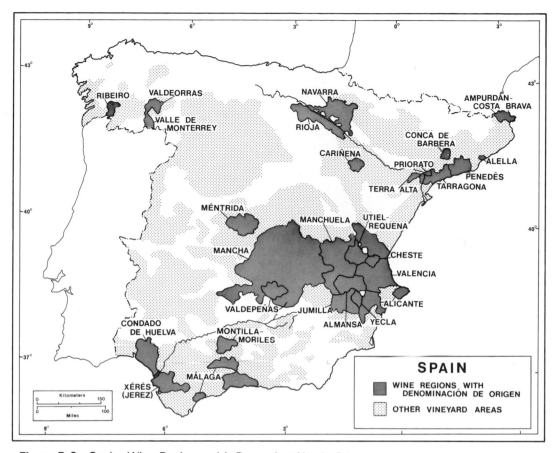

Figure 5.6 Spain: Wine Regions with Denominación de Origen

Navarra dated 1102, as the first real wine law of Spain. Actually it is Rioja's law of 1925, establishing a *Consejo Regulador de la Denominacion de Origen Rioja*, that marks the beginning of wine legislation in Spain. Rioja and Jerez long led the way in this effort, but Spain was not an E.E.C. member during the 1950s and 1960s, so that there was less pressure to extend regional rules into national laws. Indeed, comprehensive Spanish wine legislation appeared as recently as 1970, when the *Estatuto de la Viña, del Vino y de los Alcoholes* was published.

The *Estatuto* is based substantially on the French *Appellation* system. It recognizes 28 designated wine regions, each a *Denominacion de Origen*, and each controlled by a *Consejo* (Regulating Council). The role of the Council is to ensure that Spanish wine law is observed by the producers, but to do so in recognition of local conditions. As the map reveals, Spanish viticulture is dispersed throughout the country, but the designated wine regions lie in three broad zones: the temperate north, the plateau center, and the hot south (Fig. 5.6). Thus Spain's wine regions exhibit a wide range of environmental conditions, and each *Consejo* serves not only the central government but also the winegrowers in their particular regions.

Spanish regulations are quite specific and their enforcement is strict. It

Portugal may be better known for its Ports and its popular rosés, but its wine regions also produce very good table wines. The designated region (right upper corner) is Dão; the vintage is shown separately on the neck of the bottle. Older Portuguese table wines occasionally appear on the market and can be excellent values.

has been said that this has resulted in the domination of international markets by Sherry and Rioja wines, to the disadvantage of good wines from other regions. Recently the array of exported Spanish wines has widened, notably with the appearance of excellent wines from Penedés (see Chapter 8). Again the relationship between effective regulation and perceived quality is underscored, however. Spanish officials require that wines destined for export meet exacting standards; self-policing has for decades ensured the high quality of Rioja wines. When the range of exported Spanish wines did expand (including Champagne-like sparkling wines), their value was a foregone conclusion and their place on world markets assured.

It is a measure of the importance of the Port industry in Portugal that government control of winemaking is maintained not by one, but by two official bodies; the *Junta Nacional do Vinho* (National Council of Wine) in Lisbon and the *Instituto do Vinho do Oporto*, based in Oporto. The wine laws of Portugal are controlled by the *Junta Nacional do Vinho*, which enforces wine regulations in six officially designated wine regions (Fig. 5.7). Among these regions—not including Douro—only two, Vinhos Verdes and Dão, are internationally significant. In addition to its Port production, Portugal is well known for its special sparkling rosé wines; good table wines also come from the Dão region. The smaller regions clustered near Lisbon produce limited quantities of high-quality wine, but these are seen only occasionally outside Portugal itself.

Figure 5.7 Portugal: Demarcated Legal Wine Regions

While written wine laws are strict, enforcement has been patchy and has improved only recently. Individual demarcated regions have a good deal of autonomy under representative administrative bodies, whose effectiveness has varied. Social dislocation in the mid-1970s also deterred control. But the stronger hand evident in recent years has bettered the quality of Portuguese wines, reflected now by the growth of the country's export volume.

New-World Alternatives

European wine laws tend to be modeled on those of France or Germany, and the national systems have not lost their identities under the umbrella of Common Market regulations. One might imagine that wine legislation in the New World would be more easily achieved, in the absence of historic entanglements and without the domination of the great European producers. That conclusion would be wrong. Certainly New-World wine-producing countries have regulations governing their viticultural industries, but overall they have not achieved satisfactory solutions to the problems they were designed to overcome. In the United States, a convoluted attempt to establish "Appellations" was in progress in the 1980s.

South African Innovations

South African wine laws are among the most progressive in the world. This could not have been said just a decade ago, because until the early 1970s South Africa did not have a legal system resembling either the German or the French statutes. The powerful K.W.V. (Cape Winegrowers' Cooperative) dominated the industry and acted as arbiter; it rescued the industry from disaster in 1918, and in 1925 its rules for production were adopted as law by the South African (then Union) government.

For decades the South African Wine and Spirit Board, an official agency of the government, gave legal sanction to K.W.V. operations. But it acted significantly when, in the late 1960s, the need for quality-directed legislation became urgent—in part because of developments in the European Community. A committee was appointed that produced the concept of the South African "Wine of Origin," confirmed not just on a winery's label but, more important, by an official seal on the neck of the bottle. An enlarged version of the seal is shown in Figure 5.8.

The development of South Africa's legal system required the delimitation of a hierarchy of production units. Initially five levels were established, but in practice three of these have prime significance. The most prestigious is the *Estate*, closest unit in South Africa to a French château. A *Ward* is a cluster of vineyards, often near a village that gives its name to the unit. The *District* is a more specific appellation within an *Area*, but the areas have the best-known names, such as Paarl and Stellenbosch (see Chapter 9). Finally, the *Region* is the broadest regional unit, and it extends over more than one area (Fig. 5.9).

In 1972, recognition was awarded to fourteen regional designations; subsequently two additional areas were recognized, so that in 1983, South Africa had thirteen designated Areas and three Regions. Wines made in any one of these Areas or Regions may carry their label (and, more importantly, on the government-approved seal) the words *Wine of Origin*. This is only the first of five possible entries on that seal, and it is the critical one. Beneath the evidence of origin, shown on a blue band, is a red band confirming that this is a vintage wine. When the law was created, it was decreed that 75 percent of the wine in the bottle (or more) must be from the vintage of the year shown on the label. In practice, most vintage wines contain only wine made in that particular year. Beneath the red band of the vintage is a green band representing the cultivar used in making the wine. If the cultivar on the label specifies that the wine is a Cabernet Sauvignon, then at least 75 percent of the wine must be derived from that cultivar.

These three colored bands—blue for origin, red for vintage, and green for cultivar—are supplemented by two simple words of great importance. Above the bands the word *Estate* announces that this particular wine was made by one of a select group of recognized estates, representing the great names in South African viticulture. By 1982 some seventy such estates had

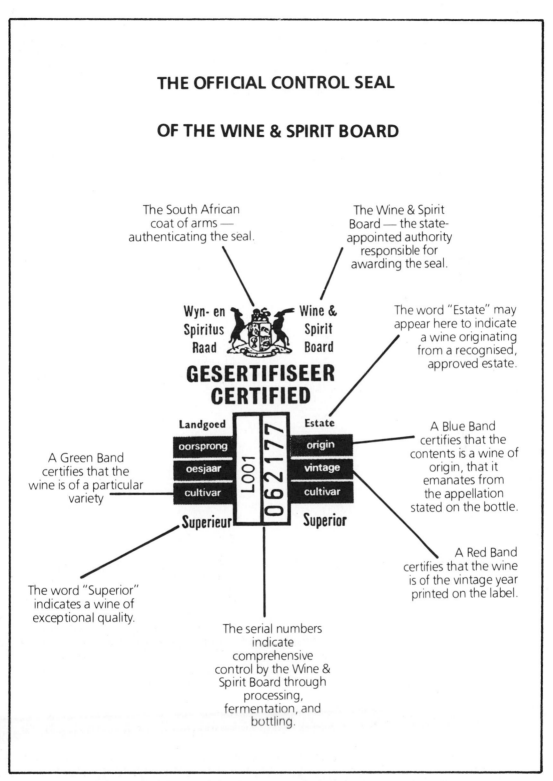

Figure 5.8 South Africa: The Official Control Seal of the Wine & Spirit Board

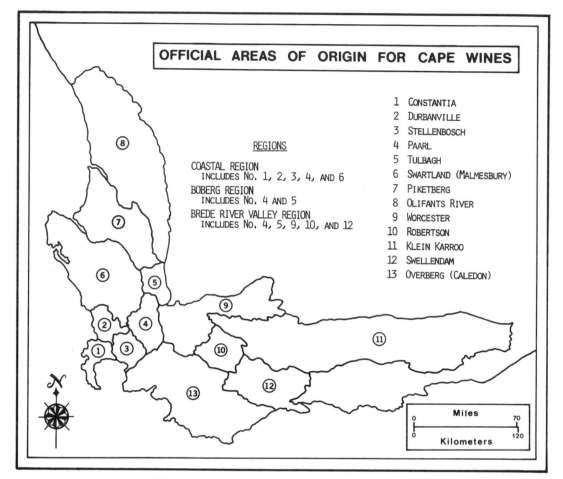

OFFICIAL AREAS OF ORIGIN FOR CAPE WINES

REGIONS

COASTAL REGION
INCLUDES NO. 1, 2, 3, 4, AND 6
BOBERG REGION
INCLUDES NO. 4 AND 5
BREDE RIVER VALLEY REGION
INCLUDES NO. 4, 5, 9, 10, AND 12

1 CONSTANTIA
2 DURBANVILLE
3 STELLENBOSCH
4 PAARL
5 TULBAGH
6 SWARTLAND (MALMESBURY)
7 PIKETBERG
8 OLIFANTS RIVER
9 WORCESTER
10 ROBERTSON
11 KLEIN KARROO
12 SWELLENDAM
13 OVERBERG (CALEDON)

Miles
0   70
0   120
Kilometers

Figure 5.9 Official Areas of Origin for Cape Wines

been awarded official recognition. A winery cannot simply proclaim that it is an estate; this is a designation based on history, tradition, sustained quality, reputation, and formal tests.

When the seal was first designed, it carried the word *Superior* as the fifth (and in many ways the most revealing) statement, beneath the three bands. Figure 5.8 represents the original seal, used until 1981, showing the *Superior* designation reserved for wines of truly exceptional quality as determined by panels of professional tasters. From 1982, a new seal was introduced for such excellent wines, with the term placed at the top, prominently displayed on a bright gold background. The distinction *Superior* immediately identifies the wine as unique and outstanding, and this of course is linked directly to its value on the market. The award, therefore, constitutes an incentive for winemakers and has the overall effect of raising quality-consciousness in the industry.

It should be acknowledged that the *Superior* designation is also a debatable aspect of South African wine law, because wines do improve in the bottle, sometimes after inauspicious beginnings, while others fade after promising much. The testing and tasting of wines submitted for evaluation is done scrupulously and under the most guarded conditions, however, and the system's advantages undoubtedly outweigh the negatives.

The consumer is well protected by the W.O. seal, because it confirms officially what the label asserts—and if the label confuses, the seal does not. At a glance it indicates the comparative qualities of the wine and its degree of finesse. This awareness—and some slight knowledge of the South African map—are among the best guides to the wines of any wine region available today.

A winemaker who does not wish to submit his or her wine to the system just described may bottle that wine without applying for a seal. Such wine may be quite good, but what its label claims is not officially confirmed. It is then up to the consumer to decide whether price and quality merit further purchase.

American "Appellations"

Viticulture and winemaking in America are centuries old, but this lengthy history has not produced mature and stable wine legislation. Certainly there have been controls, and the United States Treasury Department has long supervised the wine industry through its Bureau of Alcohol, Tobacco, and Firearms (BATF). But there has not been continuity. Rules concerning wine labeling changed significantly as recently as January 1, 1983, when a set of regulations first announced in 1978 became compulsory and superseded previous legislation. In 1978 BATF began a massive task: to invite and judge recommendations for the establishment of American "Appellations," so that the United States might ultimately have what so many other wine-producing countries have had for decades: a hierarchy of officially recognized regions whose names will become firmly linked to the character and quality of the wine they produce.

From the beginning there were doubts about this effort. There were obvious shortcomings in the plan; among these was the lack of involvement by geographers who are skilled in regionalization. Then, in the midst of this enormous project, BATF was targeted for abolition during the Reagan administration, its functions to be divided among other government agencies. Wine specialists, even those who prefer a minimum of government involvement in the industry's affairs, were concerned that years of education (of government representatives) would now be wasted. Just as the special place of wine among BATF's concerns seemed to be better understood, all the groundwork was endangered.[4]

The concept of appellations for American viticulture areas has been slow to materialize. In its 1978 announcement, BATF stated that any interested party could file a petition to establish an American "viticulture area." (This alone is an unfortunate designation, since BATF in its instructions to potential petitioners clearly seeks evidence for a *region*, not an area.) Five categories of information must be provided, the crucial one of which is geographic. In addition to name recognition, historic evidence, boundary description, and boundary cartography, BATF required evidence "of a geographic nature (climate, elevation, soil, physical features, rainfall) each of which distinguishes the viticultural features of the proposed area as similar from within, and dissimilar from other surrounding areas." No specifications concerning the dimensions or production of a viticultural "area" were given.

The appellation system insofar as official viticultural areas are concerned is part of a larger framework within which all American wines will fit. A wine may be marketed as (a) a *United States* wine, always made entirely from grapes grown in the United States; (b) a *State* wine, for example a New York wine or a California wine; (c) a *Multi-State* wine, with two or more contiguous states named on the label; (d) a *County* wine, vinted from grapes at least 85 percent of which were grown in the county named on the label; (e) a *Multi-County* wine, made from grapes grown within the named and adjacent counties; or (f) a *Viticultural Area* wine, originating entirely in the appellation described on the label.

The first petition for an American appellation came not from California, but from Augusta, Missouri, where a corner of Saint Charles County, about 50 kilometers (30 miles) west of Saint Louis and containing 40 square kilometers (15 square miles) of land including 15 hectares (35 acres) of vineyards, was proposed as an official viticulture area. In 1980 this proposal was approved and the name Augusta stood for the first U.S. viticulture area under the new regulations, and became the first American appellation.

The number of petitions grew quickly and exceeded sixty early in 1982, but not all of them progressed through the various stages of approval as did the Augusta proposal. From California came a four-county North Coast petition submitted by fifty-five winegrowers clustered in one of these, Lake County. This petition was rejected by BATF on several grounds, mainly involving the large size and diverse environments of the proposed region. A petition for recognition of a Napa Valley Appellation led to extended hearings and much debate over the proposed boundaries. The Amador County Winegrowers Association submitted a petition for a Shenandoah Valley Appellation based on the name of a valley in the area; this proposal drew criticism from the state of Virginia because of its historic association with the geographical name Shenandoah.

When the American appellation system was launched in 1978, winegrowers and their organizations were informed that after January 1983, only a state or county name would be permitted on a wine label if smaller and more specific viticultural areas had not by then been recognized. But the process of petitioning, followed by BATF deliberation, hearings, revisions, and related proceedings, proved to be slow and time-consuming. Many potential viticultural areas had not submitted their petitions in time for disposition prior to 1983, and some observers argued against the entire concept.[5]

The overall system of designation and appellation is combined with a set of rules regarding the three types of wine sold in the United States: *generic, proprietary,* and *varietal.* Reference already has been made to the use of such distinguished French names as Burgundy, Chablis, and Champagne for wines made in the United States that may only vaguely resemble the European original. (It is noteworthy that the state of Oregon prohibits such uses.) Eleven other "borrowed" names are sanctioned for use: Claret, Chianti, Hock, Madeira, Malaga, Moselle, Port, Rhine, Sauterne (*sic*), Sherry, and Tokay. These are the generic wines of America, and under the new regulations the European term must be preceded by a geographical one, such as "New York Moselle," "Napa County Claret," or "Green Valley Sauterne." These generic wines are the bulk, "jug" wines made and consumed in large volume; they are highly variable in quality, and their label tells the consumer comparatively little.

The proprietary wines are identified by "brand" on the label. Again the custom differs from that followed in Europe, where brand-name wines are subject to controls and tend to be identified by region or locale, for example Asti Spumante. In the United States, such association does not occur, and a brand-name wine will be the particular product of a named winery, made and identified in a certain consistent way. Franciscan's proprietary wine, Sundance, has a characteristic sweetness with which the name is associated.

The varietal wines are America's best wines, and these have long been subject to regulation. Varietal wines are wines made with specific cultivars, so that the name of the grape appears on the label to identify the wine. In France, a wine with 90 percent Cabernet Sauvignon, made in the Bordeaux region, is identified by the name of the château; the consumer is expected to know the chief ingredient of this premium wine. In the United States, such a wine would be called a Cabernet Sauvignon. Of course the name of the winery or estate is prominently displayed, but the chief cultivar also is specified.

The best varietal wines, however, frequently are blends. In Bordeaux, a number of other grapes contribute the noble wines in which the Cabernet Sauvignon is the main ingredient (see Chapter 2). In California, a wine identified as a Zinfandel or a Chardonnay also may in fact be a blend, although only the main grape variety used is shown on the label. The question always has been: in what proportion should winemakers be compelled to put the wine of the labeled cultivar in the bottle? Until January 1983, winemakers had much (sometimes misused) freedom: for a wine to be labeled a Chardonnay, only 51 percent must be derived from Chardonnay grapes. This meant that a winemaker could "stretch" a limited quantity of Chardonnay, an expensive grape, by mixing it with as much as 49 percent wine derived from inferior cultivars, and sell it as a varietal wine. In 1983 these proportions changed. Now, a wine sold as a varietal must contain at least 75 percent of that varietal. (An exception has been made for *Labrusca* varieties which, at 75 percent or more, become too "foxy"; for them, the 51-percent rule continues.) In the state of Oregon the rules are stricter still: except for Cabernet Sauvignon, wines sold as varietals must contain at least 90 percent of that cultivar.

If a winemaker wishes to produce a wine that blends two or more varietals but in such proportions that none contributes 75 percent of the wine, the label may show a combination varietal name, such as Cabernet-Zinfandel, with the percentage of each specified.

Since the label also reveals where the grapes were grown (in accordance with the regulations discussed earlier), the 1983 wine law constitutes a considerable advance in U.S. wine legislation. It must be said, however, that the majority of American winegrowers, and especially those producing prideful premium wines, always have given the consumer much label information (often far more than the law required) and have anticipated changes in wine regulations by adhering to them years before they became law. The small print on California wine labels long has included one of several statements such as "bottled by," "cellared and bottled by," "perfected and bottled by," and "produced and bottled by." The simple statement "bottled by" means that the winery may have bought the wine in bulk from some unknown (to the consumer) source and put it in bottles immediately, without contributing to it in any other way. "Cellared" or "perfected" means only that the winery named on the label fermented 10 percent or more of the wine in the bottle. "Produced and bottled by" is the strongest of these statements, requiring that at least 51 percent of the wine was fermented at the winery involved. The term "estate-bottled" was intended to provide the most comprehensive of all guarantees, but it fell into misuse and became unreliable. The new 1983 regulations have redefined the use of *estate* on the label, and it means that the winery owns or strictly controls the vineyards that produced the grapes for the bottled wine.

In one respect the 1983 law remains unchanged. When a vintage year is shown on an American wine label, 95 percent or more of the grapes must have been harvested in that year.

United States wine legislation remains in a formative stage. It is expected that petitions for viticultural-area recognition will continue to arise, even from *within* already-designated appellations. Such refinement of the system will benefit the industry; and it should be remembered that the creation of European wine laws involved decades of negotiation and experimentation. Italy is a case in point, a far older industry still organizing today. The range of environments, cultivars, wine styles, and traditions in America is enormous, in some ways greater than all of Europe's; a comprehensive wine law cannot be achieved overnight.

Wine regulations in Chile and Argentina, Australia and New Zealand, Japan, and other wine-producing countries all have elements of the laws discussed in this chapter. Such important wine laws should not only encourage productivity and quality at home, but also protect domestic industries against damaging competition from abroad. Further, wine regulations should support the export industry by meshing with laws in foreign countries. These needs are not always met by the evolving legislation, in part because wine and the wine industry are sometimes misunderstood by lawmakers. It is something of an irony that wine is linked to tobacco and firearms in a U.S. government agency; many oenophiles would argue that it does not even belong with the alcohol division of that bureau.

From Wine Laws to Wine Wars

Wine laws, it seems, are made to be broken. Strict regulations and strong control in Germany did not prevent the eruption of two major wine scandals in the early 1980s, one involving illegal sugaring of wines and the other centering on the importing into the country of tankcars full of foreign wine to be "Germanized." These are only the latest of a probably endless series of contraventions affecting not only Germany but other wine-producing countries as well. The laws are strict; they help maintain the high value of good wine. In turn, they raise the rewards of fraud.

The German experience is enlightening, because it underscores that the effectiveness of wine laws can be ensured only by the voluntary participation of all involved. Inspection and investigation can detect only a small percentage of offenses, but the winegrowers collectively have a stake in the maintenance of quality. In Germany, four successive inadequate vintages (1978, 1979, 1980, and 1981) depleted cellar stocks and made *QmP* wines scarce; the temptation to sugar the musts and raise the rank of the wines proved too great for some 2400 winegrowers, cooperative owners, wholesalers, and sugar merchants, mainly in the Mosel-Saar-Ruwer region. All those caught in the act were indicted with participation in this massive conspiracy; suspicions were first aroused by the appearance of far more Spätlese and Auslese wines on local and world markets than ripening conditions seemed to permit. The vintages of 1977, 1978, and 1979 were apparently sugared with more than 6 million tons of liquid sugar. The entire German wine industry was tainted by this violation of wine laws designed to protect the reputation of the industry.

Even before the German wine trials of 1981 came to a close, the country was rocked by still another scandal. The trials had been carried out as quietly as possible, but publicity was nevertheless world-wide, especially when some prominent persons were imprisoned. Then came the news that seventeen winemakers and merchants had been indicted for importing railroad tankcars full of foreign wine, to be blended and sugared and sold under German labels. Again the courts heard painful testimony of a wine conspiracy in this, the most rigidly controlled European region.

The German wine trials are the talk of the 1980s, but in the 1970s it was Bordeaux that made the news. A massive fraud in this prestigious French region involved several noted shippers, and the scandal was called France's "Winegate."[6] It sent major figures in Bordeaux's wine industry to jail and shocked the industry; millions of hectoliters of wine were involved. France is accustomed to small-scale offenses, usually involving small amounts of wine; in 1972, for example, French inspectors uncovered 177 offenses serious enough to be prosecuted—but these 177 cases affected only 25,000 hectoliters of wine.[7] But when the national interest and the national industry are involved, every winegrower is affected.

During the past decade the national interests of the two principal wine-producing countries in the world, France and Italy, have been damaged in another, and more serious, way. Wine scandals tend to remain internal affairs, even when foreign consumers have been hoodwinked. But wine that crosses international boundaries in large volume can have an impact on whole viticulture regions. The very E.E.C. regulations that were designed to bring order to European winemaking and commerce produced a crisis between Italy and France—a "wine war" that continued, on and off, into the 1980s.

At the root of the problem lay the large overproduction of cheap wines in Italy as well as France, declining consumption (see Chapter 6), and the Common Market's freer flow of commodities across Europe's international boundaries. As European economic integration proceeded, French markets were opened to Italian producers, and cheap Italian wine began to arrive in France in tank trucks and even in ships' holds, filled to overflowing. France's own low-priced Vins de Pays, made principally by growers in Southern France, were undercut. As the flood of Italian wine rose, so did the anger of French growers. In 1975 France experienced a series of "wine riots," when French growers and their supporters blocked roads and overturned Italian trucks. The French government responded by erecting an illegal tariff against the Italian imports (illegal under E.E.C. regulations), but the crisis continued. Eventually a regulatory agreement between France and Italy was reached, but the problem lingered.

By 1980, French wine producers were again buying large quantities of Italian wine for blending with the local product, but while the growers of the Midi were angered, they had limited political strength in a France now dominated by right-wing politics. But then the election of the Mitterrand government changed the situation and the Midi's growers once again went on the offensive.

In July and August 1981, the tactics of the 1970s resumed. Tank trucks carrying Italian blending wine were attacked and overturned; in the port of Sète an Italian ship carrying 8500 hectoliters (225,000 gallons) of wine was seized by Midi growers and sympathizers, and oil was pumped into the wine. Italian officials lodged formal protests with Mitterrand and called for E.E.C. arbitration. On August 18, 1981, the E.E.C. ruled in favor of Italy, condemned French acts of sabotage, and recommended bilateral negotiation. In October an agreement was reached once more, but not everyone was satisfied. In France, suspicions were now voiced over Italian production statistics, one of the bases for export quotas. In Italy, feelings ran high over French reaction to the success of Italian winegrowers.

Eventually the matter reached the European Court, which confirmed the E.E.C. position in favor of Italy. Renewed violence broke out in France, not without touches of irony. In Sète, again the hotbed of Languedoc, growers blew up two steel vats, each containing 28,425 hectoliters (750,000 gallons) of wine being stored in a vintners' cooperative. They were unaware until the wine flowed into the gutters that it was French, not Italian.

The Franco-Italian "wine war" illustrates an important principle in political geography: the effect of proximity and accessibility in a competitive situation of this nature. Italian producers would have had a far more difficult problem penetrating a market farther away, for example the British market, than neighboring France. The incidents involving wine-laden ships in French ports attracted much attention, but the bulk of Italy's flood of wine reached French markets on vehicles that crossed the land border between the two countries.

Political Geography of Wine

Relative location is a strong factor in geography in general, and in political geography in particular. The fact that France and Italy are neighbors intensified the "wine war" and involved whole regions in it. Proximity strengthens competition.

There are other connections between viticulture and political geography. The monopolistic intervention of powerful rulers has (as noted earlier) changed the course of viticultural development on more than one occasion, from Roman times (and perhaps even before) onward. Additional instances worthy of attention include the often far-reaching effect of international treaties, the consequences of internal politico-geographical change, and the impact of ideological change.

The aftereffect of the Methuen Treaty (1703) on the economic geography of Portugal is perhaps the best example of viticulture's role as a politico-geographical factor. The treaty confirmed an Anglo-Portuguese alliance during the struggle for the Spanish throne, giving the English a base on the Iberian Peninsula's western flank. One of the conditions of the treaty involved the lowering of duties on Portuguese wines sold in England, and the effect of this provision was that Portugal's viticulture expanded rapidly. Especially in the Upper Douro region in the hinterland of Porto (formerly Oporto), thousands of hectares of land previously used to produce grain crops were planted with vines.[8] Portugal's dependence on England as its main market was matched by its dependence on external sources for food no longer produced at home. Nor did Portuguese winegrowers and wine-makers enjoy all the advantage of the new economic order. Powerful British capitalists based in Porto bought much of the land that was converted to vineyards and controlled the export industry. The Methuen Treaty changed the map of Portugal, but it stifled economic growth in nonagricultural sectors and, in a sense, made Portugal an English dependency. It remained in effect for 140 years (the treaty was terminated in 1842), but its impact on the economic geography of Portugal has been permanent.[9] Port, the Portuguese vinicultural specialty, was developed for English tastes. The vineyards of the Upper Douro are testimony to the nearly century and a half of English involvement, also symbolized by the lodges of Porto itself.

Politico-territorial change has on occasion affected viticulture regions quite severely. Two prominent cases involve the industry in Australia and in the United States. In Australia, the vineyards of the Hunter Valley went into decline as a direct result of the formation of the Commonwealth in 1891.[10] The Hunter region produced excellent wines, but has always done so in the face of considerable environmental obstacles. As a result the price of Hunter Valley wines is never low; during the difficult years of the nineteenth century, when the region's viticulture developed, duty barriers erected by New South Wales against other Australian wines enabled the industry to survive. By the 1880s there was a boom, resulting also from the mushrooming size of the local market; Sydney already was Australia's largest city and New South Wales its most populous colony. When the Commonwealth of Australia unified the colonies and revoked internal customs and tariff barriers, cheap wines from South Australia flooded the Sydney and New South Wales markets, and Hunter Valley wines could not compete. Many Hunter Valley vineyards were uprooted, and recovery, never complete, only began decades later. The new politico-geographical map transformed the cultural and economic landscapes of the Hunter region almost overnight.

In the United States it was not a modified political map, but a changed communications system that had a major impact on regional viticulture. By the 1860s the wine industry of the Eastern United States was thriving, and Ohio was the leading viticulture region in the country, producing one-third of the entire U.S. harvest. New York and Missouri were also major producers, and the industry was spreading into neighboring areas. Eastern markets were becoming accustomed to the particular taste of the locally produced wines, and Eastern winemakers sought to prevent California wines from reaching local dealers. Although some California wines did cross the country, local wines easily prevailed—until 1869, when the first transcontinental railway link was established. Now the large Eastern markets lay within easier reach of California's merchants, and the competitive situation was changed. Not only consumers, but even some Eastern wineries bought California wines. The wineries blended their own non-*vinifera* wine with the smoother-flavored California wines, thus accommodating a market whose tastes were changing.

Had it not been for the onslaught of *phylloxera*, the Eastern industry might have gone into even more serious decline than affected several leading states. But the demand for American rootstocks kept nurseries in business and viticulture remunerative. In addition, the U.S. population was increasing rapidly, augmented by large immigration, and most of the new arrivals came first to the Eastern core area. These two circumstances gave the Eastern viticulture industry a reprieve, and by the turn of the century it was still healthy. But another threat was looming.

The impact of Prohibition on the U.S. wine industry reveals still another aspect of political geography: the effect of changing ideology. The political geography of Prohibition is familiar: first communities, then entire states declared themselves "dry" of all alcoholic beverages, and eventually (in 1920) national Prohibition became law. In this case religious fervor had an effect opposite from that of earlier times, when the church sustained viticulture even if it did not disseminate it. During Prohibition the sale of "sacramental" wines did keep some wineries in production, but decades of unrelenting pressure on thousands of congregations had their cumulative effect. Prohibition destroyed the Eastern viticulture industry and incalculably set back that of the West.

Another country whose wine industry has been afflicted by Prohibition-type pressure is Chile. The Chilean wine industry, always a promising venture, suffered especially during the political turmoil of the 1960s and 1970s. Chilean governments have curtailed the wine industry in their determination to curb alcoholism; they have legislated against the use of good farmland for vines (rather than food crops); and, most recently, vineyards were expropriated and divided up among peasants during the Allende period. Since the mid-1970s, however, Chilean viticulture has been allowed to recover, and the quality of its wines reflects the beneficial effects of stability.

A further illustration of the impact of ideological change involves the wine industry of Algeria, where viticulture was introduced (in modern times) by French colonists. The first sizeable vineyards were planted in the 1860s, and Algerian wine began to flow to France, initially in small quantities, in the 1870s. Eventually nearly 1 million French and other Southern European settlers resided in Algeria, among them growers whose vineyards in Europe had been destroyed by *phylloxera.* By the 1950s the industry thrived, producing some good and much mediocre wine, which ranked it, by volume, in a class with Portugal. In 1961 Algeria's production actually ranked it fifth in the world, after Italy, France, Spain, and Argentina, with a production of 15 million hectoliters (396 million gallons) from 360,000 hectares (nearly 900,000 acres) of vineyards.[11]

But Algeria is a Moslem society, and the wine industry always was an alien presence, its products destined not for the domestic mass market, but for foreign consumers. Throughout the French colonial tenure in Algeria, Moslem leaders voiced objection to the use of Algerian soil for the cultivation of the wine vine, and vowed that the agricultural landscape would change after the ouster of the colonists.

The Algerian Revolution (1954 to 1962) led to the departure of the great majority of European settlers, and a new political and economic posture emerged in Algiers. The vineyards abandoned by the French were taken over by the state and assigned to "workers committees." This experiment was not an unqualified success, and the state took more direct control of agriculture (and hence viticulture) in the early 1970s. One of the socialist government's stated aims was to create greater self-sufficiency, especially in food. This led to the first conversions of vineyards into cereal-producing farms, and wine production declined. When France, in its effort to protect its peasant wine producers, reduced its imports of Algerian wine, additional vineyards were uprooted in favor of grain cultivation. The viticulture area declined from about 360,000 hectares in the early 1950s to about 260,000 in the late 1960s, and fell below 200,000 hectares in the late 1970s. Production of wine, which averaged 15 million hectoliters (nearly 400 million gallons) in good years of the 1950s, plunged to 5 million hl. in the 1960s and reached a low of 2 million hl. (53 million gallons) in 1978.[12] Symbolic of Algeria's ideological reorientation also was the new market for the bulk of its wines: the Soviet Union, now the largest importer of Algeria's production.

In the early 1980s there were some signs of recovery in Algeria's wine industry, stemming from the government's recognition of wine exports as a source of foreign valuta. In 1980, the most recent year for which Algeria has published statistics, wine production was 3 million hectoliters (80.2 million gallons), a substantial gain, but still far below the country's proven potential.

Wine legislation demands the definition of areas and regions, the delimitation of boundaries on maps, and their demarcation on the ground. It creates its own political geography and, as proponents of field theory in geography would agree, generates not only a hierarchy of regions but also an organizational bureaucracy that assumes the trappings of a government-within-a-government. From a broader perspective, the world map of viticulture carries the imprints of current, recent, as well as historic political intervention. The patterns of land fragmentation that differentiate Burgundy from Bordeaux, the contrasts between the Western and Eastern wine industries in the United States, the pattern of land use in Australia's Hunter Valley, the dislocation of Algerian vineyards—all reflect spatially the political geography of viticulture under stress and change.

Additional Reading

On wine classification, legislation, and labeling:

Dovaz, M. *Encyclopedia of the Great Wines of Bordeaux.* Paris: René Julliard, 1980.

Kaufman, W. I. *The Whole-World Wine Catalog.* New York: Penguin Books, 1978.

Lichine, A. *New Encyclopedia of Wines and Spirits.* New York: Alfred A. Knopf, 1981. See individual sections under "wines laws" for various countries and regions.

Nanovic, J. *The Complete Book of Wines, Vineyards, and Labels.* San Francisco: Ottenheimer, 1979.

Paterson, J. *The International Book of Wines.* New York: Hamlyn, 1975.

Saunders, P. *Wine Label Language.* Auckland: Wineglass, 1976.

On political geography, relevant sections from:

Bergman, E. F. *Modern Political Geography.* Dubuque: W. C. Brown, 1975.

Brunn, S. D. *Geography and Politics in America.* New York: Harper & Row, 1974.

Glassner, M. I., and de Blij, H. J. *Systematic Political Geography.* 3rd ed. New York: John Wiley & Sons, 1980.

6

An Economic Geography of Wine

Christmas eve, 1980. In the vineyards of New York and New England, disaster looms. The temperature has been dropping since midday and, as darkness falls, the cold intensifies. By Christmas morning, the Christmas Eve Massacre has run its course. Temperatures have dropped as much as 60° Fahrenheit. Vines everywhere stand frozen, whole vineyards lie destroyed. Growers despair for 1981. The losses are incalculable.

On the docks of the port of New York City stand sixteen steel containers of wine, just arrived from Israel. They were unloaded a day earlier; there has not been time to place them under cover. As the temperature declines, the wine freezes, and is destroyed. When the Israeli wine is later sold to consumers, the results of the freeze become apparent, and sellers report unprecedented returns. The public resists further purchase of Israeli wine, unaware of the background. Distributors reduce their imports. Israeli wine sales to the United States show a huge decrease from 1980 to 1981, and reach their lowest volume in a decade. A freeze in North America has a deep impact on an industry thousands of miles away. Wine is a vulnerable commodity.

It is well known that wine production depends strongly upon environmental conditions in producing countries; vintage charts are constant reminders of the variability of weather. Wine consumption, too, is affected by many circumstances, including the economic climate. The state of domestic economies, levels of personal income, changing preferences of consumers, and competition from alternate beverages are just a few of the factors involved. As a result, the economic geography of wine is a volatile business, subject to fluctuations and uncertainties, variations in production and consumption patterns, political pressures, and price shifts.

During the 1970s and early 1980s the world's annual production of wine

Table 6.1 World Wine Production 1967–1981 (in millions of hectoliters)

1967	280.9
1968	279.1
1969	270.1
1970	303.9
1971	286.7
1972	281.1
1973	344.5
1974	336.1
1975	323.3
1976	322.6
1977	289.0
1978	295.8
1979	368.5
1980	351.0
1981	320.0

Note: Reports of individual countries give data in hectoliters (1 hectoliter = 100 liters), imperial gallons (1 liter = 0.22 imperial gallon; 1 imperial gallon = 4.55 liters), or U.S. gallons (1 liter = 0.264 U.S. gallons; 1 U.S. gallon = 3.79 liters).

Source: 1967 to 1976: Department of International Economic and Social Affairs (Statistical Office), United Nations, *Yearbook of Industrial Statistics*, 1976, vol. 2 (New York, 1978), p. 156. Figures for 1977 to 1980, average of several published statistics. Figure for 1981, estimate.

ranged between 270 and 370 million hectoliters (Table 6.1).* This production was achieved on a cultivated area of approximately 11 million hectares (about 27 million acres), representing approximately three-quarters of one percent of the cultivated land in the world.[1] The cultivated area under vines is growing in several countries, notably the Soviet Union; it is stable in others and declining in some, especially in North Africa. Increases in the production of the United States and Southern Hemisphere countries notwithstanding, Europe's domination in world viticulture continues. In the mid-1960s Europe's share (not including the Soviet Union) of world production was about 70 percent; in the late 1970s and early 1980s it remained the same, approaching three-quarters of total production in some years. Thus year-to-year variations in Europe's harvest, resulting from changing weather conditions, overshadow trends that might represent the dispersal of productive capacity. France alone, even in a mediocre year, produces more wine than all the vineyards of North and South America, South Africa,

*Measurement of the harvest presents several problems. Much wine is locally (even domestically) produced and consumed, and this production is incompletely recorded. In some countries the data provided to UN and other agencies are unreliable and conflict with statistics from other sources.

and Australia combined. France and Italy, alternately the two leading producers (Italy has led each of the last five years), together account for as much as 45 percent of the total world vintage.

As Table 6.1 shows, world production reached an all-time high in 1979, when nearly 370 million hectoliters (hl.) of wine were vinted. But 1977 production was only slightly greater than the output of 1967. Average production during the fifteen years 1967 to 1981 (inclusive) was 310 million hl., an average that was not reached in two of the last five years. Wine production does not display a steady growth or predictable rate of increase. Some years produce a glut, and prices fall; other years combine a high-quality vintage with a reduced volume, and prices rise.

This is the context in which Table 6.2 should be viewed. Italy's dominance has been strengthened by the harvests of 1978 and thereafter (including 1981 and 1982), and some observers suggest that Italian statistics actually understate production. Hence Italy today is the world's leading producer of wine, while France remains a comparatively close second. French production since 1967 has displayed rather more variability than Italy's, with a recent low of 52 million hl. (1977), followed by a high of nearly 84 million (1979); Italy's production during the fifteen-year period shown on Table 6.2 never fell below 60 million hl. (1972) and reached an all-time high of 85 million hl. in 1980.

Spain remains solidly entrenched as Europe's (and the world's) third-largest producer. Spanish production doubled over the period reflected by Table 6.2, from 23 million hl. in the late 1960s to an unprecedented 50 million in 1979. The industry is expanding vigorously in Spain; domestic consumption is rising and exports are increasing. Until recently Spain vied for its third rank with Argentina and the Soviet Union, but since 1978 it has reestablished itself firmly behind France.

The Soviet Union's production of wines has risen strongly during the period after World War II, an increase that is only partially reflected in Table 6.2. In several years of the 1970s the Soviet Union actually claimed third place among wine-producing countries, outproducing both Spain and Argentina. In recent years it has ranked fourth in the world, but its reported data are unreliable, and some scholars suggest that actual expansion of Soviet production is such that it "would not be long before the U.S.S.R. became the biggest wine producer in the world."[2] That may be an overly optimistic assessment of Soviet prospects, but there can be no doubt that this is the country with the most significant growth of viticulture in the middle period of the twentieth century. It also is a country where the potential for further development remains huge. In 1982 there were an estimated 1.4 million hectares of vineyards in the Soviet Union, well over 10 percent of the total world hectarage of 11.1 million. Large areas could be added to this total.[3]

Eleven of the Soviet Union's fifteen republics grow grapes, although the zone that produced almost all the wine extends from Moldavia (on the Romanian border, historically a part of Romania) across the Ukraine (and north into Beylorussia), Russia, and into Georgia, Armenia, and Azerbaydzhan between the Black and Caspian seas. Eastward lie the Moslem Soviet republics, and most of the grapes grown there are destined for the table or marketed as raisins. Among the wine-producing republics, the Russian republic leads with about one-third of the total in an average year (11 million hl. in 1979). The Ukraine ranks next with about 6 million hl., and Moldavia with 5 million hl. Beylorussia in recent years has contributed 1.5 million hl., which is comparable to the production of the three southern republics (Georgia and Azerbaydzhan, 2 million each; Armenia, 1 million).

These Soviet production figures should be compared to those for European countries included in Table 6.2; the output of Russia alone would outrank that of most European regions. Moldavia's annual production is larger than that of West Germany. Soviet wines have begun to make their appearance on Western markets, although not always with success: the good sparkling wine from Russia, Nasdorovya, was introduced in the United States in 1974 but lost its market in 1981 after supply problems to retailers proved insurmountable.[4] The Soviet export industry is in its infancy, but the potential domestic market is huge—and this is the primary objective of Soviet wine-makers.

The next two ranking world producers—Argentina (fifth) and the United States (sixth)—are New-World viticulture regions. Other than the countries already detailed, no European nation approaches these younger viticulture regions. After Italy, France, and Spain, Portugal ranks fourth in Europe, its output recently recovered after the poor years of 1977 and 1978 (the 1979 yield was more than that of 1977 and 1978 combined). Portugal suffered from social instability during the middle 1970s, but its position has strengthened since. Yugoslavia, its production and its reputation gaining steadily, produced more than 8 million hl. of wine in 1980, and Romania, which also has a strong wine industry, exceeded 7.5 million hl. These figures, and those for the remaining European countries shown in Table 6.2, should always be viewed in comparison with the enormous production of Europe's leading countries: Italy alone produces about as much wine as all of Europe, excluding France. Table 6.2 also reveals the vicissitudes of the wine industries of individual countries. Germany's 1980 output was barely half the 1979 harvest. Spain in 1979 produced more than twice as much wine as it did in 1977. Many industries would collapse under such variability and uncertainty—and these are merely production figures and do not take into account the variations in consumption and demand that also play their role.

In the New World, Argentina has long been the leading wine producer, and for nearly a decade its annual output of wine has remained between 20 and 30 million hl. The industry has always produced a small amount of quality wine (comparable to the best of Chile and, indeed, ranking among the world's better wines), but the remainder has been bulk wine. The government, intent on encouraging the industry for domestic-market as well as export purposes, offered tax incentives and low-interest loans to growers in Mendoza Province (where about 70 percent of all Argentinian wine is made) and elsewhere, especially where previously unused land was planted to the vine. Then, in the late 1970s, the Argentinian economy went into a deep decline, weakening local consumer demand. Domestic wine sales dropped, the large cellars stopped buying bulk wine from smaller producers, and bankruptcies multiplied. The export volume was too small to support the industry in this crisis, and it was clear that only quality and reputation would have averted this misfortune. But Argentina did not have wine laws comparable to those of other major producers, and too many of its vines produced cheap, undistinguished wines. In 1981, such bulk wine was sold wholesale at 10 cents (U.S.) per liter.[5] This was not enough to repay production costs, and the Mendoza industry faced a crucial crossroads. Voices were

Table 6.2   Annual Wine Production of Selected Countries 1967–1980 (in millions of hectoliters)

	1967	1968	1969	1970	1971	1972
Austria	2.59	2.48	2.27	3.10	1.81	2.60
Bulgaria	3.08	4.36	4.35	3.64	3.75	3.55
Czechoslovakia	0.75	0.83	0.99	0.99	1.03	1.09
France	62.03	66.46	51.29	75.53	61.33	58.54
Germany (West)	5.58	5.56	5.47	9.10	5.55	6.86
Greece	3.83	4.11	4.90	4.53	4.41	4.82
Hungary	1.85	1.95	2.13	2.19	2.20	2.14
Italy	74.73	65.32	71.66	68.87	64.21	60.17
Portugal	9.94	11.20	8.33	11.62	9.07	8.59
Romania	5.24	6.79	6.85	4.32	6.35	6.27
Spain	23.31	23.31	24.62	25.61	24.33	26.56
Switzerland	0.89	0.96	0.74	1.18	0.82	0.93
Yugoslavia	5.23	6.08	7.06	5.48	5.55	6.26
Europe (Total)	201.03	202.06	192.85	218.70	192.88	190.89
Soviet Union	18.00	19.13	24.02	26.84	28.04	29.30
Canada	0.53	0.63	0.62	0.69	0.82	0.80
United States	9.41	9.45	9.85	12.67	13.63	11.98
North America (Total)	10.26	10.41	10.82	13.71	14.79	13.16
Algeria	6.45	9.95	8.71	8.69	9.25	5.75
Morocco	1.37	1.75	0.70	1.25	1.05	1.15
South Africa	3.52	3.50	4.21	4.23	5.41	5.31
Tunisia	0.98	0.99	0.85	0.57	0.97	0.99
Africa (Total)	12.48	16.36	14.66	14.94	16.87	13.41
Argentina	28.17	19.51	17.92	18.36	21.78	19.99
Brazil	1.75	1.89	1.68	1.90	1.90	2.30
Chile	4.89	5.36	4.02	4.01	5.25	6.11
Uruguay	0.84	0.84	0.76	0.91	0.91	0.90
South America (Total)	35.91	27.86	24.62	25.44	30.14	29.91
Australia	1.89	2.01	2.35	2.88	2.50	2.89
New Zealand	0.10	0.14	0.16	0.19	0.21	0.22

Source: 1967 to 1976, Department of International Economic and Social Affairs (Statistical Office), United Nations, *Yearbook of Industrial Statistics*, 1976, Vol. 2 (New York, 1978), pp. 155–56. Figures for 1977 and 1978 from Fromm and Sichel, *Data Annual* (San Francisco, 1979), p. 68. Data for 1979 and 1980 from The Wine Institute via *Wines and Vines* 63, no. 7 (1982): 49.

1973	1974	1975	1976	1977	1978	1979	1980
2.40	1.67	2.71	2.90	2.60	3.37	2.78	3.90
4.88	4.18	3.01	4.41	2.85	2.73	4.51	4.51
1.12	1.15	1.24	1.33	1.53	1.39	1.44	1.37
82.43	75.48	76.41	71.81	52.30	58.20	83.65	69.29
9.84	6.26	8.50	8.67	8.55	7.31	8.19	4.63
4.61	4.90	4.34	4.53	5.18	5.61	5.25	5.40
2.47	2.25	5.16	4.68	5.78	4.92	5.19	5.71
76.72	76.87	69.83	65.85	63.60	72.53	84.44	84.85
11.27	14.12	9.38	8.13	6.90	6.60	14.32	10.18
9.22	6.28	6.92	8.96	8.76	7.86	8.88	7.61
40.00	36.19	32.47	27.48	21.80	29.01	50.11	43.57
1.21	0.70	0.77	1.19	1.30	0.76	1.11	0.84
7.70	5.81	5.42	6.38	6.40	5.89	6.75	8.18
256.61	239.07	227.14	217.63	212.42	232.28	307.24	279.91
20.70	26.75	29.65	31.49	31.90	25.97	30.71	30.71
0.82	0.75	0.65	0.48	0.49	0.39	0.52	0.52
15.73	14.17	14.55	14.38	15.84	16.18	16.07	18.41
16.94	15.45	17.40	17.70	16.45	16.72	16.76	19.11
6.30	6.28	4.32	5.00	2.30	2.00	2.69	3.04
1.20	1.25	0.70	1.20	0.92	0.55	0.90	0.93
5.47	4.91	5.90	5.98	4.80	6.07	6.31	6.31
1.10	1.15	1.05	1.10	0.90	0.79	0.61	0.62
14.29	13.79	12.23	13.49	9.19	9.70	10.83	11.29
22.57	27.18	22.10	28.20	23.24	21.35	26.98	24.08
2.36	3.13	2.35	2.20	2.65	2.85	2.90	2.90
5.69	4.99	4.65	5.11	6.13	5.62	5.62	5.93
0.90	0.90	1.01	0.95	0.45	0.45	0.55	0.55
31.90	37.91	30.47	36.45	32.91	30.67	36.63	33.85
2.66	2.95	3.53	3.63	3.83	3.34	3.35	4.15
0.26	0.24	0.26	0.30	0.35	0.41	0.42	0.42

raised in favor of the uprooting of high-yield, low-quality grapevines to make way for noble varieties that could, over the long range, save the industry.

Despite these problems, Argentina continues to stand in a class by itself among Southern Hemisphere wine-producing countries. In an average year, Argentina produces between 70 and 75 percent of all the wine made in South America, far outstripping Chile, its nearest competitor by volume. Chile's production has remained rather steady for two decades, averaging between 5 and 6 million hl. The Brazilian industry is growing, but Brazil's output is less than half of Chile's. Smaller quantities of wine are also produced in South America by Uruguay (Table 6.2), Peru, Bolivia, Paraguay, Colombia, and Venezuela.

In the early 1980s the United States ranked sixth in production with an output that approached 19 million hl. in 1980 (the 1981 grape harvest was as much as 20 percent below 1980, so that no new record was set in that year). As Table 6.2 indicates, U.S. production doubled between 1967 and 1980. All phases of the industry expanded during the fifteen-year period: vine hectarage, domestic consumption, and exports. The strength of the U.S. industry on world export markets grew substantially, a trend that continued in 1981 when the United States sold more than 400,000 hl. (10.7 million gallons) of wine in foreign countries.

The remaining wine-producing countries whose recent output is reflected by Table 6.2 are those of Africa, Australia, and New Zealand. The decline of the Algerian wine industry, discussed earlier, has placed South Africa first among wine-producing countries on the African continent. As the table indicates, Morocco and to a lesser extent Tunisia have shared in the deterioration of the industry in North Africa; as recently as 1967 this region's vineyards produced more than twice as much wine as South Africa. In recent years South Africa alone has outproduced the North African countries combined, and its output has risen from just 3.5 million hl. in 1967 to well over 6 million in 1980.

Australia's output of wine exceeded 3.5 million hl. for the first time in 1975, a volume nearly double that of the mid-1960s. Though small by world standards, Australia's production is substantial when viewed in the context of the limited domestic market and the distances to external markets. The growth of viticulture in New Zealand is perhaps even more remarkable. From just 100,000 hl. in 1967, it had increased fourfold by 1978 and approached a half-million hectoliters in the early 1980s.

Since environmental conditions have a crucial effect on the volume of grapes produced for crushing each year, reported world yields form an undependable guide to long-range production trends. The world output in the years 1973 to 1976 was without precedent, and again in 1979 and 1980 production was large. The fluctuations reported in Table 6.1 preclude any conclusions about overall growth or decline. The number of hectares under vines may be a more reliable indicator of future production, but here the distinction between wine-grape vineyards and cultivation of the vine for other purposes is sometimes blurred, even in official statistics. Reporting agencies produce widely varying statistics relating to vineyard hectarage. One respected source, for example, reports the 1975 hectarage as 10.33 million hectares and the 1976 total as 10.30 million hectares; a second, equally responsible agency reports the 1975 and 1976 figures as 9.9 and 10.3 million respectively, suggesting a 4 percent annual growth rate.[6]

Vineyard hectarage appears to be increasing slightly from a base of approximately 10 million hectares (25 million acres), but this increase actually represents a net gain: some countries are expanding their vineyards, while others are reducing their grape areas. The major growth region during the 1970s and early 1980s has been the Soviet Union, which plans to extend its vineyards to 1.75 million hectares by 1985 (in the mid-1970s Soviet vineyards covered about 1.2 million hectares). Eastern European countries, especially Bulgaria, have also enlarged their vineyards. Smaller producers, including South Africa and Japan, still are developing their industries, and some growth is occurring in North America. But reductions are recorded in North Africa, France, and Chile. These shifts have maintained the overall growth of vineyard area, and on this basis, a continued increase in world wine production can be forecast.

World Wine Consumption

Large volumes of wine enter channels of international trade every year. Italy and France, the largest producers, traditionally also have been the largest per capita consumers of wine. With their enormous production they also are the largest exporters of this commodity. For many years Italy has been the world's major wine exporter by a large margin.

The demand for wine, of course, depends upon the per-capita consumption of individual countries (Table 6.3). In this respect some significant trends are apparent. Individual wine consumption in the traditional wine-drinking countries, Italy and France, has declined over the past decade.* Portugal, for many years the world's third-ranking per-capita consumer, has seen a major decline that has placed it fourth, behind Argentina— not because Argentina's consumption has increased, but because its decline has been somewhat less.

Consumption may be declining in the older wine-producing countries (some observers suggest that this decline is related to a demand for higher quality and results from greater selectivity by consumers); in other countries it continues to rise. In both the Soviet Union and in the United States an upward trend continues, although U.S. per-capita consumption still remains far below that of the U.S.S.R. In Germany there is as yet no sign of a decline. In Australia consumption has approximately doubled since 1970.

The consumption data in Table 6.3 should be viewed in the context of the ranking countries' total populations. World consumption of wine continues to rise, annual per-capita decreases in France and Italy notwithstanding, and for two prominent reasons. First, population increase over the past two decades compensates for a decline in per-capita consumption. Second, and more important, is the increasing consumption of wine in countries with large or substantial populations, especially the Soviet Union, the United States, West Germany, Spain, and to a lesser extent Argentina. The Soviet Union is the prime example: as recently as 1963, per-capita wine consumption in the U.S.S.R. was less than 6 liters per year. By 1969 it had more than

---

*The data problem is as difficult in the context of consumption as it is with production. Reporting by "industry" agencies often is at variance with other accounts. Table 6.3 should be viewed as an approximation and as an indication of trends rather than specifics.

Table 6.3 Wine Consumption in Selected Countries 1970–1980 (in liters per capita)

	1970	1971	1972	1973	1974	1975	1976	1977	1978	1979	1980
France (54)	107.0	108.0	106.9	105.5	104.1	103.7	101.3	102.1	96.3	92.6	95.5
Italy (58)	112.0	111.0	110.9	109.3	109.2	103.9	98.0	93.5	91.0	90.0	93.1
Argentina (27)	91.8	85.3	79.7	72.5	77.2	83.7	84.8	88.5	82.0	77.0	76.4
Portugal (10)	92.5	91.1	82.4	80.4	96.0	89.8	97.8	97.0	91.3	86.0	70.1
Spain (38)	61.5	60.0	67.0	92.0	77.0	76.0	71.0	65.0	70.0	70.0	64.8
Chile (11)	43.9	43.9	44.0	38.2	40.0	43.5	47.8	52.3	47.7	46.6	46.6
Greece (10)	40.0	40.0	40.0	37.0	36.5	38.0	39.8	39.6	42.0	41.0	45.0
Hungary (11)	37.7	38.0	38.4	38.5	34.6	34.2	35.3	34.0	33.8	35.0	35.1
Australia (15)	9.1	8.7	9.0	9.9	11.2	11.2	11.2	13.7	14.3	16.5	17.4
U.S.S.R. (265)	11.2	11.5	11.8	12.0	13.0	13.4	13.4	13.3	14.0	14.0	14.4
West Germany (62)	16.9	20.7	20.0	21.2	20.3	23.3	23.6	23.8	24.4	24.3	25.5
New Zealand (3)			7.6	8.7	9.2	8.8	9.7	9.4	11.5	11.3	11.4
South Africa (29)	9.2	10.3	10.0	10.7	11.3	10.4	9.9	9.0	8.8	8.9	9.1
United States (225)	5.0	5.3	5.6	5.9	6.2	6.5	6.8	7.1	7.4	7.7	8.0

Source: "Industrial Review," *Encyclopaedia Britannica Book of the Year*, 1971 to 1982 inclusive. Figures for 1980 adjusted to averages reported by International Wine Office, Paris. Figures in parentheses are population data to the nearest million, 1983 estimates.

doubled to 12, and in 1978 it had risen to 14. With a total population of 270 million, this represents an enormous increase in demand. Even the slight but sustained annual increase in demand in the United States, with a population of 225 million, has a substantial impact. Spain's consumption also has increased considerably (the potential of the Spanish market is revealed by the 1973 consumption figure, which reflects that year's massive harvest and plentiful, cheap wines). West Germany's per-capita consumption, less than 16 liters in 1969, exceeded 25 in 1980—balancing France's decrease over the same period.

The enormous range in the volume of consumption between such countries as the United States and Australia (where it has nevertheless tripled since 1962), on the one hand, and France and Italy, on the other, suggests the potential for further change. In the Soviet Union during the 1960s the government embarked upon a systematic campaign to increase wine consumption, with the stated intent to substitute wine for hard liquor drunk in excess by too many citizens. This effort was attended by increased production at home and imports from abroad (the Algerian connection was thus forged), and it temporarily propelled the Soviet Union into third place among the world's wine-producing countries. Elsewhere, patterns of consumption have been related to price levels (wine continues to be perceived as a luxury item in many Western countries), cultural preference (Japan's fledgling viticulture industry has not significantly changed Japanese drinking habits), and public awareness (a factor in the United States). An indication of possible future developments lies in recently changed consumption patterns of such countries as the Netherlands and Denmark, where wine use has quadrupled since the mid-1960s; Finland, Ireland, Belgium, and Norway (tripled); and Sweden (more than doubled). These changes have come after many decades of very limited wine consumption, and they occurred over a relatively short period. The potential for viticulture's continued expansion remains strong.

United States Patterns

The world wine market consists, of course, of an aggregate of national markets. In the case of the U.S. market, a number of aspects reveal what lies behind the reported statistics. Per-capita consumption figures do not, for example, state whether people are drinking more red wine and less white or vice versa, or less (but more expensive) wine that produces greater revenues than a flood of cheaper wine.

In the United States in the early 1980s, white wines dominated the statistics, and the new "light" wines (most of them white) introduced with a major advertising campaign contributed strongly to this. The strength of white wines on the U.S. market has induced growers to expand their white-grape hectarages at the expense of red varieties. The dominance of white wines is likely to strengthen for years to come.

Among the states of the country a non-state, the District of Columbia, leads in per-capita consumption with 26 liters per capita—still far below the volume in major wine-drinking countries of the world, but well above the U.S. average of 8 liters. Nevada ranks second with 19 liters, most of it consumed by the state's large tourist population. The next ranking state, California, reports a consumption of 17 liters. With its substantial population,

Table 6.4   Wine Exports of Selected European Countries (in millions of hectoliters)

	1976	1978	1980
Italy	14.14	13.56	16.18
France	6.72	7.59	8.74
Spain	6.08	3.75	5.78
Yugoslavia	0.84	1.10	2.26
Hungary	1.79	2.05	2.09
Germany (West)	1.10	1.05	1.86
Portugal	1.90	1.35	1.62

Source: Data from United Nations and F.A.O. Reports, U.S. Department of Commerce, NABI 1978 *Annual Statistical Report* of the National Association of Alcoholic Beverage Importers.

California contributed significantly to overall U.S. wine consumption. Following California are New Hampshire, Rhode Island, and Washington. New York State ranks twelfth with 11 liters per capita; lowest consumption occurs in Arkansas (2.6 l.), Kentucky (2.4 l.), and Mississippi (2.4 l.).[7]

Consumption in every individual state of the union and the District of Columbia increased between 1970 and 1980, and only a few states reported slight declines from 1980 to 1981 (based on preliminary figures). None of these declines affected states with major populations. Montana, Hawaii, New Mexico, and Oklahoma were the only states reporting a decrease in consumption of more than 2 percent from 1980 to 1981; Colorado, also reporting a decline, changed its reporting procedures and may not have experienced an actual drop in consumption.

It is noteworthy that the United States, alone among developed, Western, urbanized-industrialized societies, consumed less than 10 liters of wine per person as recently as 1980 (South Africa's consumption is almost entirely confined to its non-Black minority populations). Thus the United States continues to stand at the bottom of Table 6.3, evidence not only of its limited wine consumption but also of the enormous potential of its wine market, larger than that of Italy, France, West Germany, and Spain combined.

Wine in International Commerce

In various forms—as table wine, bulk wine, blending wine, even in the form of must—wine is exported from producing regions to markets in foreign countries. It moves in bottles, barrels, tanks, even in the holds of ships. It travels by sea, river, road, even by air. Distances of movement range from across-the-border road trips to ocean journeys of thousands of kilometers.

Although the world's largest producers of wine also are the largest consumers, a considerable volume of wine (between 40 and 50 million hectoliters per year during the 1970s) enters international trade. This amounts to 15 percent of total production in a given year, and reflects several conditions: (a) a demand for wines not locally produced, (b) a demand for low-priced wines and blends on certain markets, (c) a demand for high-priced "prestige" quality wines on certain markets, (d) the demand in countries

Table 6.5   Wine Imports of Selected Countries (in millions of hectoliters)

	1976	1978	1980
Germany (West)	7.97	7.35	9.36
Soviet Union	7.99	5.91	6.90
France	6.99	7.46	6.67
United Kingdom	3.35	3.77	4.18
United States	2.23	3.56	3.89

Source: Data from *Wine Institute Economic Research Report 1978* and *Italian Wines and Spirits* 6, no. 2 (1978); also J. Boyazoglu, "Recent Trends in the Production, Consumption, and World Marketing of Wine," *Wynboer* 565 (1978): 45.

that do not produce wines in quantity themselves, and (e) year-to-year variations in harvest conditions in viticulture regions.

West Germany, normally one of the world's three leading importers, provides a good example of large-scale demand for wines not locally produced. Germany, ranking among the ten leading exporters, exports its white wines in volume, but it produces very little red wine (Table 6.4). Its large imports (Table 6.5) represent acquisition of red table wines from Yugoslavia, Spain, Hungary, and Morocco and Tunisia, as well as smaller quantities from France and Italy. Again, French imports partially reflect wines not produced in volume at home: low-priced dessert wines from Spain, Portugal, and Greece. The Soviet Union's substantial imports of wine, mainly from Algeria, also supplement inadequate local production. During the 1970s the U.S.S.R. alternated with France as the world's major wine-importing country.

Tables 6.4 and 6.5 raise the question why France, a major producer of a wide range of wines, should also be one of the world's major importers. This situation has existed for many years and is illustrated by conditions in the late 1960s and early 1970s, when per-capita consumption in France was substantially larger than it has been more recently (Table 6.3). Italian wines and blends were bought in volume by French vintners and consumers, a good illustration of the impact of readily available low-priced wine on nearby markets. By the time a combination of high Italian production and lowering French consumption had led to the first outbreak of the "wine war," French wine imports had risen to more than 9 million hectoliters (1975). Government intervention and a bilateral agreement reduced the flow to somewhat less than 7 million hl. in 1976, more nearly the customary quantity; but French consumption continued to decline, and the conflict predictably surfaced again.

The wine industry of Argentina also has been supported by the export of bulk wine (although quality wines have made an impact on U.S. markets). Such blending wine reaches markets as far removed as Japan.

High-priced "prestige" wines from France and Germany always have had their markets in wealthier countries of the world, and while these wines contribute only modestly to the volume of international trade, they generate a larger share of the revenues exchanged. The growing appreciation for quality wines has had much to do with the rising consumption of Northwest European countries and the (albeit slower) development of the North American market.

The role of the United Kingdom as a major market for French and other European wines (and for wines from more distant markets, including the U.S.A., as well) continues as it has for centuries. Per-capita consumption in the U.K. is not large by world standards, but it has risen from just slightly more than 2 liters as recently as 1965 to 7.5 liters per person in 1980. Although this is still slightly below per-capita wine consumption in the United States, the size of the market, as measured by the total British population, and the virtual absence of domestic competition render this a major consumer. In 1980 the United Kingdom was the world's fourth-largest wine importer (Table 6.5), still outranking the United States.

More will be said about the U.S. wine market later, but it is noteworthy that the United States—now the world's fifth-largest importer of foreign wines—was still as recently as 1975 out-ranked in total volume by Switzerland. The 1970s witnessed a major increase in import volume, however, and by 1976 the United States had surpassed Switzerland in the world rankings; by 1980 America imported more than twice as much wine as it had in 1975.

Year-to-year variations in weather conditions during the growing and harvest season also affect the flow of wine in international commerce. In some years one viticulture region does better than another, and surpluses flow from the advantaged to the disappointed areas or countries, perhaps aided by lower prices resulting from the large volumes. In other years viticulture areas around the world seem to be favored, and the result is a huge harvest (as was the case in 1979). Again this is reflected by international trade. Italy, the world's largest wine exporter, sent 13.6 and 16.2 million hectoliters of wine to foreign markets in 1978 and 1980 respectively. In the copious year 1979, Italy's exports approached an unprecedented 20 million hectoliters, nearly one-third more than was average during the 1970s. And not only Italy, but also Spain (6.10 million hectoliters), Hungary, and Greece had exceptional exports in 1979, and other countries had very good sales, including France (8.03 million hectoliters).

Such relationships between good vintage years and large exports do not occur without qualification, because other conditions (existing trade agreements, price competition, and available wine type) also affect export and import volumes. But abundance in the productive viticulture regions is reflected by increases in the flow of wine on international markets.

Tables 6.4 and 6.5 reveal some significant contrasts between the two leading wine-producing countries. Both Italy and France export huge volumes of wine, although Italy's exports are often twice as large as those of France. The real difference lies in the import situation: France is also one of the world's major importing countries (in recent years it has frequently been the world's leading wine importer), but Italy's wine imports are insignificant, amounting to between 200,000 and 300,000 hectoliters, and ranking it below most of the wine-consuming countries of the world. Italy's strength on world wine markets has grown significantly in the past decade: not only does Italy continue to send large volumes of wine to its prestigious neighbor (wine wars notwithstanding, see Table 6.5), but Italian wines outsell all other foreign wines *combined* on U.S. markets.

The wide-ranging networks of wine trade are well illustrated by the commerce of Argentina. Argentinian bulk and blending wines have a strong reputation on overseas markets, because they are considered to be of very good quality within those classifications. In 1977, in the holds of ships and in steel containers some 426,000 hectoliters of Argentinian ordinary wine went to the Soviet Union, Chile, Yugoslavia, Bulgaria, and in small amounts to East Germany and to the United Kingdom. Argentina's better quality and "reserva" wines, also well regarded on foreign markets, went in lesser quantities to Paraguay, the United States, Canada, Venezuela, Brazil, Ecuador, Japan, Belgium, and Czechoslovakia.[8] Yet Argentina is only one of many countries competing for these markets; in the United States, no less than thirty countries sold their wines in the early 1980s.

United States Participation

The United States constitutes one of the world's major wine markets, and the role of the U.S. as a wine-exporting country is growing. The expansion of the domestic wine market can be deduced from the rising per-capita consumption figures and the country's population increase; in 1981, the United States imported 3.76 million hectoliters of table wine and another 600,000 hectoliters of other wines, including sparkling wines, dessert wines, and vermouths.

American-made wines dominate sales on the U.S. market, but imported wines take a significant share. California wines represent just below 70 percent by volume of U.S. sales, wines from other states take a share of between 8 and 9 percent, and the remainder—between 22 and 23 percent—represents sales of foreign wines. These figures vary somewhat according to harvest conditions and production totals in California and the major import sources, but they have changed relatively little over the past decade. California's 1973 share also was about 70 percent; what has changed since then is the modest rise of imports from less than 15 to more than 20 percent and the decline in sales of wines from other states, from more than 15 to less than 10 percent.

Twenty-two percent of the American market constitutes a large volume, and this opportunity has generated some intense competition among exporting countries. As a result, the import situation has changed dramatically during the past decade. As recently as 1973, French wines outsold Italian wines on the U.S. market, and French import volumes also exceeded those of West Germany and Portugal, its other major competitors. Then Italian wine sales began their explosive growth that first surpassed French imports (1974) and, in 1978, virtually equalled imports from all other countries combined. In 1979 Italy established itself as the dominant foreign wine source in America, surpassing the volume of all other countries together. Its market share continued to grow; in 1981 Italian wines represented 58 percent of all imported wine volume in the United States. French wine sales in the United States also increased over the period, but could not match the Italians. In 1981, France contributed slightly more than 15 percent of imported wines, Germany ranked next with about 12 percent, and Spain (6 percent) and Portugal (5 percent) followed. These are the big five on the U.S. market, contributing over 95 percent of all imported wines.

Another significant change of the past decade lies in the expressed preferences of consumers. In 1975, red wines outranked both whites and rosés in U.S. sales (domestic as well as imported wines). In the late 1970s a strong preference for white wines began to make itself evident, and by 1979 white wine sales exceeded those of reds and rosés combined. That trend continued into the 1980s, to such an extent that observers predict that white wines may, by the end of the decade, outsell reds and rosés combined by four to one. White wines, it is suggested, may outsell reds alone by twelve to one.[9]

Although the big five dominate the U.S. import market, wines from some thirty countries reach American consumers, including Japan, Eastern European countries, South American countries, South Africa, Australia, and New Zealand. None of these countries in recent years has contributed even 1 percent of import volumes, but many of these comparatively rare wines are of interest as representatives of specialized viticultural regions.

As foreign wines entered the United States and competed with American wines, U.S. wines (about 95 percent from California) began to penetrate foreign markets. The volume of U.S. exports is still small, but California wines are receiving much attention overseas and on several occasions have outranked local premium wines in blind tastings and competitions. In 1981 just over 3 percent of California's wine shipments were destined for foreign markets, or about 406,000 hectoliters. Canada, which imports U.S. bulk wine for blending purposes, is the leading importer with some 206,000 hectoliters—about half the total. The United Kingdom ranks next, with 42,000 hectoliters (1.1 million gallons), a 1981 import volume that is nearly twice as large as that of 1980. Indeed, California wines were increasing their share in E.E.C. countries' sales generally, and were opening new markets as well. In 1981 American wines were exported to about forty countries and territories in all parts of the world.

The economic geography of wine involves the movement of bulk as well as premium wines, still and sparkling wines, "light" and fortified wines. Values per unit of volume range enormously. Distances and modes of transportation vary, and so do associated costs. As Argentinian wines sell in Japan, Japanese wines reach U.S. markets; American wines sell in E.E.C. countries, which in turn compete on the American market. Australian wines reach Pacific markets from New Zealand to Hawaii and from Fiji to Singapore. South African wines are gaining on European markets (chiefly the United Kingdom) and are about to expand their U.S. sales. International trade in wine over the past decades has experienced vicissitudes, but the overall record shows increasingly vigorous activity, a rise in the volume of wine entering foreign trade (adjusted for producing conditions), and growth in the number of international transactions involving wine.

Additional Reading

The economics and economic geography of wine are best followed in current periodical literature. Among journals that keep readers informed on trends and developments are:

The Friends of Wine. 2302 Perkins Place, Silver Spring, Maryland 20910.
Wines and Vines. 1800 Lincoln Avenue, San Rafael, California 94901.
The Wine Spectator. 305 East 53rd Street, New York, New York 10022.

Several English-language periodicals, some strongly independent, are published in Europe and elsewhere. Among these are:

Decanter. 16 Black Friars Lane, London, EC4, United Kingdom.
The New Zealand Wineglass. Wineglass Publishing, P.O. Box 9527, Auckland, New Zealand.
Wine and Spirit Buying Guide. 300 Bridge Road, Camperdown, N.S.W. 2050, Australia.

Industry journals or industry-supported publications often contain useful statistics and general information, such as:

Italian Wines and Spirits. One World Trade Center, Suite 86111, New York, N.Y. 10048.
Wynboer (KWV), P.O. Box 528, Suider-Paarl 7624, South Africa.

7

Cultural Landscapes of Viticulture

To geographers, a cultural landscape has special interest and meaning. In the most general sense, the cultural landscape is the tangible summation of human pursuit in an area or region: "the forms superimposed on the physical landscape by the activities of Man."[1] Technical interest focuses on the functional relationships between the components of the cultural landscape and the interconnections that create and sustain it. To the student of wine, the cultural landscape is a fertile field for exploration and discovery. "Ultimately," wrote geographers J. P. Dickenson and J. Salt, "the geography of wine is an experience of place."[2]

No agricultural industry so transforms the natural landscape as does viticulture. In Chapter 1 viticulture is described as the most expressive of all agricultural industries, and its impress extends beyond vineyards and terraces to the homes and buildings of the winegrowers, the artifacts of industry, even the lifestyles of those who create the wines. Modest houses, ornate châteaux, even whole villages and towns are dominated, saturated by the imagery of the vine and its culture history. Wherever in the world one enters a wine-producing area, the atmosphere is unmistakably unique, a combination of serenity and civility. "In Northwest Portugal . . . the appearance of the landscape is seductive enough to soften a heart of stone—and that is what has been accomplished: obdurate granite has been transformed into soft, green, terraced slopes, outlined by trees and arbors."[3]

The vine clothes the landscape and remakes it. It is tempting to read into this scene something of the national character of those who live by the vine: the exactness and regimentation of the German vineyards; the widely spaced, machine-harvested, vast expanses of central California; the undisciplined Italian vineyards where vines "spill out everywhere, climb trees and drape their branches, run along roads and hang festooned from fences, flourish in glorious disorder beside olive trees and in fields of grain."[4] Such

Transformation of the natural landscape: meticulously tended vineyards clothe the countryside in Australia's Hunter Valley and create a unique cultural landscape.

conclusions might easily be overdrawn, but the habits of the vine do reflect centuries, even millenia of history and tradition, a long heritage of, in the words of one geographer, "living in affectionate association with the land."[5]

The versatile grapevine grows in many different shapes and forms. In the wild it is a climber and a creeper, but under viticulture it proves itself capable of standing alone as a tree, its thick trunk woody and gnarled with age; it also grows in hedgelike rows of shrubs. From ancient Egyptian times the vine has climbed arbors of various designs, and winegrowers have since created an almost infinite number of structures, ranging from simple stakes to complicated trellises, to train it. Certainly aesthetics played a role in this evolution, but more important was the character of the natural environment where the vine grew: the need for distance from overheated ground, protection from frost, resistance to high winds, a need for shade.

The art of training and pruning the vine developed over centuries of experimentation. Different cultivars, different environments, and different traditions have generated diverse methods of controlling the vine's growth.[6] A major objective of above-ground training and pruning is the development of a strong root system below, so that a single, strong trunk is desirable. Viticulturists refer to *training* as the guided development of a young vine into a desirable form and *pruning* as the maintenance of that form and the control of fruiting. Although numerous systems have been devised, they may be grouped under two main training categories: *head*-training, in which the trunk rises to a single head, from which all the arms or branches extend, and *cordon*-training, in which the trunk rises taller and arms extend from it along all or most of its length. So many methods of pruning exist that

When the vine is left to grow, uncontrolled by pruning or training, it is a climber and a creeper, often choking other vegetation. This photograph, taken in Connecticut, suggests why the Vikings called America *Vinland* (land of the vine) when they first saw it.

no classification could encompass them all—but these shape the landscape of viticulture, reflecting as they do the traditions of many generations.

Thus the vine may be given a basic T or Y shape, with two arms extending in opposite directions; another method guides just one arm from the trunk, so that all the arms along a row of vines point in the same direction. Sometimes, as noted earlier, the plant is trained to stand as a tree, small or large, without wire or trellis support. Local practices reflect special viticultural demands as, for example, in the cordon system in Eastern European countries, where the lowest cordons can be covered against severe winter cold (see Chapter 4); the use of trees in Italy; the "gable" and "factory" systems of South Africa, where the vine is guided upward by a roof-like trellis. In Northern Portugal, D. Stanislawski classified all major vine forms into three groups according to height, but this encompassed no fewer than six configurations: the independent vine, the tree-supported vine, the festoon, the arbor-supported vine, the *arjoado* (a more elaborate version of the festoon, in which vertical wires are used to guide the vine hanging between trees), and the *bardo*, a fencelike design elaborated from the arjoado in which the trees are replaced by posts. Often the identity of a grower is revealed by such traditions. The Italian grower in California, the Portuguese farmer in Argentina, the German winemaker in Australia continue to use the methods of generations; viticulturists tend to be conservative people and habits fade slowly. The cultural landscape is a key to origin and diffusion.

And whatever the training and pruning methods, vineyards nearly everywhere in the world show evidence of the growers' attention to detail. Ruler-straight rows of vines, meticulously spaced, with foliage density that does not seem to vary from one end of the vineyard to the other—this is all part of the landscape of viticulture. Since every other plant in the vineyard competes with the vine and diminishes the soil's contribution to the nourishment of the grape, the ground below and between the vines is kept clear and, to promote permeability and aeration, turned. A healthy vineyard, no matter how large, resembles a carefully tended garden. Other than a well-maintained tea plantation, there is nothing like it in the world of agriculture.

By its capacity to reach deeply for water and nutrients the vine turns the gray of the desiccating summer into the seemingly permanent green of spring. Nothing quite so resembles an oasis as a vineyard, flanked by rocky hillcrests or arid steppe. "Green vines stretching like an ocean" is the description given the vineyards of Argentina's Mendoza province, where irrigation and the vine have transformed the desert.[7] It applies as well to South Africa's Little Karroo, California's Central Valley, Australia's Murray Basin: vast flatlands with row upon row of vines stretching unbroken to the horizon, the wineries and the houses of the growers standing like islands above the verdant sea. It would be difficult to identify a more evocative embodiment of Sauer's vision of the cultural landscape as a natural landscape transformed by human hand: nothing in the vineyard is left unaffected by viticulture's practice.[8]

Viticulture and Architecture

Viticulture's association with impressive architectural landmarks is as old as its connection with religion. Monasteries and abbeys rose above the vineyards; here lay not only the power and resources, but here, too, were set the standards by which good wine was made. Vestiges of that period still grace the cultural landscape of the oldest viticulture regions, even if names have changed and (as in Germany) many a *Kloster* of vinous fame became a *Schloss* after secularization. Burgundy's Clos Vougeot remains a monument to Cistercian viticulture and architecture, and many structures less imposing but also sustaining viticulture's historic linkage still rise above the vines.

When Nicolas Rolin and Guigone de Salins founded the Hospice de Beaune, they gave further confirmation to the relationship between wine (which sustained the charity) and memorable architecture. The Grande Hôtel Dieu, built in the mid-fifteenth century, remains one of the most magnificent buildings associated with viticulture, with soaring Gothic roofs, beautifully designed and executed pinnacles, columned galleries, multicolored tiles laid in intricate designs, and a serene, cobbled courtyard. The Hôtel Dieu is an architectural treasure in a town steeped in the images of wine.

It is not surprising that the attributes of religious architecture should have been transferred to secular buildings when viticulture's seventeenth- and eighteenth-century European expansion gathered momentum. Associations and images of wealth and prestige continued, and châteaux were adorned and elaborated as though they were small cathedrals. Thus Bordeaux's heritage of primacy and wealth is expressed, especially in the communes of the great châteaux, in the elaborate architecture and the spacious, ornately landscaped grounds of the estates. Legal restrictions upon

MIS ᴇɴ BOUTEILLE ᴀᴜ CHATEAU

GRAND VIN
DE
CHATEAU LATOUR

PREMIER GRAND CRU CLASSE
1967

DÉPOSÉ

APPELLATION PAUILLAC CONTROLÉE

Many wine labels carry images of important or historic structures, as
does Château Latour, here displaying its famous tower. Note the
mention of the 1855 Classification and its *Appellation Pauillac Contrôlée.*

the percentage of land that may be placed under vineyards and wide spacing
of the vines (to ensure maximum nourishment for the grapes) create an
impression that has not changed significantly for nearly two centuries. Château
Ducru-Beaucaillou (St. Julien) was built in 1720 and embellished in 1820;
Château Latour's tower was built between 1620 and 1630; Château d'Yquem's
present structure is more than two hundred years old; indeed, Château
Lafon-Rochet (St. Estèphe) is the only major Bordeaux château to be
completely rebuilt during the twentieth century.[9] The Bordeaux region is
an architectural as well as a viticultural phenomenon, a legacy of seventeenth-
and eighteenth-century France.

Undoubtedly the Bordeaux region presents viticulture's most variegated
cultural landscape, with its impeccable vineyards and large stands of old,
leafy trees, its atmosphere of spaciousness and comfort, stately châteaux,
picturesque one-story *chartreuses,* and decorative *chais.* The Loire Valley may
contain still grander châteaux, but these do not have the same functional
connection with viticulture in the region. Burgundy does have some more-
meticulously tended vines, but it lacks the architectural interest. The overall
scenery of the Rhine region may be more spectacular. But Bordeaux's
combination of style and substance is without equal, and its landscape is a
mirror of success, security, achievement, and wealth. It may be visualized
as standing at one end of the continuum of viticultural landscapes, with the
endless green flatlands of irrigated vineyards at the other—and yet Bordeaux
and Mendoza share elements of an almost tangible atmosphere unique to
the land of the vine.

Between the cultural landscape of Bordeaux and that of the irrigated expanses of Australia, Argentina, or California lie numerous alternative expressions of the geography of viticulture. Germany's pretentious *Schlösser* rise like giant sentinels over the steep Rhineland slopes, but many German growers—like numerous others in Alsace, Burgundy, Italy, Spain, and elsewhere in the wine-growing world—live and work in modest buildings that serve as residence and winery at the same time. Some impressive and historic estates exist in Burgundy, but the majority of Burgundy's growers own small vineyards and sell their carefully tended grapes, not wines; their homes are houses, not ornate villas. In Italy, where every conceivable viticultural landscape can be found, the large château or estate is the exception, not the rule. In Spain's Rioja region, the French immigrants from Bordeaux, escaping *phylloxera*, laid out vineyards—but not châteaux. Rioja's vineyards surround *bodegas*, wine factories where the wines from many vineyards are blended and aged. Only Castillo Ygay can lay claim to château status in Rioja, its history and architecture somewhat reminiscent of the Bordeaux model.

In the New World, the cultural landscape of South Africa's viticulture region may come closer to that of Bordeaux than any other, save perhaps those valleys in California where imitations of Bordeaux architectural opulence are arising. Seventeenth- and eighteenth-century estates in the Cape-Dutch architectural style (Groot Constantia is the prototype), with their chalk-white walls, thatched roofs, and ornate facades, stand etched against the green of the vines.

The cultural landscape of California's vineyards, as exemplified by the Napa and Sonoma regions, contains evidence of its early character as well as its modern transformation.[10] Before 1900 the Napa Valley had more than 600 growers and more than 100 wineries, and the Sonoma Valley, also with more than 100 wineries, rivaled its neighbor across the Mayacamas Mountains. Before Prohibition both slopes of the Sonoma Valley were covered by vineyards, and viticulture around Sonoma, beginning with the vineyards of the mission, has a rich history. Haraszthy's Buena Vista of the 1850s, with its Italian-style hilltop mansion and its tunneled cellars; the impressive Kenwood winery, originally built in 1905; and many other substantial winery buildings marked Sonoma's nineteenth- and early twentieth-century landscape. In Sonoma itself Samuele Sebastiani figured prominently as winemaker and townsman, his winery a landmark and his name on numerous institutions. But the Sonoma region suffered severely during the onslaught of *phylloxera* and Prohibition, and also faced problems resulting from its relative location. Easily accessible from San Francisco, the valley became a popular weekend and vacation retreat; as viticulture suffered setbacks, many vineyards were taken over, subdivided, and sold as lots to city residents seeking a holiday retreat. Post-Prohibition recovery was slower than it was in the Napa Valley— but the Sonoma region has not lost its capacity to produce excellent wines, and its modern landscape reflects this.

The Sonoma Valley lies at the heart of a larger viticultural region that extends northward into the Alexander Valley; Sonoma County as a whole now contains more than 80 wineries. Its cultural landscape reflects California viticulture—its well-being, and its problems and potentials. Although viticulture here is old (by American standards), having begun when the fathers of Mission San Francisco de Solano planted vines on the site of the modern Sebastiani vineyard in 1825, much of the nineteenth-century landscape has been lost—some of it in the 1906 earthquake, which caused the collapse of Buena Vista's underground cellars as well as other structures, and more during the modernization of the post-Prohibition period. Today there are vestiges of the old, but the region (like the Napa Valley to the east) gives the impression of frontier viticulture. There are true châteaux comparable in grace and style to the best of Bordeaux; there are *chartreuses* in the California style; and there are more simple, functional wineries. Part of this landscape evinces enormous investment not only to make wines but also to create an atmosphere; another part betrays the struggle of those who cannot afford to build castles while tending costly vineyards.

One of Sonoma's true châteaux is St. Jean, a magnificent example of French-Mediterranean architecture modeled after Château Lafite. The stately, columned mansion is graced by formal gardens and fountains and flanked by meticulously tended hillside vineyards. Founded in 1973 by a group of investors who wished to state tangibly their intent to make wine of excellence, Chateau St. Jean has indeed produced award-winning wines during its brief existence, and its name has achieved a high reputation.

Among older wineries in Sonoma County is Korbel Champagne Cellars and Vineyards, overlooking the valley of the Russian River. The original brick winery, still standing, was built a century ago (1886), and several other historic buildings on the Korbel estate have been preserved, including the rough-brick brandy distillery with its characterful tower. Not far away is the unusual structure of the Hop Kiln Winery, a stone building topped by three pyramidal roofs, each capped with a redwood turret. This building dates from 1905 and has been made a California Historic Landmark since it was a focus of the county's hopgrowing industry; it was restored as a winery during the 1970s. Much older is the Simi Winery in Healdsburg, its original stone structure dating from the mid-1870s when the Simi brothers, successful winemakers and merchants in San Francisco, built the winery and called it Montepulciano. The winery thrived, then fell into disrepair during the post-Prohibition period; but it was bought and refurbished in the 1960s, its majestic main buildings surviving all the changes. Also dating from the 1880s are the original buildings at Geyser Peak and Italian Swiss Colony; expansion has necessitated modernization, but the old and familiar architectural style and building materials—rough stone and redwood—provide the kind of continuity from which viticulture regions derive so much of their special atmosphere. They also provide the temporal backdrop against which such modern edifices as Chateau St. Jean and, near Healdsburg in the Alexander Valley, Jordan Vineyard and Winery are set. The Jordan Winery, a beautiful, yellow-shaded, tile-roofed, shuttered château of French provincial character, is among those California wineries evincing enormous investment in the pursuit of quality. It dates from 1972, but its operations are based entirely on the classical château tradition, and its wines have quickly attained international prestige.

If Sonoma County's viticultural landscape reflects the historic as well as the modern, the established as well as the frontier, the Napa Valley conveys a special and unmatched blend of tradition and modernization.[11] It has been said that the Napa region's cultural landscape personifies California viticulture as does no other.

Relatively confined between spurs of the Howell and Mayacamas mountains, the Napa Valley is crowded with more than 10,000 hectares (25,000 acres) of vineyards, over 100 wineries large and small, historic ruins, and modern, elaborate establishments. The links with Napa's nineteenth-century prosperity still are part of the cultural landscape. Charles Krug built his first winery in the 1860s; Inglenook's great Gothic stone house was built in 1887; Beringer's Rhine House dates from 1876; the Christian Brothers' Greystone Cellar, largest in the world in its time, was completed in 1889; and Chateau Chevalier on Spring Mountain was built in 1891. Fragments of walls, tunnels, hand-dug caves, and equipment bear witness to a period, almost a century ago, when nearly 7000 of the Napa Valley's hectares stood under vines; that figure was not reached again until the revolution of the 1960s and 1970s.

If Bordeaux's cultural landscape is studded by the great châteaux, that of Napa is marked by frequently modest signposts that carry names of historic moment. Charles Krug came to the valley in 1861, and although his winery has long since been sold and resold, the Krug name remains attached to it. Martini, Inglenook, Beringer—these and other wineries were founded or developed by the region's pioneers, and even if they were acquired by other families or corporations the venerated names remained. This has been true even during the most recent *étappe* in the cycle of sale and consolidation: the invasion of corporate giants. Inglenook and Beaulieu are now Heublein wineries; Nestlé took control of Beringer; Sterling was acquired by Coca-Cola. While the large corporations move in, however, small family vineyards still survive, their modest, often restored houses and cellars evincing their owners' enthusiasm and affection for viticulture's noble art.

Modernization, however, and not tradition, forms the dominant impression in Napa's cultural landscape. From the stainless steel holding tanks at Mondavi's mission-style winery (built in 1965) to the cable cars that convey visitors to Sterling's monasterylike hilltop building (dating from 1973) the Napa Valley represents all that is new, efficient, hygienic, and innovative in viticulture.

Certainly efficiency is a matter of necessity, because a growing stream of visitors inundates the major wineries and creates traffic jams on "The Wine Road" (Route 29, the valley's single through road) that may be without parallel in viticulture regions anywhere in the world. This phenomenon— the emergence of a major road artery through the wine country and its crowding with visitors—has become a permanent attribute to the landscape of viticulture regions from California to Germany. Such routes become known, simply, as the *Weinstrassen*, the *Routes des Vins* or, in Rioja, the *Camino del Vino* from Haro to Logroño. In turn they affect the evolution of the regional landscape as wineries seek vantage and visibility. Modest signposts and garish billboards stand side by side along California's Route 29, and ostentatious entranceways alternate with simple driveway accesses to valley wineries.

No assessment of viticulture's cultural landscape would be complete without allusion to the lesser structures and the artifacts of industry, many of which hold much interest. Toolsheds, walls and fences, wagons and carts, and abandoned equipment still standing in the vineyards may provide glimpses of the past—and understanding of the present. Even the use of plants other than the vine has purpose: in Tuscany, winegrowers mark the rows of vines qualified to produce the best Chianti by planting a rose bush at each end.

An Old World practice diffused to the New: a bed of flowers graces the vineyard. In Tuscany, an especially venerated row of vines may be marked by a rose bush; here, at Sakonnet Vineyards in Rhode Island, a cluster of lilies stands at the end of a row of Chardonnay.

The flowering rose is at once a badge of honor and an adornment of the vineyard; when it is seen off California's Route 29 or in Mendoza, it may well reveal the Italian origins of the winegrowing family.

Central Places

Wines may be named after river valleys and administrative areas, but the key location in the region (after the vineyard itself, of course) is the town on which the local industry is centered. Central places of all kinds have long been of particular interest to geographers, because their influence extends in tangible and less tangible ways across a surrounding region that is, in turn, shaped and modified by that influence. Measuring and recording these interactions can present interesting challenges, especially when two or more central places compete for primacy in a region. Where does the dominance of one central place yield to that of another? How is this transition recorded on the landscape?

The towns that lie amid the vineyards are central places in more than the technical sense. They are the foci of the economic functions and activities in their hinterlands; they also reflect and represent the ambience of the regions they serve. In a very real way the townscape of viticulture's central place summarizes the region around: its layout, architecture, religious and political influences, merchants' and shippers' establishments, and other connections with the industry, historic and current, are manifest.

Viticulture's central places are not large. Although Bordeaux is the large urban center that dominates Gironde and its districts and communes, the classic central place of the Bordeaux region is St. Emilion. Bordeaux is an industrial and port city whose service functions for the wine industry are but a part of its overall economic operations. The ancient town of Saint Emilion, on the other hand, is an integral part of the viticulture region for which it has since Roman times constituted the focus. Vineyards extend into the town itself; great châteaux adjoin it; cellars have been hewn from the rock beneath it. Saint Emilion is the historic, economic, and ceremonial center for a major viticultural district. In the greater Bordeaux region, it is not the only place of its kind; Pauillac, Cadillac, Langon, and several other small towns have central place qualities. But Saint Emilion is undoubtedly most representative of the type. Similarly, the town of Beaune is the undisputed central place for Burgundy's Côte d'Or, as Mâcon is for that region's southern flank. Dijon, at the northern end of Burgundy, and Lyon to the south are larger, but also more diversified. Beaune (another French town of Roman origins) since the seventeenth century has been Burgundy's most expressive town, variously described as an enormous "Burgundian Commercial" and as the "Capital of Burgundian Wines." Certainly Beaune's primary role is beyond doubt; from the famous Hospice to the museum, from its labyrinth of cellars to the headquarters of the great shipping firms, from its storefront wine displays to its ubiquitous advertisements, the wine trade dominates all. As part of the cultural landscape of old European viticulture, the central places of France, Italy, Germany, and Iberia differ markedly from those of the New World. The dimensions of the towns of Napa, Sonoma, Stellenbosch, Paarl, Cessnock, and Tanunda may be comparable, but there the similarity ends. The layout, architecture, comparative youthfulness, and general ambience of these towns set them apart, their roles as foci for wine regions notwithstanding. Beaune's townscape is dom-

The architecture of viticulture: the main building of Groot Constantia, South Africa's oldest estate. The Cape-Dutch architectural style prevails throughout the wine country of the Cape, and marks not only its estates and wineries but also its central places.

inated by Burgundy's regional viticulture; Napa's townscape is dominated by prevailing norms of northern California. Saint Emilion is visibly procreated by the vineyards from which it rises; Cessnock resembles an Australian frontier town. Stellenbosch and Paarl carry their roles as central places for Cape viticulture lightly, in spite of the presence of Cape-Dutch architecture in Stellenbosch and the KWV in Paarl.

Whether old or young, the central places of the wine country are the settings for important elements of the regional culture: celebrations, festivals, fairs, and other ceremonies associated with the viticultural year. Tales, myths, and legends surround virtually every phase of the viticultural year, but none as much as the harvest. Harvest time is celebrated in some way in virtually all wine-producing regions, and the chief locales for these feasts are the regions' focal points, the towns. Growers, merchants, shippers, dignitaries, and visitors of various ranks join in the festive occasion. Adornments and decorations are brought out to grace public, religious, and wine-related buildings. Organizations of various kinds, such as the Confrérie des Chevaliers du Tastevin de Bourgogne (Burgundy) and the Confrérie Saint-Etienne (Alsace), contribute their pomp and ceremony to an event that joyfully serves the common cause. Briefly the town is transformed as historic continuities are once again confirmed. In the process, the role of the wine town as regional viticulture's nodal locus is strengthened anew.

Time remains the crucial factor in the integration of viticulture's central places in the regional cultural landscape. Europe's older centers are part of viticulture's landscape far more completely than the younger towns of the New World. The strength of the monoculture is another element: in famed

Old-World viticulture regions, vines are virtually the only cultivated plants, but in the New World, agricultural diversification may prevail even in well-known wine-producing regions. Viticulture is not the only form of farming in the Hunter Valley, nor are grapes the sole product of South Africa's Cape. Travelers along Rioja's Camino del Vino are impressed by the interspersed crop patterns in so famous a wine region. In Australia, the Cape, even in older Rioja, viticulture is diluted; the central places reflect it.

City and Vineyard

The central place is an ally of viticulture, but a nearby city also can be a formidable foe. The central places just mentioned tend to be towns of comparatively modest size, some of them large villages. But a major city positioned near a viticultural region can engulf the vineyards and convert vineland into suburb.

This is not to suggest that vineyards near older, stable cities or smaller wine towns have been free from the threat of urbanization. At one time there was, in Burgundy, a Côte de Dijon whose wines were held in high esteem. The expansion of the city of Dijon contributed to this subregion's demise—in the very heart of an area where wine reigns supreme.[12] The urban march is inexorable, fueled by a concentration of wealth that makes vineyard land, no matter how valuable, vulnerable to "development" and subdivision. As mentioned in Chapter 1, Sonoma County's vineyards north of San Francisco have suffered from the city's penetration; in the Napa region, the county government in 1968 enacted a restrictive law to stem the urban tide. The law stipulated that no subdivision of land outside the county's four towns could produce parcels smaller than 40 acres (17 hectares). Since then the determination of Napa County government officials has been tested, especially when the 40-acre minimum proved to be no insurmountable obstacle, in terms of cost, to wealthy urbanites bent on acquiring a base in the wine country. A proposed subdivision of more than 1000 acres of prime Chardonnay vineyard in the southern part of the county was rejected, and a temporary reprieve was won.

But that story is atypical. When vineyards lie in the path of expansion of a major city, coexistence tends to be temporary. In Santiago, Chile, the vineyards at Macul lie directly in the path of the city's eastward sprawl. In Cape Town, South Africa, the country's historic old vineyards have long been engulfed by the urban tide, and other vines are vulnerable. Here the process continues on the south side of the conurbation (on the Cape Peninsula, site of the Constantia vineyards) as well as the north. A major reason why the better wines of the Bucelas and Carcavelos regions of Portugal have become collectors' items is because the suburbs of the capital, Lisbon, and the resort city of Estoril have invaded the vineyards and decimated them. In Japan, in Argentina, in Germany, in Italy, as in other wine-producing countries the vine is in competition with the very markets it serves.

Landscapes of Modernization

From the Central Valley of California to the desert of Mendoza, the Little Karroo of South Africa, and the Murray Valley of Australia, irrigated viticulture has transformed the countryside. Here grapes are grown and

Mass-production: modern, large wineries take on the appearance of refineries as their steel, computer-cooled vats stand in the open. The Penfolds winery in the Barossa Valley, Australia.

wine is made in prodigious quantities, mechanized means of harvesting are pioneered, mass transport of the grapes over hundreds of kilometers occurs. Wineries are factories, and barrels are replaced by stainless steel tanks that stand in the open, rising like the pipes of a huge organ above the vineyards. Sometimes the winery is not surrounded by vines at all, but stands at an optimum relative location to receive trucked-in tonnage of grapes from as far as 300 kilometers away. The world's largest single winery, Ernest and Julio Gallo's establishment at Modesto, California, is the most prominent example of this refinerylike development in viticulture.

This is a particular component of the cultural landscape of viticulture, a comparatively modern development made possible not only by irrigation but also by temperature control in the open-air tanks.

Water supply, trellising techniques, row spacing, training to promote leaf protection, and cooling spray systems against the summer's searing heat made the mechanized cultivation of the vine possible—but the crucial breakthrough involved the application of large-scale cooling. Controlled conditions of fermentation made possible the production of creditable wine in quantities undreamed of just decades ago, and the landscape soon bore the evidence as vineyards sprawled over thousands of square kilometers of irrigable land, enormous fermentation vats towering over the vines.

The vast vineyards of California's Central Valley and Argentina's Mendoza and adjacent areas are not diversified by picturesque towns, clusters of tall trees, ornate mansions, or other adornments. This is the landscape of mass production, of ultimate efficiency, of machines.[13] The spacing of rows of vines is geared to the needs of mechanical harvesters, not to the nutrients the soil can best provide. The vineyards lie square or rectangular, separated by ruler-straight roads that maximize accessibility to the wineries. It is the most basic, the most efficient cultural landscape of viticulture, a tribute to the human capacity to modify natural environments.

Additional Reading

The literature on the topic of Chapter 7 is yet limited, but fragments of information are included in various descriptions of wine regions and wineries, such as:

Arlott, J., and Fielden, C. *Burgundy.* London: Davis-Poynter Ltd., 1976.

Baird, J. Armstrong, Jr. *Wine and the Artist.* New York: Dover Publications, 1979.

Fletcher, W. *Port: An Introduction to Its History and Delights.* London: Sotheby Parke Bernet, 1978.

Halliday, J. and Jarratt, R. *The Wines and History of the Hunter Valley.* Sydney: McGraw-Hill, 1979.

Hinkle, R. P. *Central Coast Wine Book.* St. Helena, Calif.: Vintage Image, 1980.

Knox, G. *Estate Wines of South Africa.* Cape Town: David Philip, 1976.

Latimer, P. *Sonoma and Mendocino Wine Book.* St. Helena, Calif.: Vintage Image, 1979.

Massel, A. *Basic Viticulture.* Hindhead, England: Wine Book Club, 1976.

Potter, N. *Wines and Wineries of South Australia.* Adelaide: Rigby Ltd., 1978.

Stanislawski, D. *Landscapes of Bacchus: The Vine in Portugal.* Austin: University of Texas Press, 1970.

Yapp, R., and Yapp, J. *Vineyards and Vignerons.* Shaftesbury: Blackmore, 1980.

8

An Old-World Vintage Regional Geography: From Rioja to the Rheingau

In the concluding chapters of this geographic appreciation of wine the focus is on regions and vintages. Not even an entire volume could do justice to all the world's wine-producing countries and areas *and* to the vintages of the past dozen years, and so this is an inevitably selective and somewhat personal account of favorite geographies and preferred years. Certainly it is productive to go beyond the usual and to examine some more remote and less familiar regions, where some excellent wines are made. If no commentary such as this could omit the Burgundies or the Californias, neither should it fail to review the Chileans or the Hunters. Wines from virtually all parts of the world are reaching American markets. A fascinating geography lies behind them all.

Vintage Years: A Caution

Maps normally have the virtue of neutrality: they depict and reveal, but they do not exhort (although, as political geographers are aware, they can be distorted in support of propaganda). Vintage charts, on the other hand, represent opinions and impressions. They are necessarily subjective, and frequently become the subject of debate and disagreement. For several reasons, vintage charts such as those distributed by agencies of the wine industry, by wine institutes and societies, and even by independent wine writers, should be used with caution.

In the first place, a vintage chart, even one with considerable detail, constitutes a generalization. It reflects an average that may accurately describe the wines of a substantial part of a particular region in a given year, but virtually always there will be exceptions. When the assessment of a certain vintage is low because rain came just before and during the harvest, those rains may have held off in certain places, where the wine is much better than the chart suggests. When a vintage year is awarded a high rank because conditions generally were favorable throughout the ripening and harvesting periods, there always is the potential for disappointment. Not every wine of the 1970 and 1975 Bordeaux vintages is a great wine. Some winemakers may not have done their work as well as they should. And microclimates have a way of betraying the norm.

Thus the "poor" or "mediocre" vintage actually represents an opportunity for the consumer. The average tends to depress overall prices, and a chateau that made good wine because environmental conditions in its vineyards were much better than those prevailing elsewhere that year cannot sell its wines at the higher prices it merits. The lowly vintage (unless the year really was a complete disaster) thus deserves a closer look, and bargains can be found. Conversely, and for obvious reasons, the high-ranked vintage suggests circumspection. Prices are high, and even wines from vineyards where conditions may have been less than ideal, or from estates where the wine was not made as well as it should be, are expensive.

A good example that illustrates the partial relevance of vintage charts is the 1964 Bordeaux vintage. This was an abundant year in the region, with a marvelous summer followed by a very good September. Some châteaux harvested while the weather was good, but others, especially in the Médoc where it had been slightly cool, decided to wait (Château Latour was among the early harvesters; Lafite was late). Then began local but incessant rains that were concentrated in the Médoc and lasted two weeks, and the late-pickers were in trouble. As a result, it was essential for consumers to know (a) that Saint Emilion and Pomerol escaped these problems to a far greater extent than the Médoc, and (b) that some Médoc wines were excellent while others, made from later-harvested grapes, were ordinary. Today the great wines from Pomerol and Saint Emilion of the 1964 vintage are magnificent still (especially Château Petrus from Pomerol), and from the Médoc there remains the fabulous Latour—but Lafite, Mouton-Rothschild, and many other surviving 1964s are not up to standard.

Another qualification concerning vintage charts relates to over- or under-estimates that later change—when market misjudgments already have been made. After the midpoint of the twentieth century a number of Bordeaux vintages were heralded as "the vintage of the century," including 1955, 1959, 1961, 1966, 1970, and 1975. Among these admittedly great vintages, only 1961 continues to be recognized as one of the century's two or three best; but the early and excessive adulation of the other vintages helped inflate prices (especially during the 1970s) and raised expectations that were later disappointed.

Again, a vintage sometimes turns out better than is first anticipated. A collection of vintage charts from Bordeaux of the 1960s proves the point: at first the 1962 vintage was judged to be short-lived, to be drunk when young. It was given a mediocre rating, which was perhaps not surprising in view of its immediate predecessor. But then the wines of 1962 proved to have greater staying power than was first believed, and the vintage's rank

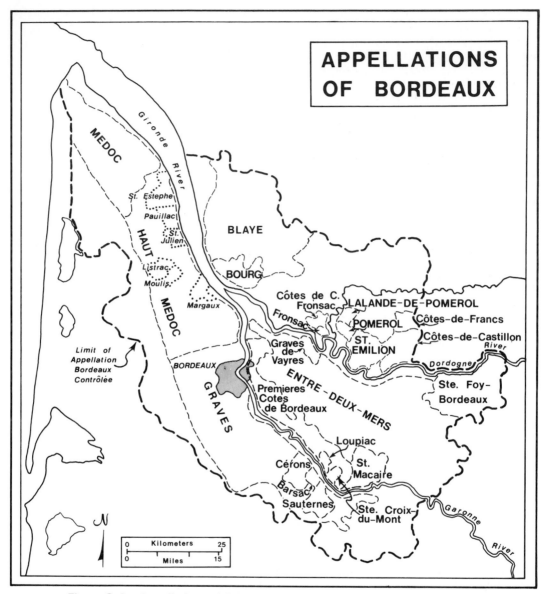

Figure 8.1 *Appellations* of Bordeaux

began to improve. By the time its full potential was recognized, much of the wine had been consumed prematurely.

For these and other reasons, vintage charts should be used with care. They have, in certain instances, become marketing devices, their ranking inflated to encourage purchase and consumption. But some vintage charts include more detail than others and are therefore more useful than usual, especially when they are prepared by independent evaluators. Some Bordeaux vintage charts differentiate between the Médoc and other districts of the region, and list red wines as distinct from white; this practice is more frequently seen in the context of Burgundy's red and white wines. The most revealing California vintage charts provide their information by cultivar as well as by region, a far more reliable guide than the overall "California" average for all wines.

Vintage charts report their rankings in numerical form, but not consistently so. Some charts, for example those of the International Wine and Food Society, use a 0–7 rating scale. A well-designed South African scale rates wines and vintages on a 9-point basis. Various other systems range from 10 to 20 points. In order to establish uniformity, all vintage charts in this chapter are on a 20-point basis. The advantage is that the larger range of numbers permits rather more discrimination than do some other systems. The charts in this and the following chapter go back as far as 1970 for practical reasons; older vintages of exceptional quality are mentioned as appropriate.

Bordeaux

The regional geography of Bordeaux is the ultimate geography of wine, a fitting locale with which to begin (Fig. 8.1). Where the Dordogne and Garonne Rivers join to become the Gironde lies an historic viticultural region centered on the city of Bordeaux, capital of ancient Rome's province of Aquitania, later ruled by English kings, recalcitrant during the Revolution, and unique in the annals of the vine.[1]

The boundary (*limite*) of the *Appellation Bordeaux Contrôlée* encloses nearly 4000 regional and local viticultural toponyms, some among the world's most famous, others obscure. Here lie the great Haut-Médoc, Graves, Saint Emilion, and Pomerol, wine districts of eminence; and communes without peer. Of the Haut-Médoc's twenty-seven communes, no fewer than six have their own *Appellations:* Saint-Julien, Pauillac, Margaux, Saint-Estèphe, Listrac, and Moulis. Flanking the Gironde's left bank are four châteaux of First Great Growth rank, and the fifth, Château Haut-Brion, lies in the shadow of the city itself. *Appellations*, famous as well as inconspicuous, and now numbering some forty, create a complex viticultural mosaic.

The compact Bordeaux region is trisected by the Dordogne-Garonne-Gironde river system, and each of the three geographical segments has distinct regional qualities. Much of Bordeaux's fame derives from the strip of land extending along the west banks of the Gironde and the Garonne, where the noble red wines of the Haut-Médoc as well as the great sweet whites of Sauternes are made. Facing the right bank of the Dordogne lies Saint Emilion and Pomerol, producers of superb red wines which, at their best, match those of the Haut-Médoc. Between the two rivers lies the appropriately named Entre-Deux-Mers, an *Appellation* that occupies much (but not all) of this less prestigious interior zone, where white Bordeaux wines predominate.

As the scale on Figure 8.1 shows, the Bordeaux region is not only compact but also quite large, extending approximately 80 kilometers (50 miles) from Soulac at the mouth of the Gironde to the southern limit of the regional *Appellation*, and about 50 kilometers (30 miles) from west to east in the latitude of Bordeaux. It is therefore not surprising that the region encompasses varied environments and numerous microclimates, and that different cultivars do better in various subregions. In the south, the *pourriture noble* ("noble

Château Haut-Brion was the only château outside the Médoc to be classified as a First Great Growth in 1855. It remains one of the region's most prestigious estates today, meriting its high rank and producing, from its gravelly soils, excellent red as well as white wines.

rot") affects the white (Sémillon and Sauvignon Blanc) grapes of Sauternes and produces the fabled sweet wines, among which those of Château d'Yquem are considered by many to be the world's greatest. The Haut-Médoc is the heartland of the Cabernet Sauvignon, but the great reds of Pomerol and Saint Emilion depend upon the success of the Merlot—here in the heartland of the Cabernet! Other approved cultivars (see Chapter 2) are used in the blending of Bordeaux's numerous styles. All these variations, of course, are related to the region's diverse climate, soil, and topography. A long, low strip of gravel dominates the Haut-Médoc and Graves; low hills supported by sandstone (with some clay) create Entre-Deux-Mers; and north of the Dordogne there is undulating relief in which limestone prevails. Geographic terms among the viticultural names reflect Bordeaux's varied physical geography: *Graves, Côtes,* and *Monts* abound.

Both red and white wines of Bordeaux come in the familiar high-shouldered bottle (as opposed to Burgundy's slope-shouldered shape). Centuries ago red and white wine were blended and the resulting light-red wine, a kind of dark rosé, was called *clairet.* Such mixing has long been illegal, but the name *claret* for Bordeaux's red wines has persisted, especially in England. The great red wines of Bordeaux are produced in the northwestern areas of the region, where conditions are more moist than in the south, more suited to the superb sweet whites. Sometimes forgotten in the assessment of Bordeaux vintages are the region's dry white wines, no match for the best of Burgundy but often very good and affordably priced. One of the best examples of what Bordeaux can achieve in white wines is the small production from a château more famous for its great reds, Haut-Brion.

Château Haut-Brion bears watching as one of those sources of good wine in mediocre years. Located in the very suburbs of the city of Bordeaux, Haut-Brion also is the southernmost of the five First Great Growths. Its vines grow in gravels as deep as 15 to 20 meters (50 to 65 feet), thick with pebbles that retain heat and, at the surface, reflect sun, and porous enough to drain away any excess water. The risk of harvest-time rain is slightly less than it is in the Haut-Médoc, and Haut-Brion's proximity to the city has the advantage that a nearby labor force is available if quick harvesting is necessary. More than once, these advantages have combined to favor Haut-Brion's wines when adverse conditions prevailed. The problem vintage of 1964 is a good example; Haut-Brion's wine has been rated superior even to the fabulous Latour, and remains rich and strong in the 1980s.

Among Bordeaux's more than 3,000 wine producers are the great names of the 1855 Classification, several hundred châteaux of less renown but substantial merit, and numerous estates of more than passing interest, including the "Petits Châteaux" from which, at times, come memorable wines. There was a time when the classified wines were virtually the sole representatives on foreign markets, but in recent decades the range of Bordeaux exports has expanded and careful research can uncover some wonderful rewards. It is not necessary to pay $100 to experience Bordeaux's special art: many an excellent wine from a respected commune will cost one-tenth of the price of a First Great Growth, and carry faithfully the Bordelais character.

RED BORDEAUX VINTAGES: 1970–1982

The Bordeaux region is subject to considerable year-to-year climatic variation that spells the difference between great, mediocre, and poor vintages. One of the remarkable aspects of Bordeaux's vintage sequence is the "pairing" of great with good years: the 1961 vintage, one of the century's greatest, was followed by the very good 1962; the 1966 vintage, undoubtedly a great one, was succeeded by the surprising 1967. The next decade opened with the very good and consistent 1970 vintage, and 1971, though spatially spotty, was good. The next-best vintage of the 1970s, the 1975, was followed by the abundant and acceptable 1976. The 1978, also a good vintage, was paired with a 1979 that was certainly better than 1972, 1973, 1974, or 1977.

1982   A good spring and a nearly perfect early summer. Large harvest indicated.

1981   Gray, overcast spring, poor July, hot and dry August. Ripening
(11)*   went well, harvest generally early but bedeviled by widespread rains. Good sugar, acid content somewhat low. Wines charming, attractive, unimpressive.

1980   Moist early summer, good weather during September and October,
(7)   but local rains during harvest. Médoc a bit better than St. Emilion and Pomerol, where Merlot fared poorly.

1979   Difficult year, cold summer, late harvest in rain. Large quantity,
(12)   low acid. Better in Pomerol and St. Emilion than in Médoc.

*Numbers in parentheses indicate ratings on a 20-pt. basis.

1978 (15)	Bad summer but much improvement from second half of August until late harvest under good conditions. Châteaux that took the risk and harvested latest had the best wines. In general, Médoc and Graves better than St. Emilion or Pomerol.
1977 (6)	Frost during flowering period: small harvest after cold and wet summer. Thin wines.
1976 (13)	A variable vintage: large harvest under poor conditions following a very good summer. Better in Médoc and Graves, mediocre in Pomerol, poorest in St. Emilion. Some very good wines in St. Julien.
1975 (17)	Early spring frost, especially severe in St. Emilion and Pomerol. Hot summer; good ripening. Disastrous hail in several Haut-Médoc communes. Very good harvest conditions. Full, rich, complex, long-lived wines.
1974 (8)	Rain during the harvest. Abundant, undistinguished vintage with a few better wines.
1973 (10)	Enormous harvest; light, round wines without much character or future.
1972 (5)	Ruinous rain during the summer; the sun did not break through until late September, preventing complete disaster. Acid, hard wines; some exceptions in St. Julien.
1971 (13)	A good vintage, small and somewhat light; fast-maturing wines. Better in Pomerol and St. Emilion than in Médoc.
1970 (18)	Great vintage, favorable conditions. Many wines will endure for decades; others are ready now.

Earlier vintages: Bordeaux wines of great vintages can improve for decades, even generations. Recent tastings confirm the magnificence of Latours of the 1920s. Among great vintages before 1970 are 1966, 1961, 1959, 1945, 1937, 1929, and 1928.

Burgundy

Geographically, Burgundy as a region differs from Bordeaux in almost every possible way.[2] More northerly and more remote from maritime influences, Burgundy is ribbonlike and elongated, not compact as is Bordeaux; its subregions lie separated and are not contiguous (Fig. 8.2). Chablis, Burgundy's northernmost subregion, lies nearly 100 kilometers (60 miles) from the Côte d'Or, and Beaujolais, its southernmost zone, lies about as far to the south. Although Burgundy has central places, including Dijon at the northern end of the Côte d'Or, Beaune (site of the famed Hôtel Dieu), and Mâcon, it has no dominant focus to match Bordeaux. Even Burgundy's relationship with its streams differs from that of Bordeaux. The Saône River flanks but does not traverse Burgundy, and where Burgundy produces its greatest wines, in the Côte d'Or, the Saône River lies many kilometers to the east.

As Figure 8.2 shows, Burgundy's five major subregions are Chablis, the Côte d'Or (consisting of the Côte de Nuits and the Côte de Beaune), the Côte Chalonnaise, the Côte Mâconnaise, and Beaujolais. These names suggest the range and variety of the wines Burgundy yields: flinty, bone-dry whites from Chablis; light, early drinking reds from Beaujolais; complex, long-lived

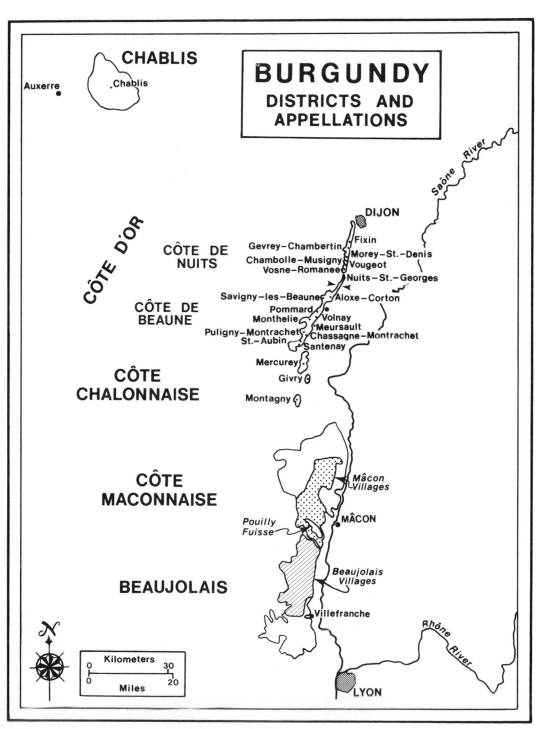

Figure 8.2 Burgundy: Districts and *Appellations*

vintages from the Côte d'Or, from slopes turned golden by the autumn. If there are those who prefer the reds of Bordeaux to those of Burgundy, there can be no question that Burgundy's whites have qualities unmatched by those of Bordeaux.

The heartland of Burgundy is the Côte d'Or, that narrow ribbon beyond compare that extends southwestward from Dijon. The Golden Slope faces southeast, overlooking the wide lowland of the Saône River; on a clear day the Alps are visible in the distance. A journey southward from Dijon passes through unassuming, picturesque villages whose names rank among the greatest in the world of wine, and past vineyards of modest dimensions whose grapes—the Pinot Noir and the Chardonnay—produce the noblest of wines. Burgundy produces only about one-third as much wine as Bordeaux, accounting for a mere 2 percent of all the wine made in France. And nearly half of this is Beaujolais; only one-third of Burgundy's tiny production comprises the great wines of the Côte d'Or, Chablis and Mâconnais. Little wonder that Burgundies are among the rarest and most expensive of wines.

The Côte d'Or divides into the Côte de Nuits and the Côte de Beaune, the dividing line lying just south of the town of Nuits-St.-Georges (Fig. 8.2). The Côte de Nuits is Burgundy's premier red-wine–producing district, and is regarded by many as the greatest of all such districts, superior even to the Médoc. That reputation was forged on the wines of earlier times, when yields per hectare were much lower (less than half of present practice), and the Pinot Noir had not yet cloned today's thinner-skinned grapes; the wines were deep, dark, even tough until time mellowed them. Some specialists regard the 1949 as the last of this breed. Yet the prices commanded by the reds of the Côte de Nuits confirm that their primacy has not faded on world markets.[3]

The most famous and noblest of Burgundy's red wines undoubtedly come from the commune of Vosne-Romanée, where small vineyards produce incomparable wines: La Romanée, Romanée-Conti, Richebourg, and La Tache among them. These labels make no mention of the village of their vicinity, the village of Vosne; they have their own prideful *Appellations.* Other excellent wines, not quite so fortunate, are labeled Vosne-Romanée (showing the village and the name of its most famous vineyard), followed by their own vineyards names, such as Les Malconsorts, La Grande Rue, or Les Suchots. As Figure 8.2 shows, Vosne-Romanée lies just to the north of the town of Nuits-St.-Georges, in the southern part of the Côte de Nuits. Nearby lie some other famous vineyards, including Echezeaux, whose difficult name (it has been suggested) inhibited its success on world markets.

The northern part of the Côte de Nuits is graced by the marvelous vineyards around Gevrey-Chambertin. As the map shows, many of Burgundy's villages attach the name of their most famous vineyard to their own (as does Vosne-Romanée); in the case of Gevrey, as with Vosne, the very best wines carry labels that make no mention of the village. Two vineyards just south of the village center, Chambertin and Chambertin-Clos de Bèze, make the most superb wines.

These two communes (villages and their surrounding vineyards), Vosne-Romanée and Gevrey-Chambertin, may be consistently the best of the Côte de Nuits, but their wines do have local rivals worthy of attention. They tend to overshadow wines that may as a result be excellent values, for example the red wines from Fixin in the north. Wines from Morey St.-Denis and Chambolle-Musigny, as well as certain labels from Clos-de-Vougeot, often reach great heights. Red Burgundy from the vineyards of the village of Vougeot (not permitted to use the *Clos* in their names or on their labels) are of lesser rank, but from Nuits-St.-Georges come wines that are quite good if not of the highest caliber. The Côte de Nuits is a treasure trove, where careful research may still uncover great values.

Just to the south of Nuits-St.-Georges lies the small village of Prémeaux, whose wines are sold under the larger town's *Appellation* (which is why it does not appear on Figure 8.2), and here begins the Côte de Beaune. A look at the map suggests that the Côte de Beaune is famous for great white as well as red wines, a versatility the Côte de Nuits cannot claim. Place names in the north tend to associate with red wines (Corton, Pommard), but toward the south the toponyms are those of white wines (Meursault, Montrachet).

Actually, white wines are made even in the northernmost commune of the Côte de Beaune, Aloxe Corton, although this commune certainly is better known for its very good reds. Here the Chardonnay stands alongside the Pinot Noir, but it is fair to say that the Pinot Noir still yields the more memorable wines, perhaps the best of the Côte de Beaune's reds. Still the whites are very good, better than anything from Savigny-les-Beaune to the south, where rather ordinary reds predominate and the whites are undistinguished. Pommard, the commune flanking Beaune, also produces red wines, many fairly good but, in part because Pommard has one of Burgundy's more pronounceable names, frequently more popular than deserved and, as a result, overpriced. Less famous Volnay, just to the south, actually produces far more interesting wines, both red and white, and Monthelie is one of those lesser-known, quality *Appellations* of Burgundy worth searching for, since its reds often are superb.

With Meursault begins the zone of white wines for which the Côte d'Or also is famous. Fully 95 percent of Meursault's wines are white, mostly (but not exclusively) made from the Chardonnay. Good as the white Meursaults are, they are overshadowed by those from Puligny-Montrachet and Chassagne-Montrachet which, by consensus, produce the noblest dry white wines made in the world. Again the simplest label is the key to quality: Montrachet itself, with Chevalier-Montrachet and, across the road, Batard-Montrachet. These and a number of other great whites are labeled by the vineyard name alone, with neither village name (Puligny or Chassagne) identified. Even the next-ranking white wines from these communes are very fine indeed, among the best the Chardonnay can yield.

At the southern end of the Côte de Beaune, St.-Aubin is rather insignificant, but southernmost Santenay is noteworthy not because of its adequate white wines, but because it produces some red Burgundies which, while not among the very best, offer excellent values.

All else in Burgundy pales against the splendor of the Côte d'Or, and certainly the Côte Chalonnaise cannot match its neighbors—but from such lesser districts can come wines of note and great reward. The Côte Chalonnaise consists of two main areas centered on the villages of Mercurey (in the north) and Montagny (in the south). Mercurey produces some reds that, in good years, are among Burgundy's bargains; Montagny's whites merit a better reputation than they have. These are names for which to look among moderately priced Burgundies.

Although the Côte Mâconnaise (also called, simply, Mâconnais after its central place, Mâcon) produces good white wines, it includes a district where

SOCIÉTÉ CIVILE DU DOMAINE DE LA ROMANÉE-CONTI
PROPRIÉTAIRE A VOSNE-ROMANÉE (COTE-D'OR) FRANCE

MONTRACHET

APPELLATION MONTRACHET CONTROLÉE

2.812 Bouteilles Récoltées

N° 01808

ANNÉE 1976

LES ASSOCIÉS-GÉRANTS

Mise en bouteille au domaine
PRODUCT OF FRANCE

73 cl

Considered by many to be the greatest of white wines, Montrachet is at once the name of a vineyard, a wine, and an *Appellation* in Burgundy. As the label reveals, only 2,812 bottles were produced in the year 1976.

whites that are merely adequate have become enormously overpriced for reasons similar to Pommard's reds—popularity overseas. Pouilly-Fuissé, undoubtedly the most visible Mâconnais wine, often is a disappointment when quality is considered in the context of price. On restaurant wine lists in the United States, Pouilly-Fuissé often is priced two or three times what it should be; expectations aroused by the high cost are unfulfilled.

Two additional subregions of Burgundy appear on Figure 8.2: Chablis in the north and Beaujolais in the south. Chablis, a town by that name surrounded by some twenty communes whose vines stand in a particularly chalky soil, produces world-famous, dry white wines from the Chardonnay grape. The name Chablis has perhaps been "borrowed" more frequently than any other, but there is no doubt regarding the real wine from Chablis: it is unmatched in its austere, dry, flinty flavor. The wines of Beaujolais are unique in Burgundy in that they are made from the Gamay grape which stands in granite-derived, clayey soil. The best come from nine villages and their vineyards: Brouilly, Côte-de-Brouilly, Chénas, Chiroubles, Fleurie, Juliénas, Morgon, Moulin-à-Vent, and St. Amour. In addition there are some thirty other designated villages or communes where good Beaujolais is made. Beaujolais usually is best drunk young, just months after the vintage. Each year the appearance of the newly vinted Beaujolais is a national event in France.

Thus the array of Burgundian wine is truly remarkable. Burgundy's magnificent reds, more expensive even than the greatest Bordeaux, have been described as the world's noblest wines. These require years of bottle aging, yet the fruity wines of Beaujolais often are at their best in the very fall of the vintage. Beside the golden, silky, soft whites of Montrachet stand the unique, straw-yellow wines of Chablis. In the world of wine there is no second Burgundy, and Burgundy is second to none.

RED BURGUNDY VINTAGES: 1970–1982

Burgundy is no less susceptible to climatic vicissitudes than Bordeaux, although the environmental problems are not always the same. Hail is a constant threat here. Ill-timed rains can afflict Burgundy as Bordeaux, but excessive cold and inadequate ripening is a more serious problem in Burgundy. Hence chaptalization occurs more frequently in Burgundy than in Bordeaux. After the harvest, the skins and juice are separated rather more quickly than in Bordeaux, so that Burgundy reds pick up less tannin; barrel-aging also is shorter, so that there is less influence from wood. Wines often are softer and rounder at an earlier stage than the harder Bordeaux, and, especially in recent decades, have been ready much earlier.

1982   Early optimism: flowering came early and went well, and the growing season was warm. No serious problems affected the harvest; the prospect is for a very good if not outstanding vintage.

1981   Early spring was warm, budding came early, then disastrous late-
(7)*   April frosts. Poor July, warm August. Severe hail in Côte de Nuits. Sporadic rain at harvest time. Small harvest. Overpriced, thin, unpromising wines. Beaujolais somewhat better.

1980   Cold spring, late flowering, poor July, variable August. Late (mid-
(9)   October) harvest, much of it in rain. Côte de Nuits better than Côte de Beaune, but mediocre, inconsistent wines. Beaujolais even worse.

1979   Cool spring weather, late development, much July cloud and rain,
(13)   but better August and September. Abundant crop despite locally devastating hail; quality uneven but good on average. Wines lack body and complexity.

1978   After an excessively cold start, conditions turned superb in mid-
(16)   August through the October harvest. Small and good yield, soft, balanced, fruity wines without tannic strength but with some elegance. Many from Côte d'Or will last a decade.

1977   Miserable summer following cold spring; damaging storms in August.
(5)   September improved but too late. Thin, light, unattractive wines betraying unripeness.

1976   Warm, dry summer; early harvest. Destructive hail in Mercurey.
(18)   Full-bodied, rich, fruity, complex wines with much future, especially from Côte de Beaune. Best Beaujolais vintage in decades.

1975   Promising early summer dashed by August-September rains and
(4)   high humidity; rot everywhere. Hail destroyed much of Beaujolais and part of Côte de Beaune. Some passable wines in Côte de Nuits; otherwise light, thin, little color.

1974   Early-season coolness followed by good summer; August hot and
(7)   nearly ideal. Vintage damaged by region-wide rains beginning before and continuing through the harvest.

*Numbers in parentheses indicate ratings on a 20-pt. basis.

1973   Good early-season conditions, but summer wet and cool. Rain during
(12)   harvest. Large crop, undistinguished wines.

1972   Variable year with warm spring and cold summer. Late harvest.
(14)   Initial impression of hard, acid wines revised as time has mellowed
         and softened them, notably those from Côte de Nuits.

1971   Bad weather during the flowering, August hail in Côte de Beaune,
(18)   and occasional summer storms did not spoil a small but excellent
         harvest, best in Northern Côte de Beaune. Full-bodied, rich, oc-
         casionally somewhat inelegant wines.

1970   Following the superb 1969 vintage, this was a good year but not
(14)   one that produced long-lived wines.

Earlier vintages: Although red Burgundies do not, on an average, last as
long as Bordeaux reds, the superior producers in the best vintage years
have created wines that have improved and sustained themselves for decades.
Great years of the past include 1969, 1961, 1953, 1949, and 1945.

The Rhône Region

The Burgundian district of Beaujolais lies just to the north of the confluence
of the Saône and the Rhône rivers, and the wine region that lies to the
south of this junction, the Côtes du Rhône, always has been in Burgundy's
shadow. But the wines of the Côtes du Rhône often are superb, and while
their prices have risen in recent years, the best from the Rhône still constitute
bargains.

The geographical region of the Rhône extends from Vienne in the north
to Avignon in the south, but the most interesting districts lie in the north,
from Valence northward. Here are the great names of Côte-Rôtie, Condrieu,
Hermitage, Cornas; but perhaps the best-known name of the Rhône, Châteauneuf-du-Pape, lies in the south, proving that very good wines are made
there as well. The grape varieties here are not those of Burgundy: the
Syrah (also Sérine) yields the wonderful, long-lived wines of the Northern
Rhône, and the Grenache (Spain's Garnacho) is blended with the Syrah in
the south. Other cultivars reflect the Southern Rhône's varied environments
and microclimates. The wines are similarly varied and provide great opportunities for the consumer; in many a year the Rhône's best are far
superior to the struggling Burgundies.

Furthermore, the Rhône region has recently had some memorable vintages.
The 1976 vintage produced some wines in the Northern Rhône that will
last until 1990 or beyond. The 1978 vintage is considered the best for
Hermitage since the 1929, and superior even to the great 1961. The 1979
vintage was very good in the Northern Rhône (although some Côte-Rôtie
wines have not shown quite as well as expected), and in 1980 Côte-Rôtie
produced some of its best wines. The 1981 season was less satisfactory;
patchy and difficult, it was affected by late rains that were least troublesome
in Hermitage in the north and in Tavel in the south. The 1982 vintage,
by midsummer, appeared to be much better than its predecessor, and the
good weather held. Whatever its ultimate quality, the Côtes du Rhône are
worth an oenophile's exploration.[4]

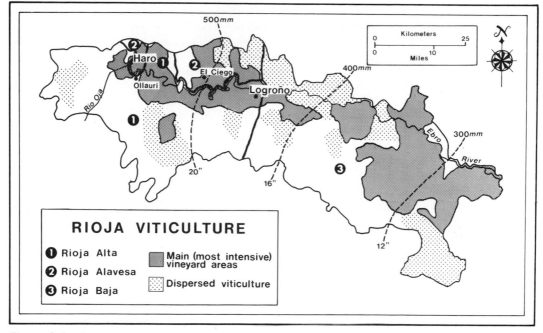

Figure 8.3 Rioja Viticulture

Rioja

It is fitting to consider Rioja after Bordeaux and Burgundy, because this Spanish wine region bears the historic viticultural imprint of France. During the spread of *phylloxera* in France, winegrowers left their dying vineyards and crossed the Pyrenees to what was, a century ago, a viticulture area in need of organization and development. The French brought their knowledge of viticultural techniques and vinicultural methodology, and in 1892 the viticultural research station at Haro was founded. Now began the campaign to improve the vineyards, to terminate any and all importing of blending wine to augment local production, to establish a monopoly over the name of Rioja on wine labels, and to promote the reputation of Rioja wines in Spain and beyond.

This is not to suggest that Rioja was unproductive before the French involvement. Indeed, some prestigious wine firms already operated there, making very good wine. But the French did make important contributions. Yet the region did not become a second Bordeaux, studded with châteaux and chartreuses. Rioja wine was and is made mainly in large *bodegas*, in some ways similar to the installations of the great shippers of Burgundy, where wine is made, blended, and aged (far longer than Burgundy) on a huge scale. As was the case in the châteaux of Bordeaux a century ago, the red wines of Rioja are aged two to five years in oak (although this practice is under reconsideration and is changing). They are sold in bottles that supposedly reflect the style of their contents: the high-shouldered "Bordeaux" bottles for *claretes* and slope-shouldered "Burgundy" bottles for *tintos*. That distinction may have been clear in the past; today it is often difficult to distinguish the different styles, and the practice is less than meaningful. Nevertheless, Rioja's red wines bear a considerable resemblance to their French counterparts, and on international markets they sell at a fraction of the price of the French originals. But Riojas are not lower-order Bordeaux or Burgundies. They have a distinctiveness and quality that rank them among the world's best wine values today, not as imitations but as remarkable wines in their own right.[5]

The Rioja region is named after a tributary (the Rio Oja) of its main watercourse, the Rio Ebro (Fig. 8.3). Its cultural landscape bears witness to a long history, with villages enclosed by protective walls situated on the hilltops. The vineyard areas, quite unlike those of Bordeaux and Burgundy, are fields of vine lying interspersed with other crops, and the individual vines standing alone as thick-trunked bushes, pruned *en vaso* without supporting wires or stakes.

As Figure 8.3 suggests, the Rioja region has quite distinct climatic zones. Its elevations are highest in the west (hence Rioja *Alta*), where the town of Haro lies at 480 meters (1560 feet). Here conditions are coolest and precipitation averages nearly twice as much as in the lower east (Rioja *Baja*), where Alfaro lies at 300 meters (975 feet). In fact, the descent from Alta to Baja involves a considerable climatic transition from Atlantic-influenced, Bordeaux-like conditions to hotter, drier, Mediterranean-type regimes. In Rioja Alta, the hills receive winter snow and some frost, the springs are mild, often wet, and summers tend to be hot but comparatively short as the early fall ameliorates the heat. Rioja Baja receives very little if any snow in winter and has a long, dry, hot summer.

The third region on the map of Rioja is Rioja *Alavesa*, consisting of two areas. This is where the province of Alava extends into the Rioja district; Alavesa wines resemble those of Rioja Alta rather than Rioja Baja production. Bottle labels sometimes (not always) state that a wine comes from Rioja Alavesa; it is likely to be found in a Burgundy bottle, but tends to resemble a full-bodied Rhône wine.

The wines of Rioja are made in large, company-run bodegas that may own substantial vineyards themselves but also buy grapes (and sometimes wine) from other growers or producers in the region. The majority of these bodegas are located in or near Rioja's two principal towns, Haro and Logroño, in the western and eastern parts of Rioja Alta respectively. The oldest of these major bodegas, of which there are now about forty, is the Marques de Riscal, founded in 1860 at Elciego. Here and at other bodegas in the region, wine is aged in stacked oak barrels (more than 37,000 are in use at Riscal alone), the length of the aging depending upon the wine's eventual rank as a table wine, a *reserva* (six years), or a *gran reserva*.

Undoubtedly the most distinctive characteristic of Rioja wines has for many decades been the strong aroma and flavor of oak, imparted by this lengthy wood aging. This was the standard technique in Bordeaux a century ago, but in Bordeaux today few wines spend as much as 18 months in wood; in Rioja, six years or more is no rarity. Twice a year or more, the wine lost by evaporation is replaced by new wine, often from a younger vintage, so that the vintage year of the original wine has somewhat less meaning than elsewhere. (*Reserva* barrels, however, normally are refilled with wine

Federico Paternina is among prominent bodegas of the Rioja region. This is a *Gran Reserva* 1952, released in the 1970s after long-term aging in Paternina's barrels. Note the Rioja seal in the upper right corner of the label.

from the original vintage.) More attention is now being paid to the virtues of bottle-aging, but a Rioja red, even a *reserva,* will not contain as much sediment in the bottle as will an equally old Bordeaux. Most of the deposit has been left in the casks.

Rioja's grape varieties for red wines include the Tempranillo, blended in Rioja Alta with the aromatic Graciano and the tannin-rich Mazuelo along with small amounts of juice from the high-alcohol Garnacho; in Rioja Alavesa the Tempranillo is more dominant and is blended in a ratio of about 10 to 1 with juice from the white grape Viura and perhaps a small amount of Garnacho. Wines made in Rioja Baja are almost always sold in the barrel, not in the bottle, and used for blending; their alcoholic content tends to be substantially higher than that prevailing in Rioja Alta or Alavesa.

Rioja wines of older vintages show their long life. Recent tastings of red Riojas of the 1920s have verified their continuing power and strength. Some bodegas release wines of considerable age, and recently a 1930s vintage came on the market. Such wines constitute magnificent opportunities for the collector.

RED RIOJA VINTAGES: 1970–1982

1982   Preliminary indications good; uncomplicated flowering, warm summer, good ripening.

1981 (16)*	Most abundant harvest in Rioja's history. Excellent weather before and during picking. Such high yields often mean mediocrity, but not for this vintage. Very good wines.
1980 (15)	Plentiful harvest, good conditions, not exceptional. Good wines.
1979 (11)	Rain at harvest-time after a satisfactory summer. Wines only fair. Some exceptions which will be good values.
1978 (18)	Vintage rated "very good" and even "excellent" by many bodegas.
1977 (5)	Disastrous year: heavy summer rains during ripening season, brief break, then deluge during harvest. Poor wines.
1976 (15)	Good conditions, some summer rain, no harvest problems. Good, sound wines.
1975 (16)	Smallish, good-quality harvest after good ripening and harvesting conditions. Very good wines.
1974 (13)	Large harvest, but conditions less than ideal during the summer. Wines only average. Some significant exceptions.
1973 (14)	Generally (and officially) rated as average, and a very variable vintage with some notable wines and many forgettable ones.
1972 (4)	A year that underscores that vintage conditions in Rioja do matter. Excessive summer heat, then ill-timed rains. Poor, thin wines.
1971 (5)	Heavy rains, then mildew, followed by widespread rot; more than 60 percent of the crop was lost. From what remained, a few adequate wines. The rest poor.
1970 (19)	The decade opened with its best vintage. Ideal conditions, substantial harvest, exceptionally good wines. Superb *reservas* and *gran reservas*.

Earlier vintages: Gran Reservas still are being released, many from exceptional years, recently including one from 1934. Among great years of Rioja's past are 1968, 1964, 1962, 1959, 1955, and 1952.

The Penedés Region

The image of Rioja dominates table-wine production in Spain, but excellent wines also are made in the remarkable Penedés region near Barcelona (see Figure 5.6).[6] Here, Spain produces very good sparkling wines such as those of Castellblanch, Freixenet, and Codorniu; but viticultural interest has focused especially on the work of the Torres family. From the Carignane (Carinena), Garnacho, Tempranillo, and Monastrell in the warm lowlands, and the Cabernet Sauvignon, Cabernet Franc, Merlot, and Pinot Noir in cooler upland areas, Torres has fashioned red wines of note. In a Paris blind tasting, the Torres 1970 Black Label ranked ahead of a 1970 Latour—a result that caused comment around the world. Unlike the Rioja winegrowers, Torres trains his vines on wires and prunes them severely, thus cutting yields but raising quality. The 1981 vintage will strengthen the Torres

*Numbers in parentheses indicate ratings on a 20-pt. basis.

reputation, and that of Penedés generally, still more; the 1980 vintage was good. The 1979 vintage is rated (by Torres himself) as fair to good, the 1978 as very good, the 1977 only slightly below the 1978, and the 1976 as very good. Three previous years (1975, 1974, and 1973) produced good vintages, and in the 1970s only the 1972 was poor; 1971 (in contrast to Rioja) was good, and the 1970 vintage, which was such a good one almost throughout the world, also rated very good in Penedés.

Tuscany

Tuscany is the quintessential Italian wine province. Here the ancient Etruscans made wine before there was a Rome; from this area for centuries has come Italy's best-known wine, Chianti.[7] Tuscany (*Toscana*) is the region of Florence and the Arno River, of Pisa and Elba Island. History pervades its cultural landscapes, but viticulture dominates it. On Tuscany's map are names hallowed in the world of wine: Montalcino, the town that stands amid vineyards of the Brunello grape that creates truly great wines, and Montepulciano, source of one of Italy's oldest and noblest wines.

Tuscany shares with the Piedmont (*Piemonte*) the honor of being Italy's viticultural heartland. Qualitatively this reality is recognized under the new D.O.C.G. classification: only wines from these two provinces have been awarded this highest rank. In the Piedmont, the Barolo and Barbaresco, tannic and long-lived wines made from the Nebbiolo grape, have been so honored. The Barolos spend years in wood and bottle before they reach their culmination as heavy-bodied, high-alcohol, intense wines that rank among the world's finest. They are at their best as *Riserva* or *Riserva Speciale* Barolos from the Piedmont's superior vintages, including the 1978, 1974, 1971, 1964, 1961, and 1958.

Three Tuscan wines have been scheduled for D.O.C.G. classification. In Tuscany the Sangiovese is the red cultivar that reigns supreme as the chief ingredient of Chianti and, cloned and under different names, of the Brunello di Montalcino and the Vino Nobile di Montepulciano. The Brunello grape that makes the great Montalcinos also is called the Sangiovese Grosso, and the mainstay of the Vino Nobile di Montepulciano is the Prugnolo, another Sangiovese relative. Thus the Sangiovese in various forms dominates Tuscan viticulture; in addition, the Canaiolo Nero, the Raspinosso, and the Mammolo cultivars stand prominently among the red grapes; the most important whites include the Trebbiano Toscano, the Malvasia, and the Canaiolo Bianco. The vines usually are trained according to a system that strings the arms vertically on wires, thus promoting exposure to the sun.

Tuscany's famous Chianti is a blend of several grapes, and although the wine is red, not all the grapes are. Sangiovese contributes from 50 to 80 percent of the volume, and Canaiolo Nero from 10 to 30 percent; two other ingredients are the Trebbiano Bianco and the Malvasia (another white grape). Sometimes a small amount of the Colorino may be added to deepen the wine's color. The role of the Canaiolo Nero is to soften the wine and enhance the color, while the white grape juice tends to lighten and enliven the wine, making it more aromatic, more flavorful, and more attractive for young drinking. Since the proportions of Chianti's ingredients vary with the vintner and with its intended aging in wood and vat before bottling, Chianti's styles differ greatly. Chianti may be marketed young (as early as March 1

A familiar name of the Chianti Classico region. Note the D.O.C. statement and the wine's *riserva* quality.

following the year of the vintage), rather like a Beaujolais; this is the Chianti that has traditionally been marketed in straw-wrapped bottles, although that practice is now declining. So, in fact, is the *governo* process that has long created these young, fresh Chiantis. This process involves the addition of concentrated juice from dried grapes, kept separately, to the fermented juice in December, thus causing a second fermentation. In this way the wine quickly acquires a special smoothness and body usually associated with long cask-aging, and is ready for consumption a scant six months after the harvest. But the *governo* process is costly and laborious, and is less common than it used to be.

Chiantis destined for longer aging at Tuscany's wineries (*fattoria*) are blended with a different intent, and in wood they become rich, full, complex wines ranking among the highest achievements of Italian viti- and viniculture. After two or three years in the barrel (respectively marked *Vecchio* or *Riserva* on bottle labels) or even more, the aged Chianti is almost unrecognizable from its youthful relative, and some Chiantis are kept in barrels and vats as much as five to eight years before bottling. Then it is marketed in a Bordeaux-style, high-shouldered bottle, never in a straw "fiasco," to mark its place among great red wines of the world.

The map of Tuscany indicates that there are seven districts of production, with Chianti Classico at the center (Fig. 8.4). The term *Classico* has special

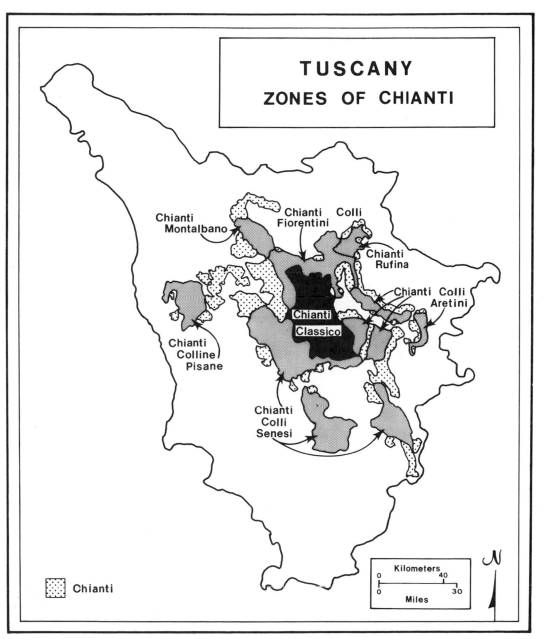

Figure 8.4 Tuscany: Zones of Chianti

Vino Nobile de Montepulciano is one of Italy's premier
wines, and one of the first to achieve D.O.C.G. recognition.

meaning in Italian viticulture, and it designates an historic heartland, a core
area, and a qualitatively superior region of production. As on Figure 8.4,
a Classico region's boundaries are clearly delimited and officially defined.
That official definition took place in 1932, although a more vaguely perceived
Classico region has existed since the early 1700s. The government did not
act until a group of growers in the Classico area founded (in 1924) the
Consorzio del Vino Chianti Classico to protect and maintain quality. This
is when the Chianti Classico symbol, a black rooster on a gold background,
was established as a sign that the bottle contains wine of approved quality.
The D.O.C. regulations for Chianti finally became official in 1967, but within
the Classico area, winegrowers often voluntarily exceed the viticultural
requirements these regulations impose. They often harvest a lower tonnage
than they are legally entitled to, in order to generate superior grapes and
better wines. A Chianti Classico must be made entirely from grapes grown
within that zone, and must be made and bottled there; it also must have a
somewhat higher alcohol content than Chianti wines from the other six
zones shown on the map.

Chianti's popularity and the slow development of protective wine legislation in Italy have combined to dilute Chianti's image and reputation. Early in the nineteenth century the demand for Chianti Classico was so strong, especially in England, that speculators sold Italian red wine of inferior quality under Chianti labels, much of it not even made in Tuscany. As a result, Chianti came to be known as a cheap, red, Italian table wine, and when quality-conscious Classico growers sought to market their wines as Chianti, consumers would not pay the price. Even the characteristic, straw-wrapped flask has been used by other winemakers, without emphasis that their wines are not from Chianti. These are the circumstances that led to the creation of the Consorzio, and the aims of this group are now taking final effect as Chianti's application for D.O.C.G. status nears approval. Certainly it has long been true that standards of viticulture and viniculture in the Chianti region are consistently among Italy's highest; wines from the six zones outside Chianto Classico (Chianti Colli Aretini, Colli Fiorentini, Colli Senesi, Colline Pisani, Montalbano, and Rufino) often are as good as the Classico version, and preference is a matter of taste, not an absolute measure of quality.

As noted earlier, two other wines of Tuscany are among Italy's first five D.O.C.G. designations. Vino Nobile de Montepulciano, a wine with ancient roots, is produced near the town of Montepulciano from a complex blend of grapes in which the Prugnolo, a Sangiovese relative, dominates. Indeed, Vino Nobile de Montepulciano is very much a Chianti-style wine, aged for three years to a *riserva* (two in wood) or for four years to become a *riserva speciale*. And in the vicinity of the town of Montalcino is made the famous Brunello di Montalcino, another memorable red Tuscan wine. This is Italy's most expensive red wine, capable of decades of improvement in the bottle; the Brunello grape, again, is a Sangiovese Grosso by a different name. There are strict controls over the very small hectarage where this cultivar may be grown and where the wine may be labeled by this name. *Riserva* Brunellos are aged five years before they reach the market, so that older vintage years are meaningful when it comes to this most prestigious of all Italian wines.

RED TUSCANY VINTAGES: 1970–1982

Italy is a large wine-producing country geographically as well as quantitatively, and vintage conditions from the Piedmont to Sicily can vary substantially in the same year. Tuscany itself is an extensive viticultural region, and it will be noted that Chianti Classico will have good conditions in years when Montalcino may not. These internal variations should be considered in the context of the vintage chart that follows.

1982   Midsummer conditions appeared favorable for a large and good-quality harvest.

1981   Very variable weather. Early frost inhibited flowering; hail during
(14)*   the summer, rain during harvest. Chianti wines average; somewhat better Brunello di Montalcino.

1980   Cool, damp spring, setting growth back as much as four weeks.
(13)   Hot, desiccating August and September. Late harvest, interrupted by rain. Mediocre wines; some exceptions.

*Numbers in parentheses indicate ratings on a 20-pt. basis.

1979   Fine weather throughout the flowering, setting, and ripening seasons;
(18)   then rain after much of the harvest had been completed. Excellent
       wines all around.

1978   Uneven year. Cold spring, small harvest. Wines scarce; some very
(13)   good Chianti, but most ordinary or less. Brunello di Montalcino
       fared better.

1977   Variable conditions. Early cold, summer hail. Small production.
(15)   Wines not plentiful, but some Chianti superb, Brunello di Montalcino
       and Vino Nobile di Montepulciano exceptional.

1976   Poor year. Much rain; light, short-lived wines. Chianti a near-
(6)   disaster; Vino Nobile di Montepulciano without promise; some fair
       Brunello di Montalcino.

1975   An excellent year. Vino Nobile di Montepulcino superb, Brunello
(18)   di Montalcino exceptional, Chianti very good to excellent.

1974   Very good vintage, especially in Chianti Classico, good also around
(17)   Montepulciano, less so for Brunello di Montalcino.

1973   Best by far for Vino Nobile di Montepulciano, average for (mostly
(11)   light) Brunello di Montalcino, fair for Chianti.

1972   Poor year in which production was very small and not good. Brunello
(7)   di Montalcino managed some mediocre wines, although some estates
       bottled none at all.

1971   Very great year for Chianti but only fair for Brunello di Montalcino,
(17)   and Montepulciano, hit by bad weather, rates (8).

1970   Very great year. Near-perfect conditions, substantial harvest, ex-
(19)   cellent Chianti, superb Vino Nobile di Montepulciano and Brunello
       di Montalcino. Small production.

Earlier vintages: Older vintages of special merit include 1967, 1964, 1961, and 1955 (for Brunello di Montalcino), 1958 (especially for Vino Nobile di Montepulciano), 1952, and 1947.

German Wine Regions

To be consistent, it would be appropriate to focus on one of Germany's eleven wine regions (see Figure 5.3), such as the Rheingau or Mosel-Saar-Ruwer. But Germany's wine regions have much in common, especially their far-northerly location and the environmental problems this produces. From Lake Constance (Bodensee) along the Rhine River and its tributaries to the Middle Rhine in the vicinity of Bonn lie vineyards on clay, slate, and limestone, glacial loess, and volcanic sand. Connoisseurs claim that they can discern from the taste of the wine the character of the soil in which the vine stood; certainly the soil contributes to the special properties of German wines. But it is the variable and difficult climate that dominates German viticulture. As indicated by the vintage chart that follows, good years are few and far between; not since 1976 has there been a truly exceptional vintage. By 1982, cellars and stocks are depleted of good wine. The sugaring scandal that erupted during this lean period had much to do with the five successive years of trouble with frosts, coldness, cloudiness, and wetness. That acceptable wines can be created even under these most difficult conditions is a tribute to the winegrowers and vintners of Germany.[8]

If one were enabled to taste the wines of only one German wine region, it would surely be the Rheingau. The vineyards of this prestigious region amount to a mere 3 percent of Germany's total, but here a combination of conditions favors virtually every vine. As the map (Figure 5.3) shows, the Rhine River turns westward from its northerly course, thus avoiding the Taunus Mountains to the north. These forested mountains form a protective wall against the cold from Arctic sources, while the Rhine, on its east-west course, acts as a reflector of sunlight all along the southeast- and south-facing vineyard slopes. Thus cradled and warmed, the Rheingau even manages to produce some of Germany's better red wines from the Spätburgunder (originally the Pinot Noir). But the region's great Riesling-based whites are its hallmark, and some of Germany's most famous names are associated with it. Schloss Johannisberg is among these: it stands for an imposing castle, a 35-hectare (86-acre) vineyard, and a legend in viniculture. It is said that the late-harvest discovery was made here by accident. According to custom, grape harvesting at the Schloss could not commence until the local ruler—in this case Prince Abbott of Fulda—gave the order to begin. In 1775, the Prince's messenger, a wine lover himself, got drunk along the way and arrived at the Schloss weeks after he should have. By then, the grapes had begun to rot on the vines but the monks, fearful of retribution, had left them there. When the harvest finally started, the half-rotten grapes produced a hitherto unknown, sweet wine, the first Spätlese. So magnificent was it that the grapes were left on the vines again the following year, but this time deliberately. Late harvests have been taken ever since, whenever the *Edelfäule* (noble rot) developed on the grapes.

Schloss Johannisberg makes famous Rheingau wine, but there are other names in the region, respected quite as much and even more so. Schloss Vollrads is among these, producing classic wines, as well as Schloss Reinhartshausen, Hallgartener Schönhell, and Gutsverwaltung Deinhard. Again the map is a useful guide, since the very best Rheingau wines are made in a zone extending approximately from Schloss Johannisberg (not far from Geisenheim) to the longitude of Wiesbaden.

Perhaps the best-known viticultural name associated with German viticulture is that of Mosel. It is curious that the French spelling of this German geographic name is often used in English-speaking countries to identify imitated wines as "Moselles," perhaps because the Mosel originates in France. But it becomes the famous wine artery only in Germany, where it forms the axis of the German region named Mosel-Saar-Ruwer—the Mosel and two of its tributaries, both vineyard-flanked.

The Mosel-Saar-Ruwer region reveals as perhaps no other the indispensability of sunshine in these northern locales. South- and southeast-facing slopes are clothed in the vine, but where the hillslope turns away from the sun or where another hill shades the slope, the land is left to wild vegetation, grass, and bush. Where the sunniest exposures also benefit from an especially favorable turn of the river, thus receiving reflected sunlight as well, lie the best vineyards, most of them in Bereich (District) Bernkastel, in the middle reach of the Mosel. Here the Riesling still prevails, producing the noble wines of Bernkasteler Doktor, most famous of the Einzellage, and several others of world repute. Above District Bernkastel, in the Saar-Ruwer District, good (which is to say rare) years persuade the Elbling grape to produce passable wines, although much Elbling goes into German *Sekt* or sparkling wine, and the Elbling, though productive, is not a high-quality grape. Below District Bernkastel, in Bereich Zell (which extends to the junction with the Rhine), the Mosel Valley's soils become richer, and the Müller-Thurgau becomes prominent, the wines fruitier and fuller but less elegant or durable. The Mosel-Saar-Ruwer, with its variety of styles, proves again that German wines cannot simply be classified into Rhines and Mosels.

Thus German viniculture provides still another opportunity for exploration and research, and every region has its adherents. Rheinhessen, largest of all with fully one-quarter of all German vineyard hectarage, produces much table wine from Müller-Thurgau and Sylvaner, but also some fine wines from the Riesling in vineyards that face the Rhine River. The Rheinpfalz region, also known as the Palatinate, has only about 14 percent Riesling and much more Sylvaner and Müller-Thurgau (each about 26 percent of the total). Some good late-harvest wines come from the Palatinate, but much more ordinary wine and, in addition, mediocre red wines in the region's warmer areas. To the west, the Nahe region straddles the Rhine tributary of that name, and its better vineyards yield very good wines with much character and body. On the other side of the Mosel (see Figure 5.3) is the Ahr region, small and northerly and known, surprisingly, for its red wines. The Spätburgunder does well in exceptionally warm years, but most of the time it must be harvested early when barely ripe, and produces hard, acid wines. Opposite the Ahr-Rhine confluence is the region known as the Mittelrhein, an area of spectacular hilltop castles, steep-sided valleys, and scenic, terraced vineyards. More than 80 percent of the grapes are Rieslings, and only about 10 percent is Müller-Thurgau; the wines here tend to be dry and distinctive.

Four regions lie east of the Rhine and south of the Main River. Franken (Franconia) is the easternmost of Germany's designated regions, and the climate is less moderated by maritime influences. Springs come quite late, the growing season often is short, and wines can be quite acid. The flagon-shaped bottle is a feature of Franconian wines. Southernmost among Germany's wine regions is Baden, located between the Neckar River and Lake Constance (Bodensee) east of the Rhine. This extensive and noncontiguous region produces nearly a dozen wines, none of them among Germany's most distinguished but including reds and rosés from the Spätburgunder, whites from the Müller-Thurgau and the less satisfactory Gutedel (France's Chasselas), and sweet, spicy wines from the Gewürztraminer. The wines of Württemberg, the region on the Upper Neckar, tend to be consumed locally, but they do hold some interest. The red Trollinger grape stands here, as well as the "Black" Riesling and, of course, the Spätburgunder. Local *Schillerwein* is made from a blend of red and white grapes, and is an unusual rosé. Last (and appropriately so) is a small region called the Hessische Bergstrasse, east of the Rhine and across from the town of Worms. With just a few hundred hectares of vineyards, this is Germany's smallest designated region, and its wines are not likely to be found on the international market. Some observers opine that the Hessische Bergstrasse should be merged with one of the adjacent, major regions.

WHITE GERMAN VINTAGES: 1970–1982

Since 1976 Germany has suffered through vintages ranging from poor to mediocre, and 1972, 1973, and 1974 also were less than outstanding.[9] The decade since 1972 has produced just one truly great vintage, and one that may be rated as very good. This, coupled with the special nature of viticulture and viniculture in Germany, indicates why prices for its good wines are so high.

1982	After five difficult years, there was a mild winter, an early flowering, and an abundant harvest. July was hot, and the summer generally warm. Even if quality was unexceptional, the copious crop was a blessing.
1981 (11)*	Great summer washed out by heavy rains of late September and early October. Most wines are QbA (see Chapter 5); the rest mainly Kabinett. Good ice wines in Mosel-Saar-Ruwer.
1980 (12)	Very small harvest, generally light wines, adequate fruit. The Prädikat wines are mostly Kabinett; some Spätlese, little Auslese. Overall an unsatisfactory year.
1979 (14)	Quality in some regions better than average. Large harvest in Rheingau, where quality was good; very good in Mosel. Mainly Kabinett and Spätlese. Merely adequate.
1978 (10)	Problem year, below-average quantity, mostly QbA wines. Very small amount of Prädikat, most of it Kabinett.
1977 (9)	Wines of rather low quality, high in acid; some fairly nice dry wines. Quantity somewhat above average.
1976 (20)	Very great year, one of the century's best, quantity slightly below average but quality great, especially for Auslese wines. Weather near-perfect throughout.
1975 (16)	Cold, wet April, warm June, hot August, rain in September. Average harvest, good year but wines somehow undistinguished, although Prädikats at all levels.
1974 (9)	Bad year, cold summer, rain throughout the harvest. Small quantity, unripe grapes, no Prädikats.
1973 (13)	Large harvest following a late spring, hot summer. Rain just before picking. Fruity, short-lived wines, low in acid, unexciting.
1972 (8)	Poor year. Late budding, cold summer until heat wave in August. Late harvest under cold conditions. Wines all QbA, no Prädikat.
1971 (19)	Almost perfect spring and summer, especially in Mosel; very great year with exceptional quality and above-average quantity. Many Prädikat wines. Excellent balance; long-lived wines abound.
1970 (15)	Complicated vintage. Good summer, then cool, rainy October. Ripening delayed; some grapes still on the vine in December. Winegrowers who harvested early had adequate wines. Those who harvested late had great wines.

*Numbers in parentheses indicate ratings on a 20-pt. basis.

Additional Reading

Descriptions of Old-World wine regions abound. Some of the better discussions consist of segments of larger volumes dealing with entire countries.

Anderson, B. *Vino: The Wines and Winemakers of Italy.* Boston: Little, Brown, 1980.

Bode, C. G. *Wines of Italy.* New York: Dover Publications, 1974.

Dovaz, M. *Encyclopedia of the Great Wines of Bordeaux.* Paris: Julliard, 1981.

Flower, R. *Chianti: The Land, the People and the Wine.* New York: Universe Books, 1979.

Hanson, A. *Burgundy.* New York: Faber & Faber, 1981.

Livingstone-Learmonth, J., and Master, M.C.H. *The Wines of the Rhone.* London: Faber & Faber, 1978.

Penning-Rowsell, E. *The Wines of Bordeaux.* 4th ed. New York: Charles Scribner's Sons, 1981.

Read, J. *The Wines of Spain and Portugal.* London: Faber & Faber, 1973.

Roux, M. P., et al. *Vineyards and Domains of Burgundy.* Dallas: Publivin, 1973.

Sichel, P. *The Wines of Germany.* Rev. by F. Schoonmaker. New York: Hastings House, 1980.

Yoxall, H. W. *The Wines of Burgundy.* New York: Stein & Day, 1978.

On the most recent vintages, the best sources are the many wine periodicals now available, including *The Wine Spectator, Decanter,* and *The Friends of Wine.* Some books describe older (pre-1980) vintages in detail. The most informative is

Broadbent, M. *The Great Vintage Wine Book.* New York: Alfred A. Knopf, 1980.

9

A New-World Vintage Regional Geography: From Napa to New Zealand

The alternation of variable vintages—from the disastrously poor to the sublime and back again to the mediocre—is the phenomenon that makes vintage charts for European wine regions relevant and often useful. As a result the vintage chart has become something of a symbol, the *sine qua non* of truly prestigious wine regions. By extension, some observers have postulated that wine regions elsewhere (notably in the New World) are neither as meritorious nor deserving of vintage assessments. "It is silly to fuss about vintage years when discussing the wines of South Africa or Australia since there the weather is always perfect," wrote a leading British authority on wine.[1] In actual fact, the natural environment can be an ally as well as a formidable foe of winegrowers in the New World as well as the Old. As more wines from New-World wine regions reach American and European markets, some knowledge of vintage conditions in those areas will prove to be very useful indeed.

The geography of New-World wine regions highlights some less-familiar names. If California's wine-producing counties are not well known to many Europeans, American oenophiles are not well acquainted with such toponyms as Aconcagua, Mendoza, Stellenbosch, Hunter, or Henderson. Yet the wines from these and other Southern Hemisphere wine regions hold much interest, and often are quite admirable.

California

As much as 90 percent of all the wine made in the United States is produced in California. This enormous total, however, includes a large volume of bulk

Vineyards in the Napa Valley seen from the Sterling Winery, California. The break in surface from the valley floor to the adjacent slopes is quite distinct in this, the narrow northern part of the valley.

and jug wine—the latter the *vins ordinaires* of America. No one should cast aspersions on California's mass-produced wines; they are superior to similar products from many other world wine regions, including France. The standards set by the largest operation of them all, the winery of Ernest and Julio Gallo at Modesto, underscore the qualitative potentials for the mass market. In 1981, Gallo made 5 million hectoliters (more than 130 million gallons) of wine, which is comparable to the entire production of Greece or Hungary for that year. Gallo's ultramodern, computerized winery assures consumers of a level of quality that is by no means common for ordinary wines. And some of Gallo's newer varietal wines, marketed at *vin-ordinaire* prices, have won awards. The quality of jug wines, from Gallo as well as from United Vintners' wineries, Almaden, Masson, and other large producers, has risen steadily and is remarkable.[2]

But the oenophile who is interested in the Great Growths of Bordeaux and the top *Appellations* of Burgundy will focus, in California, on several comparatively small districts where the region's premium wines are made. California's territory as a whole is larger than some entire countries that produce wine, and so California's wine regions are widely dispersed (see Figure 4.2). Even the premium wine-producing areas are noncontiguous, separated by mountains, urbanized areas, and lands devoted to other kinds of economies. Using the county names as identification, Figure 9.1 indicates (upon comparison with Figure 4.2) where the smaller, quality-oriented wineries of California are concentrated. Napa County in 1983 had approximately one hundred wineries, Sonoma County more than eighty and, south

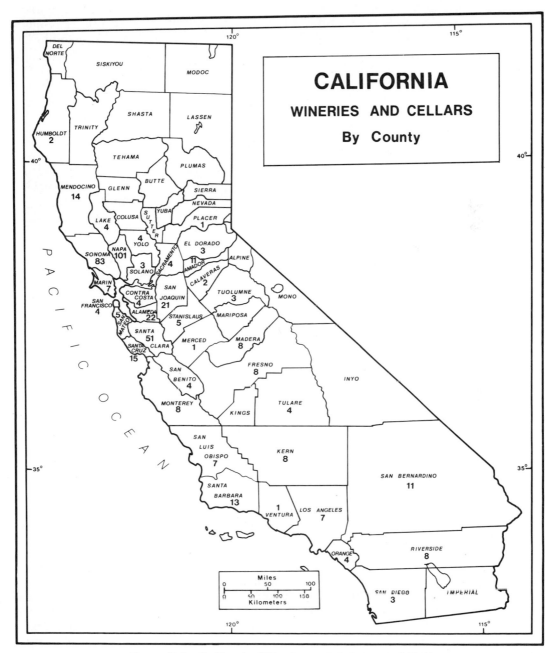

Figure 9.1 California: Wineries and Cellars, by County

of San Francisco Bay, Santa Clara ranked third with about fifty. This is not to suggest that these are the only counties where the best of California's production takes place. The cool northern environs of Mendocino County have yielded some memorable vintages, and in the south, excellent wines come from quality wineries in Santa Barbara and San Luis Obispo counties. Nor is the interior of California solely the domain of bulk production. In the foothills of the Sierra Nevada, the wineries of Amador County have produced Zinfandels to rival California's best. In fact, California's viticulture frequently holds surprises in store when upstart wineries, favored by local microclimates and liberally funded, unexpectedly burst on the scene with excellent wines.

Nevertheless, the regional name that dominates California viticulture is that of Napa.[3] North of San Francisco across the bay, Napa County is one of California's smallest, but on the land that slopes gently toward the Napa River stand some 10,000 hectares (25,000 acres) of vines with premium cultivars—Cabernet Sauvignon, Chardonnay, Pinot Noir, and Zinfandel— dominant. Among the Napa Valley's hundred wineries are many of the great names in American wine: Chateau Montelena near Calistoga in the north; Charles Krug and Louis Martini near St. Helena; Beaulieu near Rutherford; Robert Mondavi near Oakville. These estates lie on or near America's premier wine route, Highway 29, and other noted names, including Heitz and Stag's Leap, are not far to the east and west of it.

The Napa wine region is quite faithful to the course of the Napa River, so that the viticulture zone is elongated and comparatively narrow. In the north it fades into the slopes of Mount St. Helena astride the boundary with Lake County; in the south its Carneros district, often foggy and cool, overlooks San Francisco Bay. The low hills of Carneros and their special microclimates give particular character to the Chardonnay and the Pinot Noir.

The Napa region sometimes is called the Bordeaux of America, and comparisons between Napa's best and Bordeaux's greatest inevitably arise. Occasionally these comparisons produce stunning results. In 1976, at a Paris tasting to celebrate the U.S. Bicentennial, Cabernet Sauvignons from two Napa estates—young wineries not among the region's venerables—triumphed over the best of Bordeaux and Burgundy. Such successes notwithstanding, it is better to appreciate Napa's noblest wines for their own sake rather than in a Burgundian or Bordelais context. From the Cabernet Sauvignon, the Napa's wineries at their best produce a fabulous wine, not an imitation of Latour or Haut-Brion. The Zinfandel generates magnificent, long-lived, complex, deep red wines that fortunately have no French equivalent for inappropriate comparison.

West across the Mayacamas Mountains lies Sonoma County, its vineyard hectarage even larger than that of Napa, its environments more diverse, its number of wineries second only to Napa's. The historic Sonoma region's big four cultivars are the same as those of Napa, and they produce impressively—but this was not always so. General Vallejo and the legacy of Agoston Haraszthy notwithstanding, the Sonoma region until as recently as 1960 was a producer of bulk and jug wines, and Napa wineries bought their grapes there. Then Sonoma's potential for quality was recognized, and the viticultural mosaic began to change. Certain old wineries, long dormant, revived under original or new ownership. Others changed their vinicultural emphases. New estates made their appearance and set the highest of standards.

Old and new in the Sonoma Valley: modern facade atop
the old stone structure at Sebastiani Vineyards.

The environmental range of the Sonoma region generated a diversity of
wines and styles.

In the south is the "real" Sonoma Valley, where the earliest viticulture
in California north of San Francisco was established. Here Haraszthy's Buena
Vista estate has been restored and expanded, and Sebastiani's winery is one
of those that changed their emphasis from bulk wines (a mainstay as recently
as the 1950s) to premium-wine production. Northward lies the Alexander
Valley, its heat summation (see Chapter 4) transitional from Region II to
Region III, thus producing excellent Cabernet Sauvignon and Zinfandel.
Jordan's Vineyard and Winery, founded in 1972, is a prominent example
of massive investment and remarkable results; it was Jordan's 1976 Cabernet
Sauvignon with which President Reagan celebrated his election in 1980.
Still farther to the north (and to the west) is the elbow-shaped Russian River
Valley, a district of varied climates and diverse soils, producing a wide range
of wines that includes Korbel's sparkling "champagnes" and Italian Swiss
Colony's mass-produced reds and whites.

The list of Sonoma County winery names bespeaks the region's historic
ties, its bulk-wine period, and its modern resurgence. Hanzell's estate of the

The Jordan Vineyard and Winery, modeled on a Bordeaux château, has produced a series of excellent Cabernet Sauvignons, among which the 1976 was made famous by President Reagan's selection of it to celebrate his election victory. The 1977 was intense and powerful; the 1978 is arguably the best of the series.

1950s copied as faithfully as possible a Burgundian vineyard; Jordan imitated a Bordeaux château. Chateau St. Jean was established in the early 1970s and concentrated on quality white wines, for which it rapidly achieved fame. Gundlach-Bunschu was among the unproductive older wineries (1858) until it was swept up in Sonoma's revival. Pedroncelli emerged from its bulk-wine period to make notable Cabernets and Pinot Noirs. Compared to self-secure Napa, Sonoma still is part of California's viticultural frontier.

RED (NORTHERN) CALIFORNIA VINTAGES: 1970–1982

Vintage charts for California's premium wines often rate years by cultivar, a sensible procedure. Conditions for later-ripening varietals may not be the same as for earlier-ripening grapes, so that the Cabernet Sauvignon may not fare as well as the Zinfandel in the same year.

At one time it was held that California's climate varies so little from year to year that vintage charts would be unproductive. This may be so in the Central Valley, but not in the Napa or Sonoma regions (nor in other near-coastal wine-producing areas), where untimely rain, drought, severe cold, excessive heat, and other environmental factors have placed certain vintages far below others. The variations may not be as great as they commonly are in Burgundy or Germany but—as the following summary indicates—they certainly matter.

1982   Cool spring and early summer, maturity late. Rainfall in late June; excellent summer conditions indicated an exceptional vintage until rains at harvest time (damaging hail in Mendocino County) severely dimmed the prospects.

1981   Good spring, scorchingly hot June, no relief in July or August
(14)*   when the usual fogs failed to develop. Very early ripening; August harvest. Comparatively light wines, somewhat low in alcohol. Cabernet Sauvignon better than Zinfandel in general.

1980   The numerical rating is an average; there was triumph and disaster.
(15)   Earliest, longest flowering in memory; uneven ripening. Cool summer, much fog. Then high heat during a late harvest, grapes suddenly ripe en masse, some overripe before picking. Some grapes had superb sugar and acid levels; others were over- or underripe. Wines very mixed.

1979   Winter rains extended into spring; flowering limited but no frost
(14)   damage. Following a good summer, late rains. Low acid, variable quality; some exceptions.

1978   Large volume. Rain just before the harvest; grape sugars somewhat
(16)   low but no rot. Above-average vintage, but not great. Wines may not be as durable as first anticipated.

1977   Severe drought. Yield per acre was down, but high intensity.
(17)   Scattered rain during the harvest, no serious damage to quality. Superior year. Excellent Zinfandel.

1976   Heat wave in early summer. Yield down, but quality high. Some
(16)   wines lacked acidity. Both Cabernet and Zinfandel yielded fine wines.

1975   Variable year. Cool, long growing season. Red wines good but early-
(15)   maturing. No long-lived wines.

1974   Great year for red varieties: cool summer, warm and dry fall, near-
(18)   perfect harvesting conditions. Excellent Cabernet Sauvignons; Zinfandels from Amador County made an impact.

1973   Spring rains heavy, but did not affect flowering; favorable summer,
(16)   large crop. Considering the high yield, quality was good.

1972   Poor year. Spring frosts, severe heat wave, heavy rains during
(8)   harvest; very low yield. Disaster for late-ripening Cabernet Sauvignon.

*Numbers in parentheses indicate ratings on a 20-pt. basis.

1971   Some consider this the decade's worst vintage for reds; spring frosts,
(7)   cool summer. Zinfandel a bit better than Cabernet Sauvignon.
       Nothing long-lived.

1970   Severe spring frosts; half the potential crop wiped out. Good, warm
(19)   summer and fall yielded good sugar, great acidity in surviving
       grapes. Best of the reds among the finest ever, concentrated, long-
       lived. Will last into the 1990s.

Earlier vintages: It is something of a tragedy that so many fine California
red wines of older vintages were consumed so young, their long-lived potentials
unrecognized until too late. Among rare but still-superb older wines are
those of 1969 (forgotten because it was sandwiched between two great
vintages), 1968 (now ready), 1965, and 1964.

Argentina

Argentina is one of the world's five leading producers of wine, and the
largest producing country in the Southern Hemisphere (and in the Western
Hemisphere as well). Argentinians themselves have traditionally been prodigious consumers of their own wine, so that Argentina never has exported
as large a part of its production as other major producers. And much of
what Argentina does send abroad is bulk or blending wine, known on world
markets for its high quality (for its class) but with its identity lost behind
Japanese, Russian, and other foreign labels.

The best Argentinian wines, the *viños finos* as they are called at home,
do reach overseas markets (sometimes as *reservas*) in small quantities, and
their reputation is considerable. In recent tastings in Europe and North
America they have ranked well; and their positions on the tasting charts
should be viewed in the context of their price on the world market.
Argentinian Cabernet Sauvignons or Malbecs may not outrank the best from
France or California (although three 1974s stood ahead of Mondavi's 1974
and just behind the acclaimed Chateau Montelena recently), but their cost
to the consumer is a fraction of that of their competition.[4] Measured simply
as value for money, the Argentinian wines are in a class by themselves.

This is all the more remarkable when the Argentinian environment for
winemaking is considered geographically. Argentina's vineyards and wineries
lie concentrated in its northwestern provinces, in the lee of the high Andes
Mountains, on stony and sandy soils at elevations exceeding 1000 meters
(3300 feet) and more. Annual rainfall here ranges from a mere 200 to 300
millimeters (8 to 12 inches), and where the climate does not classify as BS
(steppe), it is desert (Fig. 4.1). Yet the environment provides opportunities:
underground drainage channels, artesian wells, snow-derived irrigation waters
from the Andes, and thousands of deep wells provide the moisture necessary
to sustain the vine. From its original heartland in Mendoza Province (still
with the great majority of wineries and vineyard hectarage), viticulture has
expanded into areas as far north as Jujuy and as far south as Rio Negro
(Fig. 9.2). In 1980 Mendoza had more than 1300 wineries and San Juan
about 370; it is a measure of their dominance that the four northern
provinces (La Rioja, Catamarca, Salta, and Jujuy) together had somewhat
fewer than 100 wineries and the two southern provinces (Neuquen and Rio
Negro) about 150.[5] Yet these frontier zones of viticulture are of special

ENVASADO EN ORIGEN   PRODUCT OF ARGENTINA

RED TABLE WINE

TRAPICHE

Montaña Fina

SOFT FLOWERY AND DELICATE

IMPORTED BY VINOS ARGENTINOS
IMPORTS U. S. A. INC., NEW YORK, N. Y.
ELABORADO Y EMBOTELLADO EN MENDOZA POR ESTABLECIMIENTO A EXP. 01019
ALCOHOL 12,5% BY VOLUME - NET CONTENTS 750 ml.

Argentinian table wines have proven their quality during various international tastings. The Trapiche label is one of the more successful, a red wine that constitutes a very good value.

interest, because some very good table wines are made here. In the north, the vineyards clothe the cooler slopes of Andean foothills; in the south, they challenge, oasislike, the dryness of Patagonia.

Mendoza, however, remains the core area. The provincial capital of the same name has been likened to Aix-en-Provence, with its "endless tree-arched streets and ubiquitous parks."[6] The comparison may be extended to the surrounding countryside, a seemingly endless expanse draped in the soft green of the vine. Mendoza Province contains well over 70 percent of Argentina's 360,000 hectares (890,000 acres) of vines; neighboring San Juan is a distant second with less than 20 percent. If this is not the kind of landscape readily associated with premium wines, appearances deceive: amid a mass of bulk wine produced by huge, refinerylike operations are produced quality table wines created from long-adapted cultivars, in special vineyards meticulously irrigated, the vines carefully tended and the harvest taken with the utmost care. Then Argentinian winemakers prove that they are capable of producing very good wines that can compete on world markets.

Argentina's best reds are produced from the Malbec, the Syrah (the grape that also creates the great Rhônes), and a clone of the Cabernet Sauvignon.

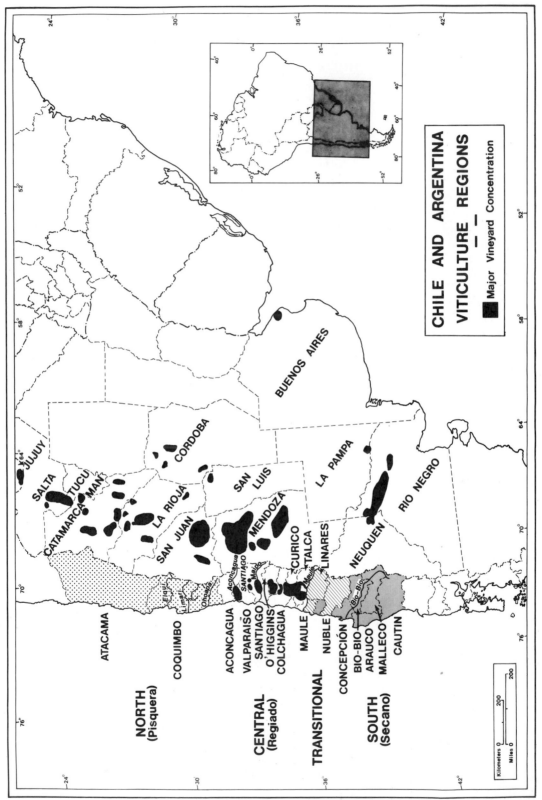

Figure 9.2 Chile and Argentina: Viticulture Regions

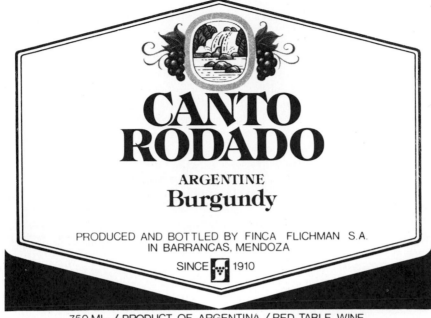

CANTO RODADO

ARGENTINE
Burgundy

PRODUCED AND BOTTLED BY FINCA FLICHMAN S.A.
IN BARRANCAS, MENDOZA

SINCE 1910

750 ML. / PRODUCT OF ARGENTINA / RED TABLE WINE
IMPORTED BY INTERNATIONAL VINTAGE WINE CO., NEW YORK, NY

Finca Flichman is among reputable Argentinian wine-exporting firms, making good varietal wines and modestly priced blends such as this "Burgundy," a successful wine on the North American market.

The whites are sometimes regarded as less successful, although the Chardonnay and the Sylvaner (labeled as a Riesling) do make adequate wines. The wines preferred by Argentinian consumers are not likely to succeed on world markets, but judicious blending creates the best *viños finos* for export. More than 60 percent of exported wines are reds.

Argentinian viticulture contains elements of Italian, Spanish, and French winegrowing. Both Spanish and French vine-training systems are used, yields per unit area are huge, and the larger wineries are versions of the Spanish bodegas. Indeed, most are called just that: the commonly seen Argentinian wines on the American market, Andean and Trapiche, are made by the Mendoza winery *Bodegas* y Viñedos Peñaflor. The practice of oak-aging for several years has prevailed in Argentina as in Spain but, again as in Iberia, it is being reconsidered and modified. The bodegas buy their wines from thousands of smaller producers (more than 35,000 in Mendoza alone) to supplement production from their own vineyards. While Argentina's wineries have traditionally concentrated on mass production for the domestic market, some are oriented toward the making of *viños finos* for export. Among distinguished names are those of Weinert, Bodegas Toso (for good Cabernet Sauvignon), and Lopez (noted Malbecs), as well as Finca Flichman (Syrah and Merlot). The number of winegrowers who wish to raise Argentinian quality consciousness also is on the rise. The wines that have satisfied domestic consumers for generations are not conducive to a specialized, quality-conscious industry. This entails risks, as was dramatically underscored by the 1981 economic crisis in Mendoza, which threatened to put thousands of smaller winegrowers out of business. Overproduction coupled with national recession collapsed the prices of ordinary wine, and the cycle toward destruction of the industry was under way.

Viticulture, however, is one of Argentina's three largest industries, and in some form it will survive and improve. The adage that vintage years do not matter in New-World wine regions certainly seems to apply here, where irrigation dominates so strongly. But in fact even Argentina has superior vintages. It should be noted that, in the Southern Hemisphere, a vintage is harvested (on the average) in March; the ripening season comes during the northern winter. Thus the 1982 vintage began its budding and flowering during late 1981, but of course a vintage is numbered by the year the harvest takes place, whether March or September. In Argentina, environmental conditions leading to the vintage are marked by the high variability of precipitation that comes with low annual averages, the occasional exceptionally cold winter (July temperatures normally go down to freezing), and the sometimes damaging heatwave. Only the most general and impressionistic rating of vintage years can be made, however. Years that would be ranked 17 and above (since 1970) include 1974, 1976, 1979, and possibly 1982; ratings from 13 to 16 characterized 1971, 1973, 1975, 1977, and 1980; and 12 and below, 1970, 1972, and 1981. These indices relate only to environmental conditions, but far more important is the skill of the winemaker. Some of Argentina's lesser vintage ratings have relevance mainly to the mass-production of ordinary wine; in those less favorable years some very good *viños finos* were nevertheless produced. Given the circumstances—cultural, economic, environmental—under which Argentina's viticulture has developed, its achievements are truly remarkable.

Chile

Chile is blessed with natural advantages Argentina lacks: a zone of true Mediterranean climate that becomes humid-temperate (Cf) toward the south and steppe (BS) toward the north (Fig. 4.1). Add to this the waters of a series of streams that flow from the Andes into the Pacific and provide excellent opportunities for irrigation, plus a varied soil pattern, and it is clear that Chile should be able to produce excellent wines. The global *phylloxera* attack somehow spared Chile, and Silvestre Ochagavia in the 1850s brought French know-how and French vines into his adopted homeland.

This combination of blessings has had noteworthy results, although ideological and political conditions have not always been ideal for viticulture in Chile, and the industry never has lived up to its potential. Part of the problem is undoubtedly geographic: Chile's 115,000 hectares (285,000 acres) of vineyards lie stretched out along a narrow zone from Atacama in the north to Cautin in the south, a distance of about 1500 kilometers (nearly 1000 miles). While variety is desirable, such attenuation and its attendant diversity—in terms of environment, viticultural needs and practices, cultivars, and traditions—is problematic. Some wineries and their vineyards always have been in the path of innovation and change (for better or worse); others lie remote and tradition-bound. Government policies have not been especially supportive of the industry; compared to Argentina's Instituto Nacional Vitivinicultura, which maintains strict control but also promotes and publicizes, Chile's official wine-related agencies are much less responsive. A very small proportion of Chilean wine is exported, although the flow is increasing,

The firm Concha y Toro is one of Chile's leading wine exporters, and various wines from its cellars are seen on foreign markets. This label indicates that the wine contains Cabernet (Sauvignon); the vintage appears on the neck of the bottle.

but there has been no major, national effort to penetrate foreign markets. Yet Chile's wines are of very good quality and are attractively priced, the reds more consistently so than the whites.

Chile's elongated and fragmented viticulture region may be divided into four districts (Fig. 9.2): the North or *Pisquera* District, the Central or *Regiado* District, a transitional zone, and the South or *Secano* District. The North is called the *Pisquera* because here, under conditions of high heat, are made the distilled Pisco wines, Chilean brandies. The major cultivars are Muscats, and in addition to brandies the North yields Sherry- and Port-like wines.

South of Coquimbo lies the Central District, the zone of seven provinces that contains Chile's most important viticultural areas, including about half the total vineyard hectarage. This is the Mediterranean zone with its winter rains and summer drought; precipitation increases from north (where it is about 300 millimeters or 12 inches) to south; near the Maule River, the approximate southern limit of the district, it is more than double this amount. During the growing and ripening season the vines must be irrigated to supplement natural moisture, and the important vineyards lie in the lowlands of the major rivers. The Central District produces Chile's finest wines from cultivars that include the Cabernet Sauvignon, Cabernet Franc, Merlot, and Malbec (here called the Côt Rouge) for the reds, and the Sémillon and Sauvignon for whites. In the areas emphasized on Figure 9.2 lie the most prestigious wineries of Chile, including Concha y Toro, Undurraga, Cousiño Macul, Santa Carolina, Santa Helena, San Pedro, and Linderos.

The Central District may be divided into two areas: the irrigated river-

A Chilean *Gran Reserva* in the making: the cellars of Undurraga, one of the country's leading wine houses (photograph by Edwin W. Snider).

valley vineyards just described and, in the hills near the coast, an irregular zone of unirrigated vineyards. These unirrigated vineyards, covering somewhat less than 10,000 hectares (25,000 acres), produce wine for local consumption from the most ordinary varieties, principally the País. The País is a grape of Spanish origin, modified by its lengthy presence in Chile. Among red grapes, it is by far the most commonly planted, evincing the Chilean industry's orientation toward the domestic market: in 1979, 70 percent of the area under red cultivars stood under País. Cabernet Sauvignon ranked next with 17 percent.

South of the important Central District, that is, beyond the Maule River, lies what Figure 9.2 labels the Transitional Zone, consisting of Linares, a part of Maule, and Nuble. Again this zone (also called the South-Central District) may be divided into a river-valley irrigated zone and a near-coastal unirrigated zone. Among the better wines, the whites now make their appearance in the river-valley area, including those made from Sémillon and Sauvignon grapes (the so-called Rieslings never have been a success). Much greater hectarage is devoted to ordinary wine production from the País in the unirrigated coastal area, where thousands of small producers own modest vineyards. This has been one of Chile's problem areas in that production here is large, domestic consumption is limited and has not risen, and economic alternatives here are few. The response has been to encourage winegrowers to convert part of their vineyards to grapes suitable for distillation, since brandy is popular in Chile and elsewhere in South America. There are, however, environmental difficulties as well. Rainfall in this part of Chile is quite high, in places exceeding 1000 mm. (40 inches), and the summer-dry regime breaks down. As a result, winegrowers' options are limited.

The South or *Secano* District is Chile's viticultural frontier, a zone of environmental and economic difficulties where rainy, cloudy summers often inhibit the ripening of grapes, soils are not among Chile's best for the vine, and yields tend to be small. Frequently the resulting wines, mainly from the País, cannot reach prescribed minimum alcohol levels and must be blended with bulk wine from northern areas in order to be marketed. Under such circumstances it is remarkable that there are as many as 8000 hectares (nearly 20,000 acres) of vineyards in this zone, but this includes gain-and-loss figures that constantly affect the South as some winegrowers give up while others make a new attempt.

From the preceding it is clear that no comprehensive vintage assessment would be of any value at all; even within the Central District there are significant variations. In addition, the early 1970s were affected by domestic political pressure. Vineyards were expropriated, vines were left to grow wild and harvests failed to take place, winery equipment and organization broke down. Indifferent wines from the period may reflect social rather than environmental dislocation. The late 1970s have witnessed recovery and the confirmation of the quality of which Chilean winegrowers are capable.[7]

In 1970, the first year of the new political order, Chile had one of its lowest yields in two decades (4 million hectoliters); it also was a mediocre year climatically. Other less successful vintages were the 1971 and 1972 (large but ordinary) and 1975. Fairly good to good years were 1973, 1978, 1979, 1980, and 1982; the best of the decade appear to have been 1974, 1976, 1977, and (perhaps) 1981.

South Africa

The principal wine regions of South Africa are among the most scenic in the world. Hugging the southwestern tip of the continent to form an L-shaped zone, South Africa's vineyards lie etched against the spectacular mountains of the Cape, cradled in valleys of unsurpassed beauty (Fig. 9.3). If such magnificent scenery leads to high expectations, South Africa's wines do not disappoint. From unique Pinotages and Steins to excellent Cabernet Sauvignons and surprising Rieslings, the range and quality of the Cape's wines are often beyond the expectations of oenophiles.

The natural environment at the Cape has the variety to make such achievements possible. As Figure 4.1 shows, a Mediterranean climatic regime prevails in an area centered on Cape Town, extending inland to encompass the premium-wine–producing districts of Constantia, Durbanville, Stellen-bosch, and Paarl, and extending into Malmesbury (Swartland). The soils of this area are based on sandstone, granite, and shale, and in many locales are ideally suited to viticulture. Summer heat is ameliorated by prevailing southeast winds off the cool ocean waters. This combination of circumstances permits the production of the finest South African table wines, including the Pinotage (see Chapter 2), Cabernet Sauvignon, Shiraz, Cinsaut, and Hermitage among the reds, and Stein (an adapted Chenin Blanc), Riesling, and Colombar among the whites.

Northward and eastward, conditions change. Rainfall diminishes, and the

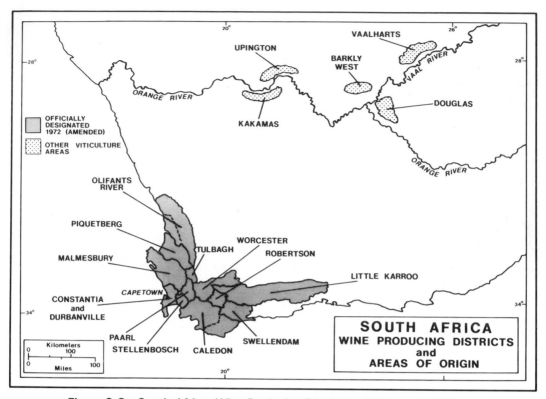

Figure 9.3   South Africa: Wine-Producing Districts and Areas of Origin

summer period is much warmer. In the Tulbagh area, high mountain ranges, snow-capped in winter, surround valleys exhibiting a variety of microclimates. Annual rainfall averages only some 350 millimeters (14 inches), so that irrigation augments the natural water supply. In addition to the Stein and Clairette Blanche, cultivars for sweet wines make their appearance as well, such as the Palomino and Muscat; the Tulbagh area produces very good Sherry-type wines.

Still farther from the core area, South African viticulture begins to resemble other fruit-growing regions where irrigation of extensive, flat fields makes harvests possible. In both the Olifantsriver and Little Karroo areas, the vineyards stand among orchards and groves producing apples, peaches, apricots, and citrus fruits. Here the emphasis is on fortified wines and distilled products. In addition to good Sherry-type wines, South Africa produces notable Port-style wines and excellent brandies.

Viticulture also is expanding in a South African region far from its original heartland, in the basin of the Orange River and its tributary, the Vaal. Centered on the town of Uppington, these striplike vineyards adjoin South Africa's major rivers in a steppelike environment, their survival and yield made possible by irrigation. Formerly this was exclusively a raisin-producing zone, but today the Sultana and Muscat varieties are joined by the Chenin Blanc and Colombar. Geography is a strong factor in the success of this viticultural frontier; while it does not produce premium wines, its comparative proximity to the populous Witwatersrand and Johannesburg is sufficient advantage to make its bulk and distilling wines competitive.

Vineyards interspersed with stands of trees in the area between Stellenbosch and Paarl.

The heartland of South African viticulture is one of the world's foremost wine regions, the comparative obscurity of its finest wines notwithstanding. At its core lie Stellenbosch and Paarl, the Napa and Sonoma of the Cape. As Figure 9.3 shows, the Stellenbosch area adjoins False Bay, thus lying open to maritime influences; its vineyards are flanked by mountains towering thousands of feet above the verdant valleys. The flanks of these mountains provide the heavy granite-based soils that carry many of Stellenbosch's finest vineyards, while lighter sandy soils dominate in the valleys. Here, too, many vineyards produce well. The Stellenbosch area yields many of South Africa's greatest red wines, especially from the Cabernet Sauvignon but also from the Pinotage. The Cabernets are rich, deep, complex, and often require as much as a decade or more in the bottle to reach their best; as in California they have often been consumed far too young, so that few examples of the best vintages of the 1960s and early 1970s remain. The Pinotage, in some ways the Cape's Zinfandel (although, unlike the Zinfandel, it is a *métis*), creates distinctive red wines ranging from light, early-drinking styles to heavy-bodied, tannin-rich, slow-aging breeds. Among the whites, the Stein yields fruity, well-balanced wines, and the Riesling produces good, dry wines.

The town of Stellenbosch is a true viticultural central place (see Chapter 7). The University of Stellenbosch is the University of California, Davis, of South Africa, with faculty members specializing in viticulture and oenology. In addition to its university, Stellenbosch is the site of the Government Research Institute for Viticulture and Oenology. The town also serves as headquarters for three large corporate firms, including the famous Stellenbosch Farmers' Winery, makers of Zonnebloem, Oude Libertas, and Chateau Libertas wines. The Oude Meester firm produces another well-known brand, now appearing on the American market: Fleur du Cap. Gilbey's, third of

GEPRODUSEER EN GEVUL IN DIE REPUBLIEK VAN SUID-AFRIKA

ZONNEBLOEM

1977
OESJAAR

1977
VINTAGE

STEIN

DIE STELLENBOSCH–BOEREWYNMAKERY BPK.
OUDE LIBERTAS,   STELLENBOSCH

PRODUCED AND BOTTLED IN THE REPUBLIC OF SOUTH AFRICA   S.A. LITHO LTD.

The Zonnebloem label is a product of the Stellenbosch Farmers'
Winery and has a strong reputation. The Stein (Steen) is one of South
Africa's unique wines.

Stellenbosch's large firms, markets the Bertrams brand. But what makes the
Stellenbosch area especially interesting is the large number of prestigious
estates that have official recognition, now two dozen. Among famous names
are Kanonkop, Rustenburg and Schoongezicht, and Delheim.

Adjacent to Stellenbosch is the Paarl viticultural area, also centered on
a town of the same name as the district. The town of Paarl is the headquarters
of the Cape Winegrowers Cooperative, the KWV (see Chapter 5). As in
many villages in France, the vineyards stand even within the urban confines
amid buildings and beside streets, emphasizing Paarl's special role. From
the Paarl area come many of South Africa's finest white wines; the Stein
does especially well here. Like the Pinotage, the Stein can be harvested and
vinted to produce a fragrant, early-drinking wine, or it is picked somewhat
later to create a more lasting, complex wine of balance and depth. In
addition to the Stein, the Paarl area carries substantial stands of the Riesling,
and other white varieties are being planted; the viticultural pattern is changing
in response to changing tastes and preferences. The reds also are asserting
themselves more as the Cinsaut, Pinotage, and Cabernet Sauvignon are
undergoing expansion.

The KWV dominates Paarl viticulture, although a famous name here,
Nederburg, is a product of the Stellenbosch Farmers' Winery. The great
majority of the growers sell their grapes or wine to the KWV or to one of
several other, smaller cooperatives. There are far fewer estates than in
Stellenbosch, but Backsberg ranks among the country's better-known winemakers.

South Africa's viticulture industry began in the shadow of Table Mountain, and today the oldest areas—Constantia and Durbanville—are being invaded by urban sprawl. The country's oldest estate, Groot Constantia, survives as a government-owned property managed by its institute in Stellenbosch. Groot Constantia's wines are of high quality and, its bureaucratic operation notwithstanding, deserve their ranking among the country's finest.[8]

RED CAPE VINTAGES: 1970–1982

South Africa's Cape is a wine region where a single vintage assessment will not apply to all areas. Although environmental vicissitudes may be less severe than in Burgundy or Germany, the Cape does have its adversities, one of which is an occasional spell of scorching heat just before the harvest. Such trouble may be quite localized: the Northern Paarl may be affected, but not Stellenbosch.[9]

1982   Large harvest following good winter rains and a moderate summer without extremes of heat or wind. Cabernet Sauvignon was harvested late, and not before some early April rains caused decline in sugar levels. Good Pinotage.

1981   The 1980 winter rains were insufficient in the coastal districts; then
(13)*   it was cool and wet from flowering to ripening. Much rain in January, just before harvest and again during harvest of Cabernets. Reds lack adequate sugar; whites better. Disastrous rains and floods in Karroo region where sweet and fortified wines are made.

1980   Substantially larger harvest than 1979, but quality mixed. Red wines
(15)   have rich, deep color and good alcohol but rather low acidity and may not be durable, although promising Cabernets and good Shiraz do exist. Good whites; very good sweet-style wines.

1979   Somewhat larger harvest than 1978; the grapes had good acid and
(17)   many long-lived Cabernets were made. Trend toward preference for lighter Pinotages evident in the bottling of majority lighter-style wines.

1978   Good to very good year for red wines from the coastal districts,
(16)   many of which still are improving. Several 1978s have won international recognition.

1977   Conditions far better in Paarl region than in Stellenbosch. Unusually
(11)   cool summer; late-ripening Cabernet Sauvignon did not do well. Good Steins.

1976   Much better for reds than whites; very good year for Pinotage as
(16)   well as Cabernet Sauvignon. Warm summer, no excessive heat.

1975   Late flowering, cloudy summer, comparatively cool weather; grapes
(12)   did not ripen satisfactorily. Wines (red as well as white) rather thin, light.

1974   Great year for Cabernet Sauvignon, Pinotage, and other red va-
(19)   rieties. Excellent red wines resulting from ideal summer, especially in the Stellenbosch area.

*Numbers in parentheses indicate ratings on a 20-pt. basis.

The *chai* at Groot Constantia, oldest of South African wineries and completely restored.

1973   Very variable year; few good reds, although whites fared better.
(13)   Cabernet Sauvignon did not ripen adequately; Pinotage fared rather better, but no distinguished wines.

1972   Great year for red wines, very good for whites. Some regard this
(18)   as the best year of the decade, but the reds of 1974 may improve longer.

1971   Not a year for long-lasting wines. Variable weather, inadequate
(13)   ripening. Comparatively light wines, many rather thin.

1970   A very good year. Cabernet Sauvignon produced beautiful, balanced
(17)   wines of distinction and long life. Those who argue that Pinotages are best drunk young may be persuaded otherwise by one of few surviving 1970s.

Earlier vintages: Far too many of South Africa's red wines were consumed while still young, and the greatness of earlier vintages has unfortunately been recognized from all too few surviving bottles. Among those are the 1968 and the 1966, only now at their best.

Australia

By the time the first vines were planted in Australia, Cape viticulture was more than a century old. Still today, South Africa produces more wine per

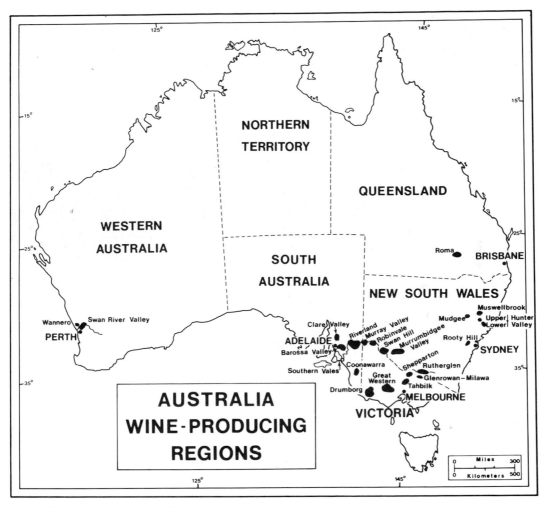

Figure 9.4 Australia: Wine-Producing Regions

year than Australia (see Table 6.2); indeed, South Africa in most years outproduces Chile for second place in the Southern Hemisphere. But Australia has unmatched potential, and viticulture's future downunder—in quality as well as quantity—is obviously bright.

Viticulture is widely dispersed throughout the southern latitudes of Australia and occurs in scattered locations such as the Swan River Valley in the hinterland of Perth, in uplands of Tasmania, in the suburbs of Adelaide, and in the heat of Queensland.[10] Some vines may even be seen near Alice Springs in the Northern Territory's great desert, so that viticulture occurs in all of Australia's major political divisions. But the great majority of the vineyards lie in only three states, in the southeastern corner of the country (Fig. 9.4). Australia's viticultural heartland lies in a roughly rectangular region south of a line from Muswellbrook (north of Sydney) to the Clare Valley in South Australia (north of Adelaide).

As the map indicates, Australian viticultural areas are numerous, frag-

No chateaux in the Hunter: at this modest winery, some of Australia's noblest wines are made. Tyrrell's, founded in 1858, still greets visitors in this wood-frame building. The main winery is in the background.

mented, and tend to have well-defined identities, so that regionalization is difficult. Indeed, Australian observers themselves use various systems to order the pattern, employing geographic proximity, similarity of wine styles, and other criteria in doing so. Some clustered viticulture areas are sufficiently similar to permit generalization (for example, the Barossa-Clare-Adelaide-Southern Vales areas in South Australia), but others, such as Coonawarra and Mudgee, lie comparatively isolated and are quite distinctive. The map, thus, should be seen in the context of Australia's changeable and evolving viticulture: not only is expansion occurring and in prospect, but patterns within existing wine regions are changing as grape varieties are replaced with others, new wineries are established, old wineries are taken over, and corporate penetration proceeds. Australia still is a viticultural frontier.

The present chapter focuses on prominent wine regions of world significance, and few would argue that at least two such regions are among Australia's numerous viticulture districts. Each of the two most prominent is located within easy reach (but neither is threatened by the sprawl) of a major city. About 160 kilometers (100 miles) north of Sydney lies the Hunter Valley, an historic region where Australian viticulture first became more than an experiment, and just 50 kilometers (30 miles) from Adelaide is the Barossa Valley, where premium wines of several kinds are produced.

In some ways the Hunter Valley epitomizes Australian viticulture. James Busby, the industry's crusty pioneer, brought 400 European vines to the area in the early 1830s, and from these cuttings arose the first successful vineyards of New South Wales. By 1840 there were 80 hectares (200 acres) under vine in the Hunter Valley, and soon the Hunter's wines were sent to Sydney (a laborious road-and-boat trip, since no rail connection was established until the 1880s). Vineyard hectarage grew rapidly, reaching 1000 in 1868 and approaching 1800 just three years later.[11] Remarkably free from serious disease and not afflicted by *phylloxera* (the Hunter has been spared), the wineries thrived.

But the region does not yield its wines easily. Rainfall around Pokolbin in the heart of the Hunter Valley averages about 675 mm. (27 inches), and summer temperatures are high, so that evapotranspiration losses are severe and water stress is a frequent problem. The desiccation caused by scorching westerlies is ameliorated somewhat by humid air from the nearby Pacific Ocean, and there is fairly high incidence of cloud cover, but the humidity takes its toll in mildew and rot. Furthermore, the rainfall regime is highly variable, and diaries of Hunter winegrowers are full of laments about poorly timed rains. The years 1975, 1976, and 1977 were marked by severe winter droughts that inhibited budding and flowering, and in 1977 the drought lasted throughout the summer ripening period, only to yield to rain at the worst possible time, during the harvest.

Successive years of poor environmental conditions have caused many a Hunter winemaker to abandon the vineyards, and economic and political change, as well as changing consumer preferences, also have had serious impact from time to time. Over its century and a half of wine production, the Hunter has seen numerous ups and downs, the ups always clouded by uncertainty and the downs sometimes threatening to exterminate the whole industry.

Yet the Hunter survives, and the original core area now must be called the *Lower* Hunter since, approximately 80 to 100 kilometers to the northwest, an Upper Hunter wine region is emerging. Certainly the Hunter Valley's winegrowers have proven their determination to overcome the most difficult of circumstances. As a result, the Hunter is an Australian national treasure, a hill-fringed oasis amid eucalyptus trees, bush, and brown-gray grass, described by one observer as "one of Australia's great visual experiences."[12] The countryside, somewhat rolling even in the riverine lowlands, is enlivened by streams and dams; meticulously tended rows of vines, green and prospering, gently confirm the natural topography and stand starkly etched against the gray, sometimes dusty environs.

The Hunter Valley produces both red and white wines, and among the whites certain late-harvest wines have attracted international attention. Many would opine that the Hunter's reds constitute the region's most remarkable achievements, however. Traditionally the Shiraz (Hermitage) has been the dominant cultivar for red wines, and the Sémillon for whites, but in recent years the Cabernet Sauvignon has been making a growing contribution. The Pinot Noir has made its appearance (and a 1976 Pinot Noir from Tyrrell made world headlines at a Paris tasting, where it outranked some notable Burgundies); the Chardonnay also is increasing in hectarage. The second-place position of the Hunter's "Rhine Riesling" among white cultivars is clearly threatened.

In its comparatively rare years of near-perfect conditions, the Hunter Valley produces magnificent red wines, and the prospect of new achievements in blending Shiraz, Cabernet Sauvignon, Merlot, and Malbec promises much for the future. Whether the Hunter's tough environment can nurture the Pinot Noir remains a long-range doubt, but what has already been accomplished is evidence of the Hunter winemakers' talents. Among great names in the Hunter Valley are Tyrrell, Drayton's, Elliotts, Lake's Folly, and

Tulloch, but no short list adequately represents the variety of historic and new establishments in the area.[13]

RED HUNTER VINTAGES: 1970–1982

The middle period of the decade of the 1970s was dominated by a severe and persistent drought, but the period began and ended well.

1982   Rains during the spring and summer: the drought finally broke. Warm, even hot, ripening weather. Good harvest conditions. Intense, fruity, full-bodied wines, perhaps classics among Hunter vintages.

1981   Drought again affected the growing season. Water stress; very early
(17)*   harvest, but intensity high. Low yield, deep and complex wines that will develop into characteristic Hunter reds.

1980   Persistent drought during the ripening season, fairly moderate
(16)   temperatures. Then untimely rain. Best wines complex, balanced, long-lasting; others ordinary.

1979   Perhaps the best vintage of the decade. Preceded by good winter
(20)   moisture. Full flowering, large harvest, yet excellent quality. Great wines for long cellaring.

1978   Dry weather throughout the ripening season; then rain at harvest-
(15)   time, presaging a wet winter. Fortunate growers had harvested early-ripeners just before the rain. Break in the wetness permitted later-ripeners to be picked. Wines good but not outstanding.

1977   Preceded by a dry winter; summer dry throughout; yields down.
(18)   Intense, powerful wines that will endure. Disastrous harvest rains in the Upper Hunter.

1976   Middle of a persistent dry period, then rains at harvest-time. Problem
(15)   year, variable; some good wines, especially among the whites.

1975   Elegant reds and only slightly lesser wines from this vintage, one
(17)   whose quality has come to be appreciated over the long term.

1974   A year that defies generalization. The whites were superb, with a
(15)   (19) rating; the reds, rather undistinguished, even thin, many rather light. Some exceptions.

1973   After a variable growing season, the rains came the first week of
(16)   February, before the great majority of the grapes were harvested. Good fortune: the growers waited for a dry spell and it came; no rot; good vintage, better for reds.

1972   Adequate but undistinguished wines, superior to the 1971s but not
(14)   among the decade's best for reds; whites were great.

1971   Disaster. Persistent rains, clouds, cool. Few grapes ripened properly;
(8)   only one or two noteworthy red wines from Cabernet Sauvignon.

1970   One of the best years of the decade, comparable to 1979. Conditions
(19)   ideal for ripening; no harvest rain. Long-lived wines, many of which are still developing.

*Numbers in parentheses indicate ratings on a 20-pt. basis.

EST. 1844

Penfolds

KOONUNGA HILL
Selected Bin
CLARET

This is the second release of Koonunga Hill Claret which is
made from a blend of Shiraz and Cabernet Sauvignon grapes
grown at Penfolds' Magill and Barossa Valley vineyards.

Only premium quality material has been used in the blend and
while the wine is ready to drink now it will benefit considerably
with further bottle age.

PENFOLDS WINES PTY. LIMITED
SYDNEY · MELBOURNE · ADELAIDE · BRISBANE · PERTH · F/10068

750 ml · WINE MADE IN AUSTRALIA

Penfolds is among Australia's large wineries with establishments in several parts of the country and vineyards from
which grapes are harvested for special blends. As the label
indicates, some grapes for this "Claret," a Shiraz-Cabernet
Sauvignon combination, come from Penfolds' vineyards in
the Barossa Valley.

Earlier vintages: The best of the Hunter Valley's red wines can develop for
many years. Among older vintages still to be admired are the 1969, 1965,
1959, and 1954.

It is one of the ironies of Australian viticulture that the country's most
famous red wine comes not from a premier red-wine region, but from the
cellars of a winery that is prominent in the heartland of white wine. This
wine is Grange Hermitage, made by Penfolds, and it is a blend of dominant
Shiraz with a smaller amount (5 to 15 percent) of Cabernet Sauvignon, aged
in American oak barrels and released after as much as five or six years of
bottle age. It is a wine of world class, and the 1975, recently released, is
obviously years from full development.

The success of Grange Hermitage proves that Australia's other historic premium-wine–producing region, the Barossa Valley, is not just a white-wine region. Indeed, Barossa vineyards owned by Penfolds have produced some of the Cabernet Sauvignon that has gone into this wine (much of the Shiraz now comes from nearby Clare, but the sources of the components vary from year to year). The Barossa is a versatile wine region, and its emphasis on white wines has as much to do with its culture history as with its physical environment.

The Barossa's German connection was established very early, even pre-dating viticulture's introduction. The first immigrants arrived as religious refugees from German Silesia in the early 1840s, and the first vines were planted in 1847. Some of the pioneer names from that period still are on the map: Seppelt's Seppeltsfield winery, for example, is an historic landmark that commemorates Joseph Seppelt's pioneering venture of the 1850s. The cultural landscape today strongly reflects the introduced European traditions, including "the cleanliness and order of the valley . . . a lesson to the rest of [Australia]."[14]

The physical geography of the Barossa explains its cultural versatility. The valley proper, more than 30 kilometers (20 miles) in length and, on an average, about 7 kilometers (4 miles) wide, is the most Mediterranean zone of the region climatically (see Figure 4.1), with rather low rainfall and a long, often hot and quite dry summer. Here the soils are dominantly red loams and here, from early on, the winegrowers planted varieties for fortified wines such as the Grenache, Pedro, and Mataro, in addition to the Shiraz. The hillslopes surrounding this valley floor are somewhat moist and, because of their elevation and exposure, rather cooler. Here the soils are varied, and include sandy Alfisols, with limestone in the subsoil (see Figure 4.3). On these slopes the Barossa long has supported various types of Rieslings for white wines, and some Shiraz.

The state of South Australia is the country's leading wine-producing state, accounting for as much as 60 percent of all the nation's annual wine production, and the Barossa Valley is South Australia's viticultural heartland. Concentrated in the valley are not only hundreds of growers, many of families who have cultivated the vine here for generations, but also a number of large companies, wine firms that mass-produce wines with grapes bought from the small growers. In addition there are limited-production, quality-oriented estates, so that the viticultural mosaic of the Barossa comprises every dimension of the industry. As such, the region has not escaped the problems also felt in the Hunter Valley, notably the change of consumer preference from sweet and fortified wines (and red table wines) to lighter white wines. This caused the large corporate firms to press smaller Barossa growers to change varieties to meet this situation, but the smaller growers were reluctant. The new varieties would not bear as heavily as the old, and there was uncertainty over the duration of the new demand. While the small growers resisted, the large firms began to purchase grapes in other areas and brought them to their Barossa cellars for fermentation. This, in the view of many observers, weakened the reputation of the Barossa, but the situation has stabilized and the region continues to prosper, its reputation intact.

Among the large producing firms in the valley are such names as Orlando-Gramp (another historic name: Gramp was first among Barossa vintners in 1850); Kaiser-Stuhl, a cooperative involving more than 500 growers in the

The large establishment of the cooperative Kaiser-Stuhl winery in the Barossa Valley. The German influence in Barossa Valley architecture remains strong.

Barossa and nearby Eden valleys; Seppelt, among the largest Australian wine companies with two estates in the Barossa (Seppeltsfield and Château Tanunda); Yalumba, known for many decades as maker of excellent aperitif and dessert wines; and Penfolds, major purchaser of Barossa growers' grapes and maker of a wide range of respected wines. These large firms are not simply bulk-wine producers; as in the case of Penfolds' Grange Hermitage, they have quality components that create wines made by several of Australia's leading winemakers. Thus wines from these firms regularly rank among the medal-winners at official tastings. In the Barossa Valley as elsewhere, smaller wineries retain their prestige as well, including such names as Henschke, Basedow's, and Château Yaldara. Some of the valley's old family firms have been taken over by larger corporations, but other operations are still being launched or sustained by enthusiasts who can afford to do so. The Barossa may be old and venerable among Australian wine regions, but it remains an exciting place.

The wines that come from the Barossa are truly astounding—both for their diversity and for their quality. "Champagnes," "Rhine Rieslings," "Spätleses," "Moselles," "Sauternes," "Clarets," "Sherries," "Ports," and "Burgundies" stand beside rosés, a wine labeled "sangria," a "Passionwein," and even a *Schillerwein.* In addition there is virtually every conceivable varietal wine, including Shiraz or Hermitage, Cabernet Sauvignon, Pinot Noir, Grenache, Frontignac, Sylvaner, Gewürztraminer, Chenin Blanc, Chardonnay, and various blends also involving the Tokay, Mataro, and Carignan. While this remarkable (and incomplete) list reflects the Barossa's versatility, it should be noted that many of the wine firms producing these wines do import grapes from other viticulture regions. Certainly the variety of Barossa wines sometimes has the effect of obscuring what it does best, and in recent years the valley has been seriously challenged by another South Australian region, the Clare Valley. Some observers feel that the Clare Valley has in fact overtaken the Barossa in quality, but such claims have been made before during the region's long history. Only time will tell whether the Barossa's primacy is really in doubt.

BAROSSA VINTAGES: 1970–1982

The Barossa's vintages vary more sharply than those of the Hunter Valley. Environmental conditions on the valley floor and against the hillslope rim can differ considerably during a particular year, so that some vineyards will prosper while others do not. There also is year-to-year variation of some magnitude, as expected in this Mediterranean-transitional zone.

1982	Nearly ideal conditions: good spring rains, excellent harvest period with warm days and cool nights. Red wines, especially those from the Shiraz, will be exceptional; other reds will be very good, with depth and good color. White wines will be good to very good.
1981 (14)*	A good year, although cold weather affected the ripening and the harvest was very late. Few outstanding wines, but mostly sound.
1980 (16)	A large harvest with good to very good quality. In general, the red wines of the Barossa were better than the whites.
1979 (17)	Satisfactory conditions virtually throughout the season resulted in the best vintage overall between 1976 and 1982. Red wines have depth, good color, and good balance, and will have long life.
1978 (14)	An uneven vintage resulting from gray skies and cool weather during the ripening season, and patchy rain during the harvest.
1977 (15)	A good but unexceptional year for both red and white wines. The harvest was the largest recorded in the region, contributing to the comparatively ordinary quality of the vintage.
1976 (19)	A truly superb year for Barossa's red varieties: balanced, complex, deep wines. Great for whites. Nearly ideal conditions throughout the vintage.
1975 (12)	A variable year to follow the disaster of 1974. Not an especially good year; mediocre wines among which the reds fared somewhat better than the whites.
1974 (6)	The poorest year in the Barossa for a long time. Cold weather during the flowering, cloudy summer, ill-timed rains. Whites as undeveloped as reds. No passable wines.
1973 (17)	A very good, even great year throughout South Australia, with excellent balance and fully ripe grapes producing fine whites and very good reds; the whites were better.

*Numbers in parentheses indicate ratings on a 20-pt. basis.

1972   An exceptional and superb year with virtually perfect flowering,
(19)   ripening, and harvesting conditions. Penfold's Grange Hermitage
        did not develop as well as anticipated.

1971   A mediocre year at best, and the Barossa fared less well than most
(9)   Australian regions in 1971. Untimely rains, poor harvest. No
        distinguished wines; reds poorer than whites.

1970   A good year, if not really great. Elegant, well-balanced, round, and
(14)   full whites; some noteworthy reds.

Earlier vintages: Among the Barossa's best vintages before 1970 were the
1967 and (especially) 1962.

New Zealand

What the New Zealand viticulture industry lacks in size it more than makes
up in interest (see Table 6.2). In the past decade there has been enormous
expansion, and despite some setbacks the quality of New Zealand's best
wines has risen markedly. The potential for further development is strong,
and the key lies in the proof that New Zealand can yield wines that can
compete with the best.

Perceptions of New Zealand as a remote, high-latitude archipelago, with
insufficient warmth for quality viticulture, still survive. The map should
dispel such misconceptions: New Zealand's North Island lies substantially in
the same latitude as Australia's Victoria. Its largest city, Auckland, lies very
slightly south of the latitude of Adelaide and well to the north of that of
Melbourne. The line of latitude that approximately bisects New Zealand's
North Island is (in the Northern Hemisphere) that of Bordeaux. The wine
country of Germany extends farther to the north than the southernmost
tip of New Zealand reaches to the south.

Other factors do come into play. New Zealand is an island country, and
maritime influences play a powerful role in its climatic regimes; there are
no protective mountains capable of holding off the Antarctic airmasses. So
New Zealand's climes are cool for latitudes so low, but they are not frigid
and (see Figure 4.1) they classify as Cfb in the Köppen system. This is
similar to much of Southeastern Australia and a large area of Western
Europe. Hawkes Bay, for example, has a heat summation of 2470, warmer
than many Burgundy locations and very close to that of Bordeaux (see Table
4.1). Conditions, thus, have something in common with Burgundy and
Germany—but New Zealand has numerous microclimates and supports not
only Burgundy's Pinot Noir and Germany's Müller-Thurgau, but also Bordeaux's Cabernet Sauvignon and South Africa's Pinotage.

Thus New Zealand viticulture is no mere appendage of Australia's, although
the indefatigable James Busby brought European cuttings here as he did to
Australia. Certainly Australian money is invested in New Zealand winegrowing, but environments and economics ensure that the enterprise retains
its identity. Long-latent opportunities were seized in the 1970s, when im-
provements in grape varieties, equipment, and vinicultural methods produced
far better wines than had been the norm. These wines found ready markets,
and vineyard hectarage expanded. During the decade of the 1970s the
vineyard area increased as much as 400 hectares annually, and exceeded

New Zealand winegrowers have produced some successful blends of the Cabernet Sauvignon and the Pinotage. The Pinotage does very well in New Zealand's comparatively cool environments; the Cabernet yields rich and complex wines in the best years.

5400 in 1981. In 1980 there were some 400 commercial wineries with a total of 5.5 million vines.[15]

The geographical distribution of New Zealand's wineries is not confined to North Island (Fig. 9.5). Indeed, the largest single vineyard is at Blenheim, South Island, and some vines are grown near Nelson and even on the Canterbury Plain in the hinterland of Christchurch. But the majority of the vineyards do lie on North Island, where most of the remarkable expansion has taken place in recent years. In addition to the older vineyards and wineries in the Henderson Valley near Auckland, the Kumeu-Huapai area, there are impressive developments near Te Kauwhata and Hamilton on the Waikato River, near Thames, around Gisborne (also the Tolaga Bay area) in the northeast—where *phylloxera* has recently made an unwelcome appearance—as well as farther south in the Hawkes Bay region. Smaller vineyards face the west coast of North Island between Wanganui and Wellington, the capital. So wide is the distribution of vineyards and so fast-growing the hectarage that fears have recently been expressed that over-

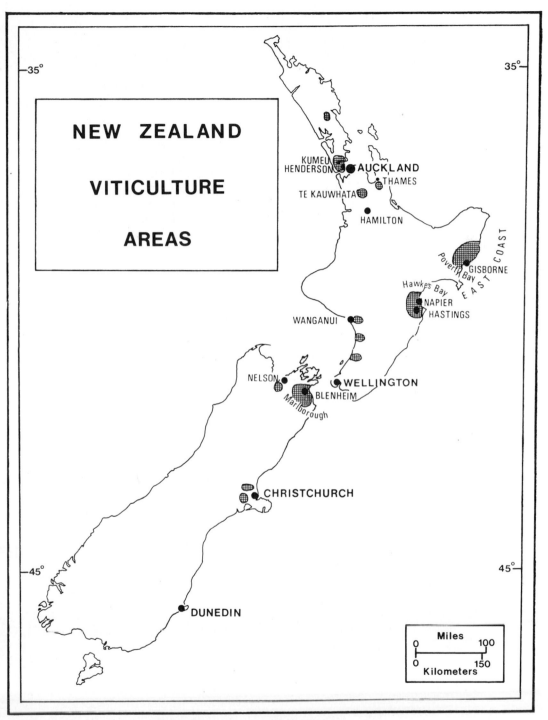

Figure 9.5 New Zealand: Viticulture Areas

Source: Modified from J. C. Graham, *Know Your New Zealand Wines* (Auckland: Collins, 1980).

production may occur, especially in view of New Zealand's stable population numbers and the recent lack of significant growth in per-capita consumption.

Good quality and successful exports are two elements of the solution to such a potential problem, and New Zealand has made progress in both areas. In the past, undistinguished bulk Sherry-type wines constituted a significant part of New Zealand production, and unattractive red and white table wines, made from inferior hybrids, contributed much of the rest. Today *vinifera* varieties occupy more than 90 percent of the vineyards, led by the Müller-Thurgau (also called the Riesling-Sylvaner, and there is some doubt regarding its exact ancestry), with nearly 2000 of the country's 5400 hectares. In New Zealand, this grape produces a characteristic, fruity, slightly sweet wine through the process called backblending, the addition to the wine of un-fermented grape juice with its natural sugars. The Palomino, the Sherry grape, still ranks second to the Müller-Thurgau, now producing Sherry-style wines far superior to those of an earlier period. The Chardonnay has made its impact, and more recently the Sauvignon Blanc has yielded some memorable wines. The Chenin Blanc is a mainstay, though not of outstanding repute under New Zealand's cool conditions.[16]

The area devoted to red cultivars is much smaller, but the results are noteworthy. One might wonder what could be possible in New Zealand if domestic and foreign tastes tended toward red wines as they now favor whites. In better years (notably 1976) the Cabernet Sauvignon, the largest red variety yet with a mere 250 hectares in 1981, proves that it can yield excellent wines. The Pinotage stands second with about half the Cabernet's hectarage; while it produces a fine wine, it also has been successfully blended with Cabernet Sauvignon to produce an unusual, round wine. For the Pinot Noir (fewer than 100 hectares) a bright future may well be in prospect: when time matures the vines, most of which are yet young, its wines may come to rank second to none in New Zealand.

New Zealand wines appearing on foreign markets tend still to come from one or other of the "Big Seven," the companies that dominate the industry: Cooks, Corbans, Glenvale, McWilliams, Montana, Penfolds, and Vidal. Their investments and, overall, their pursuit of quality have markedly raised the level of viticulture in New Zealand. But interest naturally focuses on smaller wineries dedicated to the creation of the best of which the country is capable—true premium wines that can match the world's finest. Nobilo Vintners (Huapai) have made excellent Pinot Noirs and Cabernet Sauvignons (the 1976 Cabernet Sauvignon was a magnificent wine); Delegats, Selaks, Collard Brothers' Sutton Baron Vineyards, and others less visible than the moneyed giants contribute strongly to the country's rising reputation in the world of wine.

New Zealand viticulture is recording the final chapter in a saga of global diffusion that began nearly five centuries ago. In the process it is proving again that this noble art and science hold an endless fascination.

NEW ZEALAND VINTAGES: 1970–1982

Vintage ratings have come to mean more as the industry has grown. In certain years, vintage conditions are quite similar over all or most of the country's wine regions; in other years there are regional differences expressed in the varying quality of local wines.

1982   A very good ripening season through mid-February was marred
         by rain during the harvest of early-ripening varieties. Yield down
         significantly in the Gisborne area.

1981   Very good vintage overall, best since 1976. Yield of white varieties
(17)*   somewhat down, reds normal. Good sugar through warm late season,
         although localized rain delayed picking in some areas. Good red
         wines.

1980   A notable improvement over 1978; good conditions in virtually all
(15)   the wine regions. Cool summer but long sunny spells, good sugar
         in the grapes. Good wines.

1979   Poorest year of the decade. Cool, wet ripening season; late harvest,
(9)   but wines still show effect of inadequate sugar. Light, rather thin
         reds; ordinary whites. Little regional variation.

1978   An adequate, rather ordinary year, without notable high or low
(14)   points. Good color in Cabernet Sauvignons. Whites undistinguished
         but sound.

1977   Variable year; warm ripening period but intermittent rain. No long-
(13)   lasting wines among the reds. Whites lacking in acid, fairly dull.

1976   Near-ideal conditions in one of the three best years of the decade.
(18)   Warm, dry ripening period after uneventful flowering; excellent
         harvest conditions. Deep, dark, well-balanced reds; excellent whites.
         Proof of the country's potential.

1975   High temperatures throughout much of the development of this
(15)   vintage. High alcohols, and the wines are not very well balanced.
         Reds rather rough, harsh; whites better.

1974   A great year that produced sound, robust Cabernets that may
(19)   develop for more than a decade; award-winning Chardonnays; other
         whites excellent as well.

1973   A good year of unexceptional reds not destined for long cellaring
(14)   and pleasant, fruity whites.

1972   A good to very good year, much regional variation. Complex reds
(16)   of depth and durability and excellent whites.

1971   Mediocre at best, this vintage resembles other Southern Hemisphere
(12)   1971s in not being among the decade's most satisfactory.

1970   The decade of the 1970s opened with its best year. In general,
(20)   ideal flowering, ripening, and harvesting conditions. Complex, bal-
         anced reds of depth and distinction; excellent white wines.

Additional Reading

While information on California wine regions is substantial, material in
English on Argentina and Chile still remains comparatively scarce, and
segments of encyclopedias covering the entire world remain the most ac-

*Numbers in parentheses indicate ratings on a 20-pt. basis.

cessible sources. Literature on South Africa and Australia is substantial and readily available. Among global coverage:

Burroughs, D., and Bezzant, N. *Wine Regions of the World.* London: Heinemann, 1979.

Sutcliffe, S. *André Simon's Wines of the World.* New York: McGraw-Hill, 1981.

Among regional approaches:

Abel, D. *Guide to the Wines of the United States.* New York: Cornerstone Library, 1980.

Adams, L. D. *The Wines of America.* 2nd ed. New York: McGraw-Hill, 1978.

De Jongh, F. *Encyclopedia of South African Wine.* 2nd ed. Scarborough: Butterworths, 1981.

Halliday, J., and Jarratt, R. *The Wines and History of the Hunter Valley.* Sydney: McGraw-Hill, 1979.

Olken, C., et al. *The Connoisseurs' Handbook of California Wines.* New York: Alfred A. Knopf, 1980.

Potter, M. *Wines and Wineries of South Australia.* Adelaide: Rigby, 1978.

Saunders, P. *A Guide to New Zealand Wines.* Auckland: Wineglass Publishing, 1981.

Vintage information for New-World countries is not as readily available as it is for European regions (except for California, where the monitoring and reporting are constant). Among useful sources are (in the United States) *Wines and Vines* and *The Wine Spectator;* for Europe, *Decanter;* for South Africa, *Wynboer* (partially in Afrikaans, published by the KWV); for Australia, *Wine and Spirit Buying Guide;* for New Zealand, the *New Zealand Wineglass.* Numerous industry and winery newsletters also provide valuable insights.

Notes

Chapter 1

1. D. Stanislawski, *Landscapes of Bacchus: The Vine in Portugal* (Austin: University of Texas Press, 1970).

2. D. Stanislawski, "Dionysus Westward: Early Religion and the Economic Geography of Wine," *Geographical Review* 65 (1975): 427–44.

3. O. D. von Engeln, "Geography of the Ithaca, New York Region," *Annals of the Association of American Geographers* 16 (1926): 124–50; P. C. Morrison, "Viticulture in Ohio," *Economic Geography* 12 (1936): 71–85; E. H. G. Dobby, "The Economic Geography of Port Wine," *Economic Geography* 12 (1936): 311–23; L. Hewes, "Tontitown: Ozark Vineyard Center," *Economic Geography* 29 (1953): 125–43; C. Olmstead, "American Orchard and Vineyard Regions," *Economic Geography* 32 (1956): 189–36.

4. A. John, "Sixty Million Bottles of Italian Goodwill," *Geographical Magazine* 51 (1978): 169–76; W. B. Fisher, "Wine: The Geographical Elements," *Geographical Magazine* 51 (1978): 86; W. B. Fisher, "French Wines with an English Connection," *Geographical Magazine* 53 (1981): 753; H. J. de Blij, "Geographic Dimensions of the Japanese Wine Industry," *Wines and Vines* 63 (1982): 60–65.

5. R. Fredericks, "Nineteenth Century Stonework in California's Napa Valley," *The California Geographer*, vol. K (1969): 39–48; J. N. Gruber, Jr., "The Northern Virginia Wine Industry," *The Virginia Geographer* 14 (1981): 1–10; D. G. Holtgrieve and J. Trevors, *The California Wine Atlas* (Hayward: Ecumene Associates, 1978).

Chapter 2

1. E. Hyams, *Dionysus: A Social History of the Wine Vine* (New York: Macmillan Co., 1965), p. 16.

2. It has been determined relatively recently that three American species of *Muscadiniae* exist. A. J. Winkler et al., in *General Viticulture* (Berkeley: University of California Press, 1974), identify two (p. 18). P. Galet, in *A Practical Ampelography* (Ithaca: Cornell University Press, 1979), adds *Vitis Popenoi* to the subgenus (p. 218).

3. M. A. Amerine and V. L. Singleton, *Wine: An Introduction* (Berkeley: University of California Press, 1977), p. 27.

4. A. J. Winkler et al., *General Viticulture*, p. 20.

5. M. A. Amerine and V. L. Singleton, *Wine*, p. 27.

6. H. Huang, "Viticulture in China: A 21-Century Legacy of Cultivation," *Wines and Vines* 62, no. 10 (1981): 28.

7. P. Galet, *A Practical Ampelography: Grapevine Identification*, trans. by L. Morton (Ithaca: Cornell University Press, 1979), p. 29.

8. P. M. Wagner, *Grapes Into Wine* (New York: Alfred A. Knopf, 1981), p. 25.

9. G. Knox, *Estate Wines of South Africa* (Cape Town: David Philip, 1976), p. 24.

10. W. James, *Wine in Australia* (Melbourne: Sun Books, 1978), p. 141.

11. M. A. Amerine and V. L. Singleton, *Wine*, p. 159.

Chapter 3

1. E. Hyams, *Dionysus: A Social History of the Wine Vine* (New York: Macmillan Co., 1965), p. 16.

2. E. Isaac, *Geography of Domestication* (Englewood Cliffs, N.J.: Prentice-Hall, 1970), p. 69.

3. E. Hyams, *Dionysus*, p. 60.

4. R. J. Forbes, *Studies in Ancient Technology*, 2nd ed. (Leiden: Brill, 1965), p. 73.

5. D. Stanislawski, "Dionysus Westward: Early Religion and the Economic Geography of Wine," *Geographical Review* 65 (1975): 427–44.

6. C. Seltman, *Wine in the Ancient World* (London: Routledge & Kegan Paul, 1957), p. 75.

7. S. F. Hallgarten, *German Wines* (London: Publivin, 1981), p. 21.

8. W. A. Younger, *Gods, Men, and Wine* (Cleveland: World, 1966), pp. 35 ff.

9. D. Seward, *Monks and Wine* (New York: Crown Publishers, 1979), p. 33.

10. N. J. G. Pounds, *An Historical Geography of Europe 450 B.C.–A.D. 1330* (Cambridge: Cambridge University Press, 1973), p. 288.

11. H. W. Allen, *A History of Wine* (London: Faber & Faber, 1961), p. 79.

12. P. Forbes, *Champagne: The Wine, the Land and the People* (London: Victor Gollancz, 1979), p. 113.

13. D. Blackburn, "1855 List Rates Brands Not Vineyards," *The Wine Spectator* 6, no. 23 (March 1982): 19; and A. Lichine, "Classification des Grands Crus Rouges de Bordeaux," in *The New Encyclopedia of Wines and Spirits*, 3rd ed. (New York: Alfred A. Knopf, 1981), pp. 120–21.

14. H. B. Leggett, "Early History of Wine Production in California," mimeographed (San Francisco: The Wine Institute, 1941), p. 43.

15. T. Schoenman, ed., *The Father of California Wine: Agoston Haraszthy* (Santa Barbara: Capra Press, 1979). This volume contains a complete reproduction of A. Haraszthy's book *Grape Culture, Wines, and Wine-Making* (1862).

16. H. B. Leggett, "Wine Production in California," p. 62.

17. L. D. Adams, *The Wines of America*, 2nd ed. (New York: McGraw-Hill, 1978), p. 95.

18. G. Ordish, *The Great Wine Blight* (New York: Charles Scribner's Sons, 1972), p. 37.

19. Ibid., p. 159.

20. Ibid., p. 109.

21. Ibid., p. 177.

22. G. Knox, *Estate Wines of South Africa* (Cape Town: David Philip, 1976), p. 8.

23. W. James, *Wine in Australia* (Melbourne: Sun Books, 1966).

24. P. Saunders, *A Guide to New Zealand Wine* (Auckland: Wineglass, 1981), p. 7.

25. H. Huang, "Viticulture in China: A 21-Century Legacy of Cultivation," *Wines and Vines* 62, no. 10 (1981): 28.

26. H. J. de Blij, "Wine in the Land of the Rising Sun," *Wines and Vines* 63, no. 5 (1982): 60–65.

Chapter 4

1. W. B. Fisher, "Wine: The Geographical Elements," *Geographical Magazine* 51, no. 2 (1978): 86.

2. B. C. Rankine et al., "Influence of Grape Variety, Climate, and Soil on Grape Composition and Quality of Table Wines," *Vitis* 10 (1971): 33–50.

3. W. M. Kliewer and L. A. Lider, "Effects of Day Temperature and Light Intensity on Growth and Composition of Vitis Vinifera Fruits," *Journal of the American Society of Horticultural Science* 95 (1970): 766–69.

4. A. J. Winkler, "The Effect of Climatic Regions," *Wine Review* 6 (1938): 14–16.

5. A. J. Winkler et al., *General Viticulture* (Berkeley: University of California Press, 1974), p. 66.

6. Ibid.

7. H. Johnson, *The World Atlas of Wine* (New York: Simon & Schuster, 1977), p. 232.

8. C. M. Baumann and F. W. Michel, *German Wine Atlas and Vineyard Register*, trans. by Nadia Fowler (New York: Hastings House, 1977), p. 5.

9. M. S. Buttrose, "Fruitfulness in Grapevines: Effects of Light Intensity and Temperature," *Botanical Gazette* 130 (1969): 166–73.

10. P. J. Kramer and T. S. Coile, "An Estimate of the Volume of Water Made Available by Root Extension," *Plant Physiology* 15 (1940): 743–47.

11. P. Wallace, "Geology of Wine," in *Proceedings of the 24th International Geological Congress*, sect. 6 (London: 1972), pp. 359–65.

12. D. W. Gade, "Windbreaks in the Lower Rhône Valley," *The Geographical Review* 68, no. 2 (1978): 127–44.

13. R. J. Weaver, *Grape Growing* (New York: John Wiley & Sons, 1976), p. 292.

14. W. M. Longhurst et al., *Fences for Controlling Deer Damage*, Circular 514 (California Agricultural Experiment Station, 1962), pp. 1–19.

15. Y. Vaadia and A. N. Kasimatis, "Vineyard Irrigation Trials," *American Journal of Enology and Viticulture* 12 (1961): 88–98.

16. E. Le Roy Ladurie, *Times of Feast, Times of Famine: A History of Climate Since the Year 1000*, trans. by Barbara Bray (New York: Doubleday, 1971), p. 51.

17. R. A. Bryson and T. J. Murray, *Climates of Hunger* (Madison: University of Wisconsin Press, 1977), pp. 68–69.

18. J. R. Bray, "Alpine Glacial Advance in Relation to a Proxy Summer Temperature Index Based Mainly on Wine Harvest Dates, A.D. 1453–1973," *Boreas* 16, no. 1 (1981): 1.

19. H. H. Lamb, *The Changing Climate* (London: Methuen, 1966), p. 7.

20. Ibid., pp. 190–91.

Chapter 5

1. S. F. Hallgarten, *German Wines* (London: Publivin, 1981), p. 37.

2. P. Sichel, *Frank Schoonmaker's Wines of Germany* (New York: Hastings House, 1981), p. 30.

3. S. F. Hallgarten, *German Wines*, p. 360.

4. J. Forsyth, "Wine and the Labyrinth of Bureaucracy," *Wines and Vines* 63, no. 5 (1982): 36.

5. C. Goldwyn, "The Case Against Appellation Contrôlée," *The Friends of Wine* 19, no. 4 (1982): 116.

6. N. Faith, *The Winemasters* (New York: Harper & Row, 1978), p. 252 ff.

7. Ibid., p. 256.

8. H. W. Allen, *The Wines of Portugal* (New York: McGraw-Hill, 1964), p. 29.

9. G. Robertson, *Port* (London: Faber & Faber, 1977), p. 29.

10. L. Evans, *Australian Complete Book of Wine* (Hamlyn, Australia: Dee Why West, 1977), p. 31.

11. S. Sutcliffe, *André Simon's Wines of the World* (New York: McGraw-Hill, 1981), p. 440.

12. "Wine Production in the World by Selected Countries, 1975–1980," *Wines and Vines* 63, no. 7 (1982): 49.

Chapter 6

1. H. Johnson, *The World Atlas of Wine* (New York: Simon & Schuster, 1977), p. 10.

2. S. Sutcliffe, *André Simon's Wines of the World* (New York: McGraw-Hill, 1981), p. 426.

3. I. P. Gerasimov, D. L. Armand, and K. M. Yefron, *Natural Resources of the Soviet Union: Their Use and Renewal* (San Francisco: Freeman, Cooper, 1971), p. 66.

4. J. Suckling, "Soviet Wine Loses Ground," *The Wine Spectator* 7, no. 3 (1982): 23.

5. W. Long, "Argentine Vineyards Yield Grapes Galore, but No Wine Profits," *The Miami Herald*, December 6, 1981, p. 1F.

6. See G. Furlan, "World Wine Consumption Shows a Modest Increase in 1980," *Italian Wines and Spirits* 6, no. 2 (1982): 16; and J. Boyazoglu, "Recent Trends in the Production, Consumption, and World Marketing of Wine," *Wynboer* 565 (1978): 44.

7. Figures from "Per Capita Wine Consumption in the U.S., by States," *Wines and Vines* 63, no. 7 (1982): 30.

8. Instituto Nacional de Vitivinicultura, Argentina, "Wine Growing in Argentina," n.d., pp. 8 and 9.

9. V. W. Eaton, "Data Aids Vine Choice," *Wines and Vines* 63, no. 7 (1982): 52.

Chapter 7

1. C. O. Sauer, "Recent Developments in Cultural Geography," *Recent Developments in the Social Sciences* (New York: J. B. Lipincott, 1927).

2. J. P. Dickenson and J. Salt, "In Vino Veritas: An Introduction to the Geography of Wine," *Progress in Human Geography* 6, no. 2 (1982): 184.

3. D. Stanislawski, *Landscapes of Bacchus: The Vine in Portugal* (Austin: University of Texas Press, 1970), p. 197.

4. A. Lichine, *New Encyclopedia of Wines and Spirits* (New York: Alfred A. Knopf, 1981), p. 267.

5. D. Stanislawski, *Landscapes of Bacchus*, p. 197.

6. A. H. Malan, "The Slanting Trellis," *Farming in South Africa* 28 (1953): 61.

7. A. Lichine, *New Encyclopedia*, p. 80.

8. C. O. Sauer, "The Morphology of Landscape," *University of California Publications in Geography* 2, no. 2 (1925): 19.

9. E. Penning-Rowsell, "Château Ducru-Beaucaillou," *The Friends of Wine* 16, no. 5 (1979): 32.

10. R. Fredericks, "Nineteenth-Century Stonework in California's Napa Valley," *The California Geographer* vol. K (1969): 39–48.

11. M. Johnston, "Napa, Valley of the Vine," *National Geographic* 155, no. 5 (1979) 695–717.

12. A Lichine, *New Encyclopedia*, p. 196.

13. A. S. Morris, "The Development of the Irrigation Economy of Mendoza, Argentina," *Annals of the Association of American Geographers* 59, no. 1 (1969): 97–115.

Chapter 8

1. W. Davenport, "Bordeaux: Fine Wines and Fiery Gascons," *National Geographic* 158, no. 2 (1980): 233.

2. For some insights see E. Hyams, *The Wine Country of France* (New York: J. B. Lippincott, 1960).

3. M. P. Boux et al., *Vineyards and Domains of Burgundy* (Dallas: Publivin, 1973).

4. S. M. Eliot, "The Wines of the Northern Rhône," *Vintage* 11, no. 2 (1981): 3.

5. T. Mahin, "Rioja: A Different Spanish Flavor," *The Friends of Wine* 15, no. 1 (1978): 4.

6. J. Reay-Smith, *Discovering Spanish Wine* (London: Robert Hale, 1976), p. 114.

7. D. Masieri, "Tuscany and its Wines," *The Friends of Wine* 15, no. 5 (1978): 30.

8. For details see "Special Report: the White Wines of Germany," *The Wine Spectator* 6, no. 18 (1981): 21–25.

9. I. Jamieson, "German Vintage Guide," *Decanter* 7, no. 8 (1982): 25.

Chapter 9

1. Quoted from W. James, *Wine in Australia* (Melbourne: Sun Books, 1978), p. 147.

2. For a recent evaluation see C. Parnell et al., "California Crush," *Decanter* 6, no. 12 (1981): 19–49.

3. M. Johnston, "Napa, Valley of the Vine," *National Geographic* 155, no. 5 (1979): 695.

4. J. Mariani, "Argentina Versus California: A Tasting of Some Surprises," *The Friends of Wine* 19, no. 3 (1982): 106.

5. Anon., *Wine Growing in Argentina* (Mendoza: Instituto Nacional Vitiviniculture, n.d.), p. 7.

6. C. Churchill, "Argentine Wines," *The Friends of Wine* 19, no. 2 (1982): 67.

7. L. Roberts, "Chilean Wines Vie for Quality Market," *The Wine Spectator* 6, no. 21 (1982): 4.

8. An excellent commentary is published by KWV., *Wine: A Guide for Young People* (Paarl: KWV, 1975).

9. For partial details see C. Swanepoel, "Suid-Afrika Het Wynoesjare" [South Africa Has Vintage Years], *Wynboer* 565 (1978): 18.

10. R. Mayne, "Tasmania: The Next Wine State?" *Wine and Spirit Buying Guide*, August 1981, p. 45.

11. J. Halliday and R. Jarratt, *The Wines and History of the Hunter Valley* (Sydney: McGraw-Hill, 1979), p. 31.

12. K. Kemp, *Wineries of New South Wales* (Sydney: New South Wales Department of Tourism, 1976), p. 8.

13. For historical details see M. Lake, *Hunter Winemakers* (Melbourne: Jacaranda, 1970).

14. L. Evans, "The Wines of Australia," in S. Sutcliffe, *André Simon's Wines of the World* (New York: McGraw-Hill, 1981), p. 587.

15. R. Small, "The Wines of New Zealand," in Sutcliffe, *André Simon's Wines of the World*, p. 601.

16. For details see P. Saunders, *A Guide to New Zealand Wines* (Auckland: Wineglass Publishing, 1982).

Index